PANCHAYATI RAJ REFORMS IN INDIA
Power to the People at the Grassroots

About the Academy of Grassroots Studies and Research of India

The Academy of Grassroots Studies and Research of India (AGRASRI) is an autonomous, non-profit and Non-Governmental Professional Organisation, Registered under the Societies Registration Act xxi of 1860 in the year 2001, being headquartered at Tirupati (A.P.), a World renowned Hindu pilgrim centre. The Academy was formally inaugurated by Shri Mani Shankar Aiyar, a champion of democratic decentralisation movement in India, on 20th August, 2001 at Tirupati.

The Academy works to provide an environment suitable for the study and promotion of academic research, training, education and consultancy in grassroots democratic institutions for self-sufficient Village Republics in India. The Grassroots Governance Journal (Bi-annual) and Grama Sabha Magazine (Monthly) are the official publications of Academy, besides books, working papers, occasional papers and monographs.

In pursuance of the aims and objectives, the AGRASRI is organising the Bharat Ratna Rajiv Gandhi Memorial Lecture and presenting the Bharat Ratna Rajiv Gandhi Outstanding Leadership and Bharat Ratna Rajiv Gandhi Best Panchayat Awards at three levels—District, Taluk and Gram Panchayats—on 20th August every year since 2002, in recognition of Shri Rajiv Gandhi's significant achievements and services to the nation, as Seventh Prime Minister of India.

About the Editor

Dr. D. Sundar Ram is a Founder and Director of Academy of Grassroots Studies and Research of India (AGRASRI), being headquartered at Tirupati (A.P.). He is heading the Rajiv Rural Development Foundation (RRDF), Tirupati. He is Editor of The Grassroots Governance Journal (Bi-annual) and Grama Sabha Magazine (Monthy). He is a prolific writer, author, researcher and analyst. He has written extensively on Indian governance, parliamentary studies, electoral reforms, decentralisation, federalism and state politics, with over 20 books and 150 research papers to his credit. He was earlier Reader in Public Administration, Sri Subbaraya and Narayana College P.G. Centre (Acharya Nagarjuna University), Narasaraopet, Guntur District (A.P.); UGC Research Associate in Political Science at Sri Venkateswara University, Tirupati; and Parliamentary Fellow at the Institute of Constitutional and Parliamentary Studies, New Delhi.

He is a Member in many professional bodies and organisations of national repute. He is actively involved in imparting Capacity Building Training for the elected representatives of PRI's and SHG's in Andhra Pradesh state, under the aegis AGRASRI, Tirupati. He is conferred the Man of the Year Award-2004; Man of the Achievement Award-2005 and Man of the Year Commemorative Medal for the Year-2006, by the American Biographical Institute, USA.

Presently, he is the Chief Organiser of the Bharat Ratna Rajiv Gandhi Memorial Lecture programme and Convener of the Bharat Ratna Rajiv Gandhi Outstanding Leadership and Best Panchayat Awards Jury, under the aegis of AGRASRI and Rajiv Rural Development Foundation, Tirupati (A.P.).

PANCHAYATI RAJ REFORMS IN INDIA

Power to the People at the Grassroots

Edited by

D. SUNDAR RAM

Published under Auspices of

ACADEMY OF GRASSROOTS STUDIES AND RESEARCH OF INDIA, TIRUPATI (A.P.)

In Association with

KANISHKA PUBLISHERS, DISTRIBUTORS

NEW DELHI-110 002

KANISHKA PUBLISHERS, DISTRIBUTORS
4697/5-21A, Ansari Road, Daryaganj
New Delhi-110 002
Phones : 2327 0497, 2328 8285
Fax : 011-2328 8285
e-mail: kanishka_publishing@yahoo.co.in

First Published 2007

ISBN 978-81-7391-925-9

PRINTED IN INDIA

Published by Madan Sachdeva for Kanishka Publishers, Distributors, 4697/5-21A, Ansari Road, Daryaganj, New Delhi-110 002; Typeset by Sunshine Graphics, Delhi, and Printed at Nice Printing Press, Delhi.

M. V. RAJASEKHARAN

सत्यमेव जयते

MINISTER OF STATE FOR PLANNING
GOVERNMENT OF INDIA
PLANNING COMMISSION
YOJANA BHAWAN, SANSAD MARG,
NEW DELHI-110 001

Foreword

I am very happy that the Academy of Grassroots Studies & Research of India (AGRASRI) has come out with this timely compilation of scholarly papers under the title "Panchayati Raj Reforms in India: Power to the People at the Grassroots". India 'lives in villages'. We can't see India as a developed nation, unless our villages are developed and our farmers, farm labourers and poor are assured of good quality of life through access to employment, health, education and food.

For making India really a developed nation, we have to fulfil the vision of Mahatama Gandhiji, who said:

> "My idea of village Swaraj is that it is a complete republic, independent of its neighbours for its own vital wants, and yet interdependent for many others in which dependence is a necessity..."

This vision was given a Constitutional shape and sanction by late Shri Rajiv Gandhi, by empowering Panchayati Raj Institutions to function as "institutions of self-government", to plan and implement programmes of economic development and social justice. However, the aim of devolution of functions, finances and functionaries to PRIs are yet not at the best and needs more perfection.

Against this backdrop, this attempt to bring out scholarly papers by distinguished leaders on the subject, is a praise worthy contribution. I wish all the best to all those who are working hard to strengthen Panchayats to provide power to the people of this great nation.

(M.V. RAJASEKHARAN)

New Delhi
02.01.2007

Preface

India lives in villages. We have nearly 2,50,000 Village Panchayats, 5,000 Taluk Panchayatis at the Block/taluk level, and 500 district level Zilla Panchayats. Decentralisation of Institutions and powers at the Grassroots level, as it stands today, have evolved as the outcome of several developments since 1950. No doubt that the 73rd Constitution Amendment Act, 1992 was considered as a radical in nature, for its promised institutionalisation of a third stratum of governance at the grassroots level. The 73rd and 74th Amendments to the Constitution aimed at the empowerment of Panchayati Raj Institutions were a progressive step towards democratic decentralisation, generating considerable hopes that these would result in the realisation of Gandhiji's dream of *Gram Swaraj*. However, one and half decade after these Constitution Amendments, it is universally and acutely realised that the empowerment of the Panchayati Raj Institutions cannot be complete without devolution of adequate and rightful financial and administrative powers to them. Under these circumstances, it is obvious that the time has come for a comprehensive review of the working of the Local Self- Government Institutions in India.

Against this background, the Academy of Grassroots Studies and Research of India (AGRASRI) makes a modest attempt to hold a National Seminar on *Panchayati Raj Institutions in India: Real Powers and Responsibilities* at Tirupati (Andhra Pradesh) on 20th August, 2002. As a part of the ongoing debate on the 73rd Constitution Amendment Act, 1992, it was decided to map the spectrum of the real powers and responsibilities of Panchayati Raj Institutions and sum up its experiences, inadequacies and challenges, as well as the requirements and vision of the future. The present Volume is concerned with this and experts have been requested to contribute their enriched impressions and remedial measures for a fresh look in an introspective spirit at various aspects of and issues on the existing Panchayati Raj Institutions, as a self-sufficient Village Republics in India.

The Sixteen chapters in this Volume by a distinguished group of Scholars provide an overview of the changing role of the Panchayati Raj Institutions in India at the grassroots level, in the process of decentralisation and devolution of powers. Examining the administrative and political lacunae in the functioning of the *Institutions of Self-government*, this Volume explore a real insight into the issues of major haunting dilemmas of the grassroots democratic institutions in contemporary India. We know that our democracy functioning fairly well on the national stage, despite a fairly extensive planning machinery at the national and the state levels and despite crores of rupees being pumped into scores of anti-poverty and development programmes, somewhere we have not run into a ground.

Since Independence, we believed that for the overall development, village should first flourish and the people at village should prosper. As the basic unit of local-self government, the effective functioning of village panchayat is vital for good governance. However, the majority of Panchayats do not inspire confidence in people as institutions of self-government due to various reasons and problems. Providing an analytical description of the working of the Panchayati Raj Institutions since its inception in India, this timely Volume constitutes a significant contribution to the current debate on the Second Generation of Panchayati Raj reforms and draws attention to various unresolved issues and dilemmas of the grassroots democratic institutions.

In the preparation of the Volume, I have received unfailing support and encouragement from many distinguished scholars and academics. I acknowledge gratefully to *Dr. Subhash C. Kashyap*, former Secretary-General of Indian Parliament (Lok Sabha), New Delhi; *Dr. George Mathew*, Director, Institute of Social Sciences, New Delhi; Dr. G. Palanithurai, Rajiv Gandhi Chair for Panchayati Raj Studies, Gandhigram Rural Institute, Deemed University, Gandhigram (Tamil Nadu), *Dr. P.C. Mathur*, President, Indian Network for Rajasthan Studies, Jaipur (Rajasthan) and *Dr. S.P. Jain*, Chairman, Society for Good Governance and Sustainable Development, Lucknow (U.P.) for their encouragement and valuable suggestions at different stages of the preparation of the manuscript of the Volume.

As a Director of the National Seminar, I am very much thankful to *Dr. Mani Shankar Aiyar*, the then CWC Member and Hon'ble Member of Parliament (Lok Sabha), New Delhi, for taking a special interest to Inagurates the Seminar on 20th August, 2002 in Tirupati. I am also grateful to *Dr. K. Keshava Rao*, presently Hon'ble Member of Parliament (Rajya Sabha) and President of the Andhra Pradesh Congress Committee (I), Hyderabad, for his inspiring Valedictory address at the Seminar. Many thanks are due to the noted contributors, who have taken pains to revise their earlier version of the Seminar papers, for this Volume.

I am very much thankful to *Shri M.V. Rajasekharan*, Hon'ble Union Minister of State for Planning, Govt. of India, for his enriched Foreword to this Volume.

I acknowledge a numerous well-wishers and my colleagues at the Academy of Grassroots Studies and Research of India (AGRASRI), who have extended their constant support and encouragement for me in bringing out this Volume.

Last but not least, I am highly thankful to Shri Madan Sachdeva of Kanishka Publishers, Distributors, New Delhi, for processing manuscript expeditiously and bringing out the book in such a short period of time.

Tirupati D. SUNDAR RAM

Contents

List of Contributors

Dr. Mani Shankar Aiyar, IFS (Retd.), Hon'ble Union Minister for Panchayati Raj and Youth Affairs and Sports, Government of India and a well-known Champion of Democratic Decentralisation Movement in India, New Delhi.

Dr. Subhash C. Kashyap, Hon. Research Professor at Centre for Policy Research, New Delhi. He has been the Secretary-General of the Lok Sabha and Member, National Commission to Review the Working of the Constitution and Chairman of its Editorial and Drafting Committees. Also he is Hon. Chairman of the AGRASRI, Tirupati (A.P.).

Dr. L.C. Jain, Former Member of Planning Commission and Indian High Commissioner to South Africa. He is actively associated with many Grassroots Level Organisations. He is now based in Bangalore.

Dr. (Mrs.) V. Mohini Giri, Hon. Chairperson, Guild of Service and Member, Board of Trustees, Rajiv Gandhi Foundation, New Delhi. She has earlier been the Chairperson of the National Commission for Women, New Delhi.

Ms. C.B. Muthamma, IFS (Retd.), Former Indian Ambassador and Political Analyst, Bangalore.

Shri K.C. Sivaramakrishnan, IAS (Retd.), Hon'ble Visiting Professor at Centre for Policy Research, New Delhi. He has earlier been the Secretary to Government of India.

Shri M. Gopalakrishanan, IAS (Retd.), Former Special Chief Secretary to Government of Andhra Pradesh and Chief Electoral Officer, Hyderabad (A.P.).

Dr. George Mathew, Director, Institute of Social Sciences, New Delhi.

Dr. G. Palanithurai, Rajiv Gandhi Chair for Panchayati Raj Studies, Department of Political Science and Development Administration, Gandhigram Rural Institute, Deemed University, Gandhigram (Tamil Nadu).

Dr. Rajesh Tandon, President, Participatory Research in South Asia (PRIA), New Delhi.

Dr. N.S. Gehlot, Professor of Political Science, Maharshi Dayanand Saraswati University, Ajmer (Rajasthan).

Dr. Yatindra Singh Sisodia, Senior Fellow, Madhya Pradesh Institute of Social Science Research, Ujjain (Madhya Pradesh).

Dr. Y. Bhaskar Rao, Senior Assistant Director, Centre for Panchayati Raj, National Institute of Rural Development, Hyderabad (A.P.).

Dr. S. Harsha, Lecturer in Political Science, Assam University, Silchar (Assam).

Dr. (Mrs.) Nupur Tiwary, Project Co-ordinator, Rajiv Gandhi Institute for Contemporary Studies, Rajiv Gandhi Foundation, New Delhi.

Dr. D. Sundar Ram (Editor), Founder and Director, Academy of Grassroots Studies and Research of India (AGRASRI); Secretary-General, Rajiv Rural Development Foundation (RRDF); and Editor, Grassroots Governance Journal, Grama Sabha (Monthly Magazine) Tirupati (A.P.).

1

Introduction: Panchayati Raj Reforms and Empowerment of Grassroots Democratic Institutions in India

D. SUNDAR RAM

Effective decentralisation by way of empowerment of the Panchayati Raj Institutions (PRIs) is essential to achieve the goal of equitable social and economic development. Free India has been much concerned to fulfil Mahatma Gandhi's[1] promise and to implement the constitutional directive. The First Five Year Plan declared that 'from now on, the primary emphasis in district administration has to be on the implementation of development programmes in close co-operation with the active support of the people.'[2] The need for popular participation in development tasks under the Five Year Plan prompted the Congress leaders in government to look in the direction of strengthening the Panchayati Raj System in India.

A comprehensive review of Local Government and Administration in India conducted by Balwantrai Mehta Study Team in the year 1957 envisaged a three-tier system of decentralisation, namely the Village Panchayat, the Panchayat Samithi and Zilla Parishad.[3] The above scheme recommended by the Committee was endorsed by the National Development Council on 12th January, 1958, and thereafter it urged the States to work out structures suitable to each State. Accordingly, the States took action to inaugurate Panchayati Raj through appropriate Acts passed by the State Legislature.[4] It was in this context that Pandit Jawaharlal Nehru described panchayats as the 'foundations of democracy'[5] in India. He was of the opinion that the 'progress of our country is bound up with the progress in our villages.' Towards achieving this end, there is no doubt that throughout the period of 1950 to 1964, the government headed by Pandit Nehru was all along keenly interested in the decentralisation of governmental authority and in the establishment of village panchayats.

In 1978, the Janata Government headed by Shri Morarji Desai finding that the States had not managed the Panchayati Raj Institutions properly, set up a Committee with Shri Ashok Mehta[6] as the Chairman to review the working of Panchayati Raj Institutions and in particular among other things, to delineate their true role in the task of integrated rural development. The Ashoka Mehta Committee submitted its report in August 1978, making 123 recommendations to revitalise Panchayati Raj as a living and integral part of the democratic continuum. But all these suggestions and recommendations on the whole the performance of decentralised planning experiments has been rather dismal, barring a few exceptional cases.

In order to improve the participation of the rural people in the process of their development and involvement in decision-making and decentralised planning directly affecting their life, the Congress (I) Government headed by Shri Rajiv Gandhi has appointed various committees[7] to go into the various aspects of Panchayati Raj issue. Taking into account the several reports and recommendations regarding the working of the Panchayati Raj Institutions, the Government of India introduced 64th Amendment Bill to the Constitution of India. It is probably the first time in the world that a Prime Minister has proposed a Constitutional Amendment on a subject like local self-government in federal democracy.[8] No wonder, the 64th and 65th Amendment Bills were lost in the Rajya Sabha by 3 votes only in 1989. Subsequently the National Front Government introduced the 74th Constitution Amendment Bill which lapsed due to the dissolution of Lok Sabha in 1990.

Being committed to decentralisation of power and authority, and revitalisation of Panchayati Raj Institutions, the P.V. Narasimha Rao Government introduced the 64th Constitution Amendment Bill in a somewhat diluted form again in 1992 and it was passed by the Parliament in December, 1992.[9] It became an Act on 24 April, 1993 known as the 73rd Constitution Amendment Act, 1992. This Act retained the spirit of 64th Constitution Amendment Bill, introduced by Shri Rajiv Gandhi, an architect of modern Panchayati Raj System.

In pursuance of its election manifesto called the National Agenda for Governance, the NDA Government headed by Shri A.B. Vajpayee has appointed a 13-member National Commission to Review the Working of the Constitution (NCRWC) under the Chairmanship of the former Chief Justice of India Shri M.N.Venkatachaliah on 1st February, 2000.[10] After considering the various viewpoints and recommendations to the Government of India through a comprehensive report submitted on 31st March, 2002 for reconstruction of the executive, legislative and judicial aspects of the Constitutional provisions of Governance. There were 38 recommendations made by the National Commission to Review the working of the Constitution on the decentralisation and devolution, besides empowerment and strengthening of Panchayati Raj Institutions alone.[11] In addition, the National Democratic Alliance Government took keen interest in organising the All India Panchayat Adhyakshas Sammelan in New Delhi during 5-6 April, 2002 for formulating National Declaration for Local Self-Governance, a text consisting of 15-point recommendations.[12] This resolution was at the Centre of the recommendations made by the 1,600 elected heads representing 3,40,000 Panchayats of India.

In continuation of the Panchayati Raj reforms process and to improve the quality of life of the mass of the people of India, the United Progressive Alliance Government at the Centre headed by Dr. Manmohan Singh has also ensured in its National Common Minimum Programme (NCMP)[13] that all funds for poverty alleviation and rural development programme will be credited directly to Panchayati Raj bodies as per the recommendations of the 12th Finance Commission, besides devolution of functions and functionaries as well. For the first time, in the history of Indian Panchayati Raj, the UPA Government has been set up to the Ministry of Panchayati Raj to primarily oversee the implementation of Part IX of the Constitution, inserted by the 73rd Constitution Amendment Act, 1992, which has institutionalised Panchayati Raj Institutions at the village, intermediate and District levels as district units of self-government.[14] The Prime Minister Dr. Manmohan Singh set the tone through his inaugural address at the first conference of all Chief Ministers on Rural Poverty Alleviation and prosperity through Panchayati Raj on 29th June, 2004, where he asserted that effective and sustainable poverty alleviation could be achieved only by the Constitution. He said[15] : 'Panchayati Raj' is the medium to transform rural India into 700 million opportunities. The key instrument for integrating economic reforms with institutional reforms in the country side is Gandhiji's farsighted goal of *Purna Swaraj through Gram Swaraj*. This was given constitutional shape and sanction by late Shri Rajiv Gandhi's vision of empowering Panchayati Raj Institutions to function as 'institutions of self-government', to plan and implement programmes of economic development and social justice.

The 73rd Constitution Amendment Act and the first fourteen years succeeding it can be considered as comprising first generation reforms, with the central theme being creation and empowerment of strong panchayats. These reforms aimed to combine social justice with devolution with its emphasis on reservations for deprived classes of the population in panchayats and leadership positions in panchayats.[16] The objective of creating a strong base of political empowerment of ordinary people has been largely achieved, as the statistics on Panchayats would reveal.

Today, more than 21 lakh representatives stand elected to the three levels of—District, Intermediate and Village Panchayats. Of these more than 40 per cent are women, 16 per cent belong to SCs and 11 per cent belong to the STs.[17] At the Village Panchayat level, each panch's constituency comprises of about 340 people (70 families) making India the largest and most intensely democratic country worldwide.

However, the spirit of Part IX of the Constitution goes beyond political empowerment. It is essentially that elected panchayats are expected to function as units of rural local self-government. The emphasis is to empower them with certain functional mandates, give them a significant degree of autonomy and impart to them an element on self-reliance and self-sufficiency through fiscal transfers, taxation powers and tax assessments. For several reasons, the constitutional provisions alone have not been an effective trigger for the empowerment of panchayats.[18] The major reasons are : First, the Constitutional framework leaves the states to decide through legislation the extent of powers that have to be transferred to the Panchayats to function as institutions on self-government. Secondly, till recently, in spite of the mandatory provisions of Part IX relating to the creation of Panchayats many states have delayed the conduct of elections to panchayats. Thirdly, even in states that have passed strong and sweeping legislations assigning most of the powers and functions listed in the Eleventh Schedule to the Panchayats, formal transfer of functions has not been matched by the concomitant transfer of funds and functionaries for performing these functions. Fourthly, there has been very little change in the first decade after the 73rd Constitution Amendment in the way that Central Ministries dealing with the mandates of Panchayats function. When Central Ministries, which send down substantial funds for implementation of centrally sponsored schemes, ignores panchayats, it leaves very little for states to go ahead with devolution.

After 1992, the Grassroots Democratic Institutions are considered as the heart of the Indian polity and governance. In this context, a 14 years after the 73rd Constitution Amendment Act, it is universally and acutely realised that the empowerment of the Panchayati Raj Institutions (PRIs) cannot be complete without devolution of adequate and rightful financial and administrative powers to the Grassroots Democratic Institutions. It is obvious that the time has come for a comprehensive review of the working of the Local Self-Government Institutions.[19] If the 73rd and 74th Amendments constituted the first generation of Panchayati Raj reforms there is all-round realisation now of the necessity to introduce the second generation of Panchayati Raj reforms.

With respect to the second generation of Panchayati Raj reforms in India, the Union Ministry of Panchayati Raj, under the leadership of Dr. Mani Shankar Aiyar, has taken several initiatives[20] from the view point of the working of the Panchayati Raj Institutions at all levels as institutions of local self-government, in letter and spirit of the 73rd Constitution Amendment Act, 1992. In accordance with the decision taken in the Conference of Chief Ministers on 29th and 30th June, 2004, the Ministry of Panchayati Raj organised Seven-Round Tables in different parts of the country.

The second generation on reforms in devolution to panchayats aim to tackle the continuing time lag between the constitutional mandate and effective functional transfer to panchayats. From an operational perspective, second generation reforms would be characterised by a focus on building mechanisms for increased participation of the people in decision-making mechanisms for increased participation of the people in decision-making, streamlining the fiscal mechanisms that fuel the functioning of panchayats, and strengthening administrative mechanisms that enhance the efficacy and capabilities of panchayats.

In order to come up with specific modalities for operationalising the objective of the National Commission Minimum Programme, the Congress from the Seven-Round Tables comprise of 150 action points pertaining to 18 dimensions of Panchayati Raj on which effective devolution hinges.[21] Taken together, they comprise a time-bound action plan for achieving full devolution of functions, functionaries and finances to Panchayati Raj Institutions in accordance with the letter and spirit of the Constitution. The implementation of this time bound plan[22] for devolution of powers and responsibilities would call for close co-ordination between the Government of India, the States and the Union Territories, as also between the Ministry of Panchayati Raj and all Ministries of the Government of India, particularly those dealing with the 29 functions that can be assigned to panchayats under the Eleventh Schedule of the Constitutions of India.

No doubt, in the present circumstances there are a number of challenges and obstacles before the panchayati raj administration in contemporary India. Under this scenario, a need of the hour is to look at good governance in terms of its delivery to achieve overall development and social justice. For this, the whole issue of panchayati raj system is to be reviewed, policies are to be reformulated and grassroots level realities are to be recognised. This would perhaps require renewed interest in the changing structure of the grassroots democratic institutions administration from 'imposed development' approach to self-determined development approach.[23]

It may be necessary to further incorporate the following reformatory changes in the structure, composition and functions of the Panchayati Raj Institutions (PRIs), for good governance at the grassroots : First, to inculcate a participatory development approach in the minds of elected representatives of PRIs as well as the citizens of India at the grassroots. Secondly, to provide adequate training to the elected representatives of PRIs for their capacity building in transforming the panchayats into institutions of local governance. Thirdly, to introduce the (District) Indian Panchayati Raj service at All India level on par with Indian Administrative Service and minimise the supremacy of the 'Collector's Raj' in the decision-making of local self-government institutions. Fourthly, to provide autonomy to Panchayati Raj Institutions (PRIs) as per the provisions of 73rd Constitution Amendment Act to function as institution of local self-governments. Fifthly, to devolve 3F's—functions, funds and functionaries immediately to Panchayati Raj Institutions in letter and spirit. Sixthly, to strengthen the decentralised planning and provide an opportunity for more and more people to be involved in formulation of their own developmental plans through Gram Sabhas and other statutory bodies. Seventhly, to re-define the role and responsibilities of MPs/MLAs in Panchayati Raj administration and re-statement of the distribution of work between the three-tiers of the governance. Eighthly, to make effective and growing use of Information Technology in Panchayati Raj administration for quick and efficient delivery of public services at the grassroots level. Finally, to identify the real beneficiaries and disadvantaged sections of the society in a transparent way, while in implementation of various rural development programmes and welfare schemes.

The sixteen chapter in this volume by a distinguished group of scholars provide an overview of the changing role of the Panchayati Raj Institutions in India at the grassroots level, in the process of decentralisation and devolution of powers. Examining the administrative and political lacunae in the functioning of the 'Institutions of Self-Government', this volume explore a real insight into the issue of major haunting dilemmas of the grassroots democratic institutions in contemporary India.

We know that our democracy functioning fairly well on the national stage, despite a fairly extensive planning machinery at the National and the State levels and despite crores of rupees being pumped into scores of anti-poverty and development programmes, somewhere we have not run into a ground. Since Independence, we believed that for the overall development, village should first flourish, the effective functioning of village panchayat is vital for good governance. However, the majority of panchayats do not inspire confidence in people as institutions on self-government due to various reasons and problems. Providing analytical description of the Panchayati Raj Institutions since its inception in India, this timely volume consists a significant contribution to the current debate on the Second Generation of Panchayati Raj reforms and draws attention to various unresolved issues and dilemmas of the grassroots democratic institutions.

Thus, all the articles in the volume underlined clearly the fact that the devolution of powers to the grassroots democratic institutions alone would help the existing Panchayati Raj System to solve the rural problems. It is hoped that the present volume stimulates a new debate and provides a set of measures in order to bring the second generation of reforms, not merely as a weapon to streamline the Panchayati Raj Institutions at the grassroots level, but as a creative exercise in government towards the transition from representative democracy to participative democracy. What is now needed, in this 60th anniversary of India's Independence as a biggest democratic nation in the world, is a stock-taking of the Panchayati Raj experience of all states which will enable us to chart a road-map for the time-bound implementation of the philosophy of 'power to the people'.

NOTES AND REFERENCES

1. Mahatma Gandhi was an ardent exponent and devotee of Village Swaraj (self-rule). He wrote in Harijan in 1942, defining his vision of Village Panchayat in the following words :
   "My idea of village 'swaraj' is that it is a complete republic, independent of its neighbours for its own vital wants and yet interdependent for many others in which dependence is a necessity. The Government of the Village will be conducted by the Panchayat of five persons annually elected by the adult villagers, males and females, possessing minimum prescribed qualifications. These will have all the authority and jurisdiction required. Since there will be no system of punishment in the accepted sense, the panchayat will be the legislature, judiciary and executive combined to operate for its year of office. Any village can become such a republic today without much interference even from the present government whose sole effective connection with the villages is the exaction of the village revenue. Here there is perfect democracy based upon individual

freedom. The individual is the architect of his own Government." For further details, see M.K. Gandhi, *Rebuilding our Villages*, Ahmedabad, Navajeevan Publishing House, 1956.

2. The *First Five Year Plan*, New Delhi, Government of India, 1953, p. 130.
3. The Balwantrai Mehta Team affirmed that 'rural development and rural welfare are possible only with local initiative and local discretion' and offered two broad directional thrusts: first, it argued that there should be administrative decentralisation for the effective implementation of the development programme and that the decentralised administrative system should be under the control of elected bodies. For more details, See. *Report of the Team for the Study of Community Projects and National Extensive Service* (Chairman, Balwantrai Mehta), New Delhi, Government of India, Vol. 1, 1958.
4. Following the National Development Council endorsement, the Rajasthan and Uttar Pradesh took lead in passing such acts. Except for Kerala and Jammu & Kashmir, all the states had then adopted the three-tier Panchayati Raj System in India. For a penetrating analyses, See. (*i*) E.S. Venkataramaiah, 'Panchayati Raj Institutions in India' in G. Palanithurai (Ed.) *Dynamics of New Panchayati Raj System in India*, Vol. I, New Delhi, Concept Publishing Company, 2002, pp. 14-33, (*ii*) George Mathew (Ed.) *Status of Panchayati Raj in the States of India*, New Delhi, Concept Publishing Company, 1994.
5. Speaking on the occasion of the Inauguration of Panchayati Raj in Rajasthan on 2 October, 1959, he expressed his faith in the capability of the people in managing their affairs in the manner considered best by them. He said : 'It is only by providing opportunity to the people that they can be trained to shoulder responsibilities. It became imperative that a bold step be taken whereby more and more responsibility could be transferred to the people. People were not merely to be consulted but effective power was to be entrusted to them. Therefore, we decided that in every village there should be a Village Panchayat with more powers as also a co-operative society which will help its economic efforts'. For details, See. *Jawaharlal Nehru's Speeches*, Vol. IV, September 1957 – April 1963, New Delhi, Government of India, 1964, p. 93.
6. See. *Report of the Committee on Panchayati Raj Institutions* (Chairman: Ashoka Mehta), New Delhi, Government of India, 1978.
7. As young Prime Minister of India, Shri Rajiv Gandhi took great initiative for transferring power to the people at grassroots level. In this direction, his government appointed the following committees to provide the necessary suggestions and recommendations for strengthening the Panchayati Raj Institutions, as Self-Sufficient Village Republics. See. (*i*) *Report of the Committee to Review the Existing*

Administrative Arrangements for Rural Development and Poverty Alleviation Programme (Chairman : Shri G.V.K. Rao), New Delhi, Government of India, 1985. The G.V.K. Rao Committee recommended to make districts as the basic units of planning and favoured holding of regular elections to the panchayat elections. *(ii) L.M.Singhvi Committee Report* (Chairman : Dr. L.M. Singhvi), New Delhi, Government of India, 1986. The L.M. Singhvi Committee recommended for devolving more financial resources to panchayats so as to make them more viable. The Committee viewed panchayats as the base for democratic and republican operations of the nation. *(iii) Report of the Sarkaria Commission on Centre-State Relations*, 2 Vols, New Delhi, Government of India, *(iv) Report of the Sub-Committee* (Chairman : Shri P.K. Thumgan), New Delhi, Government of India, 1988.

8. While participating in the debate in Lok Sabha on the 64th Amendment to the Constitution Bill on 13th October, 1989, Shri Rajiv Gandhi said: 'I toured hundred of villages. I spoke to countless people. There in their hearts and homes I experienced the cruelty of an unresponsive administration, the oppression of an administration without a heart, the callous lack of compassion that most of our people find at the heads of much of our administration'. For a full text of Shri Rajiv Gandhi's statement of 64th Amendment Bill, See. 'Power to the People', *Rajiv Gandhi's Speeches*, New Delhi, Ministry of Information and Broadcasting, Government of India, 1989.
9. The 73rd Constitution Amendment Act, 1992 provided constitutional status to the Panchayati Raj Institutions. The Amendment also institutionalised a three-tier system of panchayats (except for states with a population of less than 2 million), with panchayats at the village, block and district levels, but, what is revolutionary in this Act 'political empowerment of women'. For more details, see. *The Constitution (Seventy-Third Amendment) Act, 1992*, Gazette of India Extraordinary, Part-II, Section-I, New Delhi, Government of India, April 20, 1993.
10. The NDA Government headed by Shri A.B. Vajpayee has constituted a 13-member National Commission, under the Chairmanship of the former Chief Justice of India, Shri M.N. Venkatachaliah and asked to provide a comprehensive suggestions and reforms. The commission asked to study in depth on three important areas—whether the political system needed to be decentralised, whether to continue with the parliamentary system and if the electoral system required a second look. For details, See. *The Hindu*, February 2, 2000.
11. For more particulars on the recommendations, See *Report of the National Commission to Review the Working of the Constitution*, (Chairman: Shri Justice M.N. Venkatachaliah), New Delhi, Government of India, 2002.

12. See. Text of the National Decentralisation for Local Self-Governance – Recommendations, *Kurukshetra*, April, 2002.
13. In order to implement the 73rd Constitution Amendment Act in letter and spirit, the United Progressive Alliance (UPA) Government has created a separate Ministry of Panchayati Raj. With this tireless efforts, for the first time in Independent India, the Panchayati Raj Institutions received all the development funds from the Government of India directly as per the recommendations of the 12th Finance Commission of India. For this purpose, all the PRI's have been opened their Bank Accounts exclusively. For more details, See. *Text of the UPA's Common Minimum Programme*, New Delhi, 2004.
14. In the history of Indian Panchayati Raj, for the first time, the Ministry of Panchayati Raj (MOPR) came into being with effect from 27th May, 2004, under the Ministership Shri Mani Shankar Aiyar, a key partner in drafting the 73rd Constitution Amendment Act.
15. For full text of the Prime Minister's Speech, See. *Text of Dr. Manmohan Singh's Inaugural Address at the Conference of Chief Ministers on Rural Poverty Alleviation and Prosperity through Panchayati Raj*, New Delhi, Government of India, 29th June, 2004.
16. For a penetrating discussion on the establishment of Panchayati Raj System in India, particularly after the 73rd Constitution Amendment Act, See. Mani Shankar Aiyar, 'The Panchayat System: A Major Innovation in Empowering People', a lead paper read out at the Conference on *Making Democratic Governments Work—Connecting Principle and Practice,* held at Ash Institute for Democratic Governance and Innovation at Harvard University, on 13th April, 2005.
17. India consists of 537 District Panchayats, 6,097 Intermediate Panchayats and 2,34,676 Village Panchayats. It has 11,825 elected representatives at the District Panchayats level, 1,10,070 elected representatives at the Intermediate Panchayats level and 20,73,715 elected representatives at the Village Panchayats level as on 30th April, 2006. For state-wise details. See *www.panchayat.gov.in.*
18. See. *Annual Report 2005-2006*, Ministry of Panchayati Raj, Government of India, New Delhi, 2006.
19. For an interesting debate, See. George Mathew, 'Ministry of Local Government in India : Need of the Hour', *The Grassroots Governance Journal*, Vol. II, No. 2, July-December, 2004, pp. 305-309.
20. As part of fresh initiatives, the Ministry of Panchayati Raj organised Seven Round-Table Conferences between July and December 2004, which covered a multiple of topics relating to as many as 18 dimensions. The details of Seven Round-Table Conferences are given below :

Sl. No.	*Date*	*Location*	*Subject for Discussion*
1.	23 and 24 July, 2004	Kolkota	Effective Devolution, Comprising Functions, Functionaries and Finances, as well as empowerment of Gram Sabhas.
2.	28 and 29 August, 2004	Mysore	Planning and Implementation, including the Questions of Parallel Bodies, Rural Business Hubs.
3.	23 and 24 September, 2004	Raipur	Reservations in Panchayati Raj, comprising Scheduled Tribes (including implementation of Panchayat Extension to Scheduled Area Act) Scheduled Castes and Women.
4.	7 and 8 October, 2004	Chandigarh	Panchayati Raj in Union Territories; Panchayati Raj Jurisprudence.
5.	28 and 29 October, 2004	Srinagar	Annual Reports on the State of the Panchayats (including preparation of a Devolution Index).
6.	28 and 29 November, 2004	Guwahati	Panchayati Raj Elections and Audits.
7.	17, 18 and 19 December, 2004	Jaipur	Capacity Building and Training for Panchayati Raj Institutions, IT enabled e-Governance for Panchayats.

21. For a complete recommendations of the Seven Round-Tables on Panchayati Raj Institutions, See. *www.panchayat.gov.in.*
22. See Mani Shankar Aiyar, 'Towards Time-bound Panchayati Raj—Tenth Anniversary Plan of Action', in D. Bandhyopadhyay and Amita Mukherjee (Eds.), *New Issues in Panchayati Raj*, New Delhi, Concept Publishing Company, 2004, pp. 18-38.
23. For useful insights and fresh perspectives on the future vision of Panchayati Raj Institutions, See *(i)* D. Sundar Ram (Ed.), *Panchayati Raj and Empowering People : A New Agenda for Rural India*, New Delhi, Kanishka Publishers, Distributors, 2007; *(ii)* D. Sundar Ram (Ed.), *Dynamics of Grassroots Governance in India : Dreams and Realities*, Vol. I & Vol. II, New Delhi, Kanishka Publishers, Distributors, 2007.

2

Panchayati Raj in India: An Instrument of Grassroots Development*

MANI SHANKAR AIYAR

Mr. President, the Director of AGRASRI, distinguished academics, friends, elite of Tirupati town, ladies and gentlemen.

Today is Rajiv Gandhi's birthday and I am truly honoured to be invited to deliver the First Bharat Ratna Rajiv Gandhi Memorial Lecture, 2002, at AGRASRI, Tirupati. This is also a somewhat emotional moment for me, because it was thanks only to Rajiv that I was able to have the opportunity of being associated with what, I regard, is the single most important and revolutionary development in the country since we proclaimed our Constitution in 1950.

It would have been much better if we were to celebrate today among the people of India rather than within this rather small group of the elite of Tirupati. Nevertheless, a beginning has to be made somewhere and it has just taken us ten years to make this beginning. Ten years after the passage of Part IX of the Constitution, if we are able to inspire about 150 people to think about Panchayati Raj on Rajiv Gandhi's birth anniversary, then you have clearly got a very, very long way to go. And what is more, I don't think we can rely at all upon the intelligentia here, in whom Dr. Sundar Ram places so much trust, to do any of this work. It will have to be done by the people who dwell at the grassroots. It will have to be done. It will have to be done by people who do not share your cultural values or your moral values either. Panchayati Raj will be a truly grassroots institution or it will remain a subject of seminars. So long as it remains the subject of seminars, I do not see much future for it. What we need to do is to get it instituted at the grassroots. Have we got it instituted the grassroots? The answer is a thundering yes. If we leave aside the one state of Arunachal Pradesh which is an exception for a reason, every other state of India has held at least one set of Panchayat elections, most two sets of Panchayat elections under Part-IX of the Constitution and others have had Panchayati Raj Institutions of one kind or another for many years before the Constitution Amendment.

Indeed, Rajiv Gandhi would be the first to acknowledge, he was the first to acknowledge it and he did not hesitate to say that he was deeply influenced by what Sri N.T. Rama Rao did here in Andhra Pradesh, what Sri Ramakrishna Hegde and Abdul Nazeeb Saab did in Karnataka, what Sri Jyothi Basu and others did in West Bengal. He was the first to acknowledge the contribution of non-Congress leaders to Panchayati Raj. But, at the same time, he was not willing to buy the Left Front myth that only the non-Congress people have got good ideas and all Congressmen are rogues. He pointed out that in Gujarat and in Maharashtra, we have continuously, since Independence, had very effective structures of Panchayati Raj.

And there are parts of India, of which very little is known, most tragically, which have demonstrated in their own way what is truly meant by grassroots development. For, I cannot think of better example grassroots development in India than a state that is exempted from Panchayati Raj and is allowed to have its own system. I refer to Nagaland and its very effective Village Development Councils.

Therefore, I think what we need to ask ourselves is not how to despair but how to go forward. Rajiv said in 1989, when he was introducing the 64th Amendment in the Lok Sabha, that we may be the world's largest democracy, but, without Panchayati Raj we are also the world's least representative democracy. We have approximately 500 elected Members of the Lok Sabha, about 300 so-called indirectly elected Members to the Rajya Sabha, and approximately 4500 MLAs. in the country as a whole. Approximately some 6000 people to represent a billion human beings. When we look at the House of Commons in UK, we find that for a country of 55 Million people that is 120th the size of India, the number of elected MPs is 100 more than in the Lok Sabha.

In my constituency I only represent about a million people, but there are countries in this world which have less people than

I have in my constituency. We have some very big one's too, the whole population of Norway is equal to three Indian constituencies. The whole population of Denmark is equal to five Indian constituencies. The whole of Sweden is equal to eight Indian constituencies. The whole of UK, and this applies also to France, is approximately equal to 55 Indian MPs. The USA is equal to just about 200 MPs. So, when we are talking about democracy in India, we are not only talking about democracy for Indians, we are also talking about democracy for 1/6th of humanity. Now, who can say how much blood has been spilt, how many billions of people have been killed so that Germany could be freed from Hitler, Italy could be freed from Mussolini, Japan could be freed from Tojo and Vietnam could be freed from the French and then from the Americans. When you think of how much struggle there has been in the world to attain a small measure of freedom, you will understand what a remarkable country you are living in.

Today, we are the most representative democracy in the world. There are now 30th lakh elected representatives. We are the only country in the world that has ensured that 10 lakh of them are women. In the USA, until Hillary Clinton gets elected sometime in the 21st century, they are never going to see one woman leader. Apart from Margaret Thatcher who has been a woman Prime Minister in UK, till today they have not had a woman as the President of France or Chancellor of Germany, but the longest serving Prime Minister of India has not been a man, it has been a woman.

I could have delivered this lecture on the basis of going through everyone of the Articles that are numbered 243, from 243A to 243Z, and then because we ran out of letters, to 243ZN. I could easily base my lecture on these matters, but for one thing. You are all sufficiently highly educated and sufficiently interested in the subject to be able to read those Articles of the Constitution yourself, and in the light of the literature on the subject, as well as your personal experience, to see what is the degree of success that we have attained in implementing Panchayati Raj.

I would also commend to your attention a document that has recently been made public, copies of which are under print and will be available to any one who cares to ask by the end of this month. This is the 37th Report of the Standing Committee of Parliament on Urban and Rural Development on the implementation of Part IX of the Constitution, that is, what was called the 73rd Amendment. I have stopped using this phrase because the bill was the amendment. It was passed ten years ago and if we are still thinking in terms of the Bill, then when are we going to think in terms of the Act. So, since the Constitution is now sanctified with Part IX and Part IXA which deals with the municipalities, I prefer the expressions Part IX and Part IXA to the expressions 73rd and 74th Amendments. This is for a substantive reason, not a reason of form. In this Standing Committees Report, you will find analysis of a very detailed kind, and data which is both official and substantial and conclusions which I hope the nation will progressively come to accept. So, I am not going to allow myself to get lost in the nitty-gritty. I would be very happy to meet with anyone of you who is more interested in specifics and talk to you about it. Alternatively, after you have read my article in the 'Economic and Political Weekly' which does go through actually virtually every Article, you can get back to me, and I would be very happy to correspond with you and share views with you. But lets look at what our Panchayats can do and understand it sequentially.

The single most important thing about Panchayats, and without that we cannot even begin to go further, is to understand the expression that is used in Article 243G which defines panchayats as 'institutions of local self-government'. They have to be, seriously, institutions of local self-government and until they become that, what you are left with is the shell. It is coming to the panchayats, the reservation for the weaker sections and the women, that's all there, but you have to fill the shell, and for filling the shell you can stand back and say it's the right coconut only when they really become institutions of local self-government. But, when we use the expression local self-government, we have limited it to local self-government for two purposes. The first purpose is for the preparation of plans for economic development and social justice, and second, it is for the implementation of programmes of economic development and social justice.

So, the panchayats, as far as the Constitution envisages, are instruments of economic development and social progress. Traditionally, they were institutions for dispensing justice, within a framework which was extremely unjustifiable, and unfortunately, there are panchayats still, today, which think their job is to grab hold of a girl from a Brahmin family who has married a boy from a Harijan family and then burn both of them together, while the villagers dance around the fire; or to drag some unsuspecting widow onto the fire and watch her burn with her husband and say 'Oh ma sati, Oh ma sati'. This is not the panchayat's job nor is the job of the panchayats to handle law and order. May be, that should be their job later, but at the moment it is not the job of the panchayat to deal with law and order. To begin to solve the problem of poverty, the measure that Rajiv Gandhi devised and put in place was constitutional sanctity to panchayati raj institutions defined as institutions as local self-government for planning and implementation.

Therefore, now that it has taken us the better part of 10 years to arrive at the stage where panchayats actually exist, what we next have to ensure is that they are given something to do. And what is it that they are supposed to do? It's a full agenda. We will think of everything they should do. If they are allowed to do planning and implementation for the 29 subjects that are listed in Schedule XI of the Constitution, that is really more than enough, much more than enough. Now, these 29 subjects are not mandatory, they are optional. But most state governments and state legislatures have been far too lazy to apply their own minds, and therefore wholesale, or virtually wholesale, those 29 subjects have been incorporated in the state legislations, and this is happening in Andhra Pradesh as well.

Everyone knows if we look at the law, what are the subjects that are supposed to be devolved to the panchayat, but what one doesn't know is whether they have been devolved or not, for the process of devolution involves the 3 Fs—Functions, Functionaries, Finances. The functions have been devolved in the law, because it says the following subjects are devolved to the panchayats, and the matter is over, its been devolved. But, if the functionaries remain with the state governments line departments, then where are the personnel available to do either planning or implementation at the grassroots? And then, if the funds are not made available for the functions that had been devolved to the institutions to which devolution has taken place, the devolution remains on paper, it doesn't become a ground reality. So, after having first asked yourselves what are the subjects to be devolved, and I really don't care for all 29 to be devolved, if you feel happy, take two, but devolve them, and devolving means you must not only devolve the function on paper. You must supplement it with the devolution of functionaries and finances.

Andhra Pradesh desperately requires primary education because primary education in your state is a disgrace. Tamil Nadu, next door, has moved far ahead to the point where, today, birth rates are the same or actually even less than in Scandinavia. How? because all girls go to school. When I say all girls, I don't mean 100 per cent but I mean something like 97 per cent–98 per cent, there are some more that get left out. They all go to school, but please remember they don't go to school to study, they go to school to eat the noon-day meal. It was Kamaraj who started it and M.G. Ramachandran who spread it, and all economists said that this is rubbish, but the minute there was a reliable, cooked, noon-day meal, all the mothers who were insisting that their elder daughter must remain at home to look after the younger child found that it was more economical to send their girl to school than to keep her at home and the little one had to also be sent.

The headmaster also arrived on time because he was illegitimately eating the food and somebody had to open the cupboard to take out the contents, the rice. They had to be given to the lady who was doing the cooking in schools. Tamil Nadu has become the owner of the biggest source of employment for distressed young widows; they have found a job which they can do, and there, it takes time to cook, it takes about four hours to get the food ready. So, in those four hours, pass your time by doing something called studies. But, if in four hours, in some way or the other, a young girl is exposed to some form of study for 6 or 7 years, at the end of it she knows enough Tamil and has picked up enough English to learn the 7 letters that are at the heart of the Tamil Nadu revolution, 'Copper T'. And every girl by the time she is getting married, knows she can control the number of children that she is going to have and it doesn't matter which is the idiot she is going to marry, she has the good sense to know- how to control the number of children, and because she has got the education, she generally tries to get some kind of job. Where, in the marriage market of 30 years ago, if a girl was employed, she couldn't find a husband, the revolution today is that unless the girl is employed, she can't find a husband. So in many areas, many of them have only one child and the root of that is the mid-day meal scheme.

In Kerala, the revolution started early when the Nayar Service Society brought to the entire Nayar community the benefits of education which the Brahmins reserved for themselves. Then came Sri Narayana Guru who ensured that girls went to school. Today Kerala has the highest literacy rate in India. Look at Goa, it is not too far away; they have, I think, outstripped even Kerala and Tamil Nadu. So, why is Andhra Pradesh so backward? One of the main reasons is that primary education, which ought to be done at the primary village level, is administered from Hyderabad. All the teachers belong to the state cadre. The school buildings are built by the State Governments and the headmaster is sent from Hyderabad. His main job is to keep the local MLA happy so that the local MLA writes to Dr. Kesava Rao or his successors, to keep me here or transfer me there, whichever the case may be, and whether the teacher or the headmaster come to school or not is not the business of the local community. The Parent Teacher Association has no role in it. The village gram sevak, what a funny name, the one thing that he doesn't do is 'seva', but the so-called gram sevak is the one who files the report which says the headmaster is a wonderful man, the children love him. Of course, they love him, they never seen him and the primary teachers on time at 7 o'clock in the morning. You will have to be there at 7 o'clock to see whether that man is there or not. The children are there but the children are not writing the report. That is why you have such a poor rate of literacy and education in A.P. Just compare it to your neighbours.

Now, primary education according to your state act is a devolved subject. According to the law, it belongs to the panchayats. But who is actually running it in the absence of functionaries? There are the teachers. There are the cooks for the mid-day meal. These are the functionaries. Unless the functionaries come under the control of the village panchayats, how is the primary school going to be properly guided? And funds, do you need the funds to build an extra classroom, to get two more teachers, to do the playground, to build a compound wall or to put in a lavatory for the girls? We found through experience that this is a very very important thing. If the mother feels that her 13 year old giri is going behind the bushes and some naughty boy is trying to peek at her through the bushes, she takes the child out of school. But, if she knows that there is a toilet to which the child can go, then she will ask the child to remain, it's a crucial element for stopping dropout rates for girls and ensuring the education of India. People think in these terms, so if you have got a limited sum of money, who is going to decide what is the priority? What is happening now is that whatever the sum of money in Hyderabad, they say so many classrooms will be built, so many toilets will be built, so many compound walls will be built and then it goes down to the district level. Then the politicians say, we can't build compound walls everywhere, so we will give one wherever somebody votes for the Telugu Desam. It's a systemic rot.

What you need to do is to send the money. Say, I don't have more, Rs. 20,000 is available, you take it, we will try to make it Rs. 30,000 next year but if you want to make it Rs. 30,000 this year, collect Rs. 10,000 from the teacher, from the village community, and do what you like with it and let the village decide whether those 30,000 are going to be used for classrooms or kitchens or lavatories or sports grounds or compound walls or more teachers or raising the salary of the teachers. If you do this, then you will get local control. It applies to primary schools, it applies to everything else that matters. Our President referred to the Ashok Mehta Committee Report in which he correctly declared that the Centre is doing many things the state should do. But the Ashok Mehta Committee Report is very outdated. It is now 20 years or more and what we know is that the villain of the piece is generally the State Government. The Centre has proved through Part IX and Part IXA, that it wants Panchayati Raj; it is the State Governments that are holding back. If primary education is entirely transferred to the Panchayat budget, then what will the Minister of Primary Education do and why should any MLA go to the Minister any more, and in the state those people will have to go and sit at the door of a harijan who has become President of the Panchayat, and that this is why Panchayati Raj is not getting its due. You need to transfer the functions, you transfer the functionaries, put all the school teachers under the charge of the Panchayat. You allow the Panchayat to decide what salary is going to get paid then we will see competition among the Panchayats.

If this country has to have a solid Panchayati Raj system, that's the way to do it. So, if we can pick these 29 subjects, fine, they are the model but you prioritize. If you can't do all the 29 at one go then, say at least some of these in this year 2004; we are going to fully devolve all three functions, functionaries, finances. 5 in this year only. For another 5, only functions, and functionaries but not finances and then say by next year finances for these 5 also. It truly requires political will to do so. It is important, and this is a point that our Report has stressed, and I hope we will pay more attention to it. It is not enough that you have a three tier Panchayati Raj system. You also have to decide what is to be devolved to which tier, because if you devolve it all only to the Zilla Parishad, then the Zilla Parishad Adhyaksha will become more powerful than today's Minister and therefore the problem will be doubled and the solution will not be found. In Karnataka, they have stipulated in great detail, which part of the devolved function is to go to which tier of the Panchayati Raj system.

And the most obvious example to give you is that there are in this country five kinds of roads. There are the National Highways which are the responsibility of the national government at the Centre. Then there are State Highways which are the responsibility of the State Governments. Then you have the major district roads, those are obviously the responsibility of the Zilla Parishad. Then you have the other district roads which should be the responsibility of the Mandal Panchayats working together within districts, and then you have roads and link roads which should be the responsibility of the Village Panchayats. So, if you have got 100 crores of rupees available for road development, the State Government should say that out of 100 crores I am keeping 50 crores on State Highways, then I am dividing the remaining 50 crores on basis of 1crore per district. Of the remaining 20 crores, I want to give 10 crores of these for maintaining other districts roads to the taluka panchayats, that is mandal panchayats. And the last 10 crores, I am not asking for much, it goes directly to the village panchayats, for these are village roads and link roads; give it to them to build it. They can easily say that this money is enough for one kilometer, but we need it for two. Then we say it is very simple. You get Shramadana done in the village, you know all the basics of laying a road for 2 km through Shramdana. You have enough money left to do the tarring for one of the 2 km. You leave it to them, you allow them to raise any funds they want, on the basis of what the Constitution, Part IX, says is 'appropriation'.

That's a special word we put, 'appropriation' means you raise revenues which you don't send to the state consolidated fund but use it yourself. Now, let me give you an example. Lets say that village panchayats decide that every person who owns cattle must give so many rupees tax per head of cattle. Now, the rich man in the village says, what is this rubbish, I have to pay more and this fellow does not have a single cow, he is going to get away free, why should I pay then? You say that all the money we raise, we will use for a veterinary centre in the village, then the same rich landlord says that the biggest beneficiary of the veterinary centre will be me, because I have got the largest number of cows and if the Harijan doesn't pay, what does it matter, he doesn't have a cow anyway. So, there are techniques that are available, appealing to the self-interest of villagers as well as the self-interest of individuals, by which you devolve, and clearly say which function is to be done at which level. If you can, you start getting a logical system of administration, and then you say that the assistant road engineer shouldn't get posted in the village, what's he going to do there. He must be posted at the district headquarters and his junior engineer, may be let him go to the Mandals. But as far as the village thing is concerned, let us have a job, not in the village, how many roads get built in the villages, let it be in the Mandal headquarters. This job will be to travel `to all the village panchayats and help them with construction of their roads and it applies to everything else. Agricultural extension, irrigation, maintenance of culverts, bring every subject under this. But, if you have to do this successfully, you have to identify which part of which function is going to be performed at which level, and then devolution of finances must follow that pattern, and the devolution of functionaries must follow that pattern. Once you do this, then the panchayats at all 3 levels actually get empowered.

And that brings me to what has agonised A.P. The answer to 3-tier, 5-tier, ZPTC, MPTC which is the nonsense argument promoted entirely in this state and no other state of India because you made a mess of what you needed to do. You imposed the new Panchayati Raj system on the old Panchayati Raj system, the Mandal came into existence as the alternative to the village. Now, under our 3-tier system, since you have to have village panchayats you should do away with the Mandal and how can we do away with the Mandal? In two ways. You are welcome if you want to define village panchayats as Mandals, nobody stops you, in which case you go back to your Mandal system but your Mandal is your lowest tier. Either the Mandal is the lowest tier, or it doesn't exist here.

The other way is that you can also constitute your intermediate panchayat at a much higher level than the village, and call it a Mandal if you like. I have no objection, you can use any word you want, but that is the only way of getting away from the A.P. sickness, which is that this is the only state of India which has defined the constituency of a directly elected Village Panchayat President as being exactly the same as the Mandal Panchayat representative and then defined the constituency of the Zilla Parishad member as the constituency of the President of the Mandal. It's a completely self-inflicted wound, and then you call this a 5-tier system, where are the 5-tiers? One-tier is the Village Panchayat, one-tier is the Mandal Panchayat and one-tier is the District Panchayat. Please tell me where are the other 2-tiers? You call members of the Panchayat a tier, this is an abuse of the English language and it is a gap of logic and common-sense. It is like saying that we have got a 500-tier Parliament system because there are 500 Members of Parliament and yet amazingly everyone in A.P. from your Chief Minister and MLA, including Congress MLA's down through to the smallest journalists in Tirupati, they all say 5-tier without asking themselves, where are the 5-tiers? There are only 3-tiers and if the rest of the country is happy with 3-tiers, why are you not happy with 3-tiers? You won't be happy with it, because the ZPTC and the MPTC member look like tiers, because their constituency is the same as the President of the lower level. Where else in India do you have this system? Nowhere, it is only Andhra Pradesh that has this system, and that is because you don't know whose children you are. Are you N.T. Rama Rao children or Rajiv Gandhi children, make up your minds. You can't be both, and I said at the start here that Rajiv Gandhi was deeply influenced by N.T. Rama Rao because the mandals that he envisaged were instruments of development.

And Rajiv said, anybody who takes the development process to the grassroots level is to be emulated, not to be criticized, so N.T.R. was one of his gurus but like every good 'shishya' is supposed to not just repeat what the guru teaches but think about it, Rajiv said, if you have a Mandal Panchayat without a Village

Panchayat then how do you get a proper gram sabha going. In a Mandal you have got several thousand inhabitants, and if these inhabitants are supposed to constitute the gram sabha, there's no way in which you can gather all these people together, so what do you have left? You have a panchayat, an executive body, but with no legislature to check it. That is called dictatorship, and today if the Sarpanches of AP are a set of dictators, if the Mandal Panchayat Presidents are a bunch Pervez Musharraffs and if the District Panchayat Presidents in A.P. are a collection Hitlers, it is because at the village level this gram sabha is not empowered. And in the Mandal, the MPTC man has no work to do because he is given no work to do, and in ZPTC and ZPs members have no work to do because they are given no work to do. What you have created are 3 little dictators who want to be on the right side of government servants, all of whom are named by the Chief Minister. There is an unholy nexus which has developed between the Village Panchayat's elected President and the nominated gram sabha. Then, the other nexus is between the Mandal Panchayats elected Presidents and the BDO. And at the top another nexus-elected Zilla Parishad President and the Collector or the BDO. These 3 sets of dictatorships have ruined the name of Panchayati Raj, because for most people it is even worse than it was in the past. Not only that, this empowerment, re-empowerment of the bureaucracy in A.P. goes by the name of 'Janmabhoomi'. All those who did not take 'Janma' in this 'Bhoomi' have been empowered. And the bane of this country is that in Delhi we have Ramajanmabhoomi and in Hyderabad Janmabhoomi; between these two there is a complete ruination of the Panchayati Raj process that is going on. We can only solve it if we get back to the spirit of N.T.R. I am pro father-in-law and anti son-in-law. N.T.R. was a genius in saying, lets us have elected representatives at the grassroots. His definition of grassroots may be different to mine but the concept was the same.

Let us have elected representatives at the grassroots who will deal with the problems of people who live at the grassroots. Now, I don't know whether N.T. Rama Rao ever actually read the Sarkaria Commission Report, but in this Sarkaria Commission Report, there's one little line that fascinated me when I came across it, which says something to the effect that most people spend most of their lives concerned with the problems of their neighbourhood. The Iran-Iraq war is not of deep interest in the villages in Tirupati.

Nor is the battle between Sonia Gandhi and Atal Bihari Vajpayee, a very serious matter in the local village. What is the problem in the local villages is what in Tamil Nadu we call scarcity of water and electricity. Is there a street light, is there a water handpump; is it functioning; can we ride up to the main road. These are the problems of the people and only the people know what the solutions to those problems are. If you give them the authority to solve them, they will solve them.

I have a very personal example on this, which I would like to share with you. I was a Member of Parliament from Tamil Nadu constituency of Mayiladuturai from 1991 to 1996, and it was after I was defeated in 1996 that the first set of Panchayati Raj elections were held there and when I got re-elected in 1999, we had had three years of Panchayati Raj. Then elections were held to local bodies in 2001. So we now got a second set, and it is my practice to wander from village to village. That's about all I do, and when I go to a village I do my best to avoid the agraharam, partly because for no fault of mine, I was born a Brahmin and largely because there are no Brahmins left in agraharams because they all fled to California. But I avoid the agraharam. I avoid the more prosperous parts of the village and I head straight for the dalit basti which is mostly Hindu dalits but sometime Christian dalits. So, I concentrate when I visit the villages, I actually visit the Harijan Basti's in village after village. When between 1991 and 1996 I was an MP, the standard complaint before I got out of the jeep was "no light, no water". So much so, that if the villagers were feeling a little shy about speaking, my own chaps would say for them "no light, no water". It did become a ritual that in every village there would be neither light nor water. And this I found extraordinary because Tamil Nadu is very highly developed with regard to infrastructure for light and water.

There is not a village in my constituency which does not have a street that is not connected with electric poles. There is electricity everywhere, I mean, at any rate there is infrastructure for electricity everywhere. And although the situation has worsened somewhat owing to the dog in the manger attitude of Karnataka which is not giving us our share of water, at that time 10 years ago, with the handpump in almost every village, you could get water, and there were handpumps everywhere and there were overhead tanks everywhere. Every side I looked around me, thousands of crores spent by a very development conscious state government under successive development conscious Chief Ministers.

There is provision everywhere for light and water and yet everywhere you go "no light, no water". So I started trying to examine why this was, and then I discovered the truth of the matter, which I use to often speak about in explaining why we need Panchayati Raj. There was no light because the tubelight in the village street would burn out. But nobody in the village had the right over the funds, government funds, to replace that tubelight. So they couldn't buy it because the government had not given them the money and if they bought it from their own funds, the government would ask why have you touched government property. So, the village officer, we call them village officers what you call gram sevaks, used to make an account every year, budget how many tubelights were needed and forward it to the BDO at the middle level, what we call the 'union' and what you call the 'mandal'. Then all the requirements of the village streets would be added together for the block and it would be sent to the district. The District Collector would then add up all the tubelights that were needed in the district and send it to Chennai, where they would count up all the requirements of all the districts, which would be a nice big some of money. At this point, the Secretary in the Ministry concerned, would go to Bangalore or somewhere and hold negotiations with Mysore Lamps about how many tubelights to buy at what price. By this time, it was lakhs of tubelights. And the negotiations would move forward, may be on the telephone to Chennai, telling the Minister who had said, 'Not one rupee more than 50', that those fellows were saying 'Not one rupee less than 60'. So, the negotiations would continue, it would come down to, '54 is the maximum we are ready to pay' and those people would say, 'No, no, no, 56 is the least at which we can give it'. At which point the Minister would telephone his Secretary and say 'You come back, I will handle the negotiations myself'. And he would carry with him 2 suitcases, one of which would be full of his clothes and the other would be empty, and he would arrive there and sit down and have a discussion. And, when this discussion ended, the price would be fixed at 55 per tube light and the Minister would return with his clean clothes having become dirty and his empty suitcase having become full. Somebody had to pay for that full suitcase, so what he would do is, 'OK, two lakh tube lights, send them one and a half lakh, who is going to sit and count one by one how many there are'. So, so many tubelights have got left behind in Mysore Lamps. The remaining were distributed district-wise. When they had been distributed district-wise, the Collector would then distribute whatever he had received, block-wise.

After they have been received by the BDO he allocates them for the Panchayats where he has his own village gram sevaks. And, he gives to each of them 2 tube lights. This gram sevak says to himself, 'Who knows how many have been given to me?' So, he sells one in the bazaar and takes one with him to the village. He puts it up in the village, there is wild excitement because light has returned after one year. But, there is one little boy who has forgotten completely as to what it was like to have a tube light in the street. So he gets up, he looks up at night, he sees there is a huge tower in the sky and to check out if this is true, he picks up a stone and he flings it and the tube light goes and for the next one year there is no light.

Now, Panchayati Raj in Tamil Nadu is much worse than in Andhra Pradesh because they never had an N.T. Rama Rao there, but one of the rights that has been given under Panchayati Raj, is the right to the village Panchayat President to buy tubelights. The other right that has been given to the village Panchayat President is to buy 5 rupee washers for hand pumps. In this term as an MP from the same constituency of Mayiladuthurai, going to the same villages, and visiting the same dalit bastis, nobody is saying "no light, no water". Now, because of this drought, I heard again for the first time in 3 years some concerns being expressed about water, but 'no light' is not being said anywhere.

To my mind it proves that if you endow the panchayats with powers of the kind that they should be exercising, then you will secure the results that you are looking for. So, this devolution of the 3 F's must be made with a full recognition of what it is the Village Panchayat should be endowed with. There are some things which should not be endowed. There are, for instance, environmental considerations.

Recently, 'The Hindu' has a story which breaks my heart, because after having been involved with Panchayati Raj for 12 years, I do not know the answer to that problem. There is a woman village panchayat president in some village in Tamil Nadu who wanted to increase the revenues of the village panchayat. She discussed it with her fellow panchayat members and they decided that certain trees that they believed were not of much use them be cut and sold, and that money should be used for panchayat development activities. So armed with this resolution, she made arrangements with contractors for those trees to be cut and for the proceeds thereon to be credited to the panchayat account. The Collector has now come to know that these trees were cut. Infuriated that the environment was wrecked, he has dismissed this lady. She was removed from her position. There is no politics in this because she is an AIADMK Panchayat President. The Collector is serving in an AIADMK Government, so we are not talking politics. He is fulfilling his responsibilities to the environment and she is fulfilling her responsibility to the panchayat, and for the 32 trees that have been cut, she has lost her job whereas most Prime Ministers of India have kept their jobs after having cut or drowned 32 lakh trees for every dam. Nor, do I as an opponent of non-sustainable development believe that trees should be felled. I am therefore opposed to what this lady did.

But, I, as a Member of Parliament, am in favour of letting the village decide whether a tree should be cut down or not cut down. And I don't know how to resolve this. But, back to the story that is given in 'The Hindu', I was reading it just before coming down here. I think it's on page 3. The Collector is saying she has to know what the rules are. And she says, 'But there are 84 government orders, which am I supposed to obey?' Now you ask yourself, do you want an elected panchayat President to be a bogus IAS officer who understands 84 orders but does not know 84 words or do you want somebody who understands 84 words but cannot read what your 84 orders are. These are things we have to think of and say very strictly, for example, that the preservation of trees is the responsibility of the Collector, not the responsibility of the Panchayat President, and that, if, therefore, the Panchayat decides to cut the trees, it is the job of the gram sevak to tell the Collector that they are about to cut the trees and the Collector can come there and stop them from cutting trees. But the Collector does not implement his own order. The poor woman cannot read that order. She takes a decision which is entirely in concurrence with views of all the elected panchayat members, and for all I know the money raised by 32 trees being felled is much more important to the village than the shade that the 32 trees give. The answer to the problem, obviously, is that if she wants to cut 32 trees to raise so many thousands of rupees, and you want to preserve those trees, then give out those thousands of rupees then she won't cut those trees. That's true Panchayati Raj—but the way it is being implemented, is by an English speaking Collector who knows how to put on a tie, has passed out first in Mussoorie and has all the qualifications that are completely irrelevant to the job he is doing. And this woman, just a woman, has become President, who has made her President? That, partly on one hand, is Rajiv Gandhi, because he reserved the seat. But the second hand is hers, because there must be any number of women who wanted to become the President of that Panchayat. She has beaten them all. She has become the President of the Panchayat. And, what do I care whether she is educated or uneducated, what do I care whether she is a literate or an illiterate. What do I care that she probably came to that village when she was 13 or 14 years old, having been illegally married to some drunkard. At that stage, she came there and she lived there. She has now reached the age of 40, God bless her, I hope she will go till 80, but she would live all her life not knowing much more than the courtyard of her home, the street on which she lives. And the direction which she gives, goes up to the panchayat. Does she know that village or does the MP for Mayiladuturai? What do I know about that? What can Mr. K.C. Pant sitting in Delhi know about it? What can Prof. Hanumantha Rao sitting in Hyderabad know about it? So this devolution is also of mindset. Against your 3 F's–I want to add an M to it—it is the mind. You trust them, you say, they can do the job better which you have given to them. And to assess them, I think, we must progressively get the IAS and the provincial service out of the district and levels below that.

In each district let us have a District Panchayat Service, where the typical career path will be a boy or girl of age 21 or 22 becoming a Village Level Officer and at the end of his or her career, one of them, like one of us in my batch, becomes a Foreign Secretary and the others do not. Like that, one of their batch becomes the District Collector.

Now, you don't have this sickness in Tamil Nadu as you have it in Uttar Pradesh, but I don't know what the situation here is. There is a huge transfer industry in Uttar Pradesh, they are constantly transferring their officers, because it's a big state and today you are sitting in Muradabad, you have just put your child into school, five minutes later you are told to go to Robertsganj, before you can reach Robertsganj, you receive your transfer orders to Gorakhpur. For the sake of your family, you turn to the Chief Minister to say, 'Anything you want, Sir', or 'Madam'. You ask, 'What do you want'? and you are told, 'I want you to do the following illegal things, and your child can continue with its education', or you say, 'I am going to beat the system by putting my child in Nainital in the boarding school'. And your wife is crying that she can't see the children, and she can't see you, because you are wandering around the district. So you say, 'OK, let the wife go and sit in Nainital'. And what does this man do, sitting in a village without family, without friends, with nobody there who speaks his language. So the whole system is breaking down.

We need to have a District Panchayat Service, so that this evil of transfer based political corruption is controlled, if not abolished. Because, if you threaten a man with transfer from one panchayat to another, within the same district, he is not going to be concerned. Also, by the time he becomes the District Collector, he will know the district like the back of his hand. Now, the British system was, "If he knows it like the back of his hand then, because he is an Indian, therefore he can't be relied on. Let us have an Englishman who does not belong to this, who is not a Hindu, not a Muslim, not a Brahmin, who is not a dalit, who is therefore 'nispaksh'. He is above the whole system and he will evenhandedly meet out justice". After what all of you have suffered with these IAS District Collectors and the PCs, BDOs and all these corrupt fellows at the Patwari level, is this the way to run this country? I would much rather have an elected Sarpanch doing corruption, than have a non-elected village patwari doing corruption.

However, this can be solved if you have a gram sabha that functions like a legislature to which all decisions have to come. Lord Mountbatten was Governor General in Council. He had to get his Council, at least, to agree. That Council is the panchayat. All panchayat members must be involved in all decisions and all decisions taken by panchayat as a whole must be ratified by gram sabha. Then only you will get democracy at the grassroots. And to have a gram sabha that is reasonable the village panchayat has to comprise say 300, 400 adults. If it is bigger than that, if you start having a Mandal Panchayat as your lowest level where you have 2000 members, how can you have a meeting of 2000 people? So, if you do have a Mandal Panchayat at the lowest level and I am not going to stop you if that's what you prefer and that's what Karnataka have said they have preferred because of the Ashok Mehta Committee report it was Ashok Mehta who introduced this Mandal concept. But I would say, whatever the size of your Village Panchayat, if it's too big, follow the Kerala example of neighbourhood sabhas, that is a ward sabha. In Kerala, every ward has a gram sabha. Now, this is an ingenious answer to the problem, because I was astonished to learn from a Panchayati Raj expert from Kerala, that these are altogether less than 1000 village Panchayats in Kerala. And I was astonished, because in my own constituency I have 451 Panchayats. So, if in one Parliamentary Constituency, I have 451 and in an entire state, they have only double that number, obviously, their village panchayat populations are very, very large. But, they have solved this by saying that the Panchayat President and the village panchayat, with the bureaucrats concerned, will go from one neighbourhood sabha to the other, one ward sabha to the other. And the same system is being implemented in Rajasthan also.

So, we need to move towards effective people's control, and for effective people's control, there is a model Act which we already have. It is meant only for 5th Schedule areas and Andhra Pradesh has one of those areas where you have the 5th Schedule, but is not being implemented there, like it is not being implemented anywhere else. But the Act exists. That Act, which was passed by Parliament is called the Provisions of Panchayat Extension to Scheduled Areas Act, 1996. It was passed in 1996. It gives three functions to the gram sabhas, which, I think, we should be made universal, not just for Scheduled Areas but for everyone. One, it says that no plan can be implemented unless it is approved by the gram sabha. So the plan is implemented after the approval of the gram sabha. This applies also to the drawing up of projects and programmes. So, anything you want to do, you first go the gram sabha, you say, "I intend to do this", and if the gram sabha says "Yes", you can go ahead and do this. Second comes beneficiary identification. Now, this can also be extended to area beneficiaries, not just people. If there is going to be a well dug, where should it be dug, that kind of a thing, plus the usual beneficiary identification for an anti-poverty programme. That this self-help group should get the money, not that one; this Harijan widow should get the money, not that zamindar's wife, that kind of a thing, beneficiary identification. And third, authorization for the issue of utilization certificates. Now, this is to take care of the fact that the money which has been sanctioned and released to build a road is not then pocketed by the village patwari, the sarpanch and the contractor between them and the road doesn't get built. The gram sabha says that yes, the job has been done, it has been done well, so we authorize the issue of the utilization certificate, without which they cannot get additional funds. If these 3 functions are given to gram sabhas everywhere, you will get meaningful results.

Now, under the Janmabhoomi, you have a gram sabha. But it is convened by the bureaucrat, it is not convened by the politician. It is convened for huge numbers, there is nobody there to check whether the resolution was passed or not, and the bureaucracy certifies that at the gathering came all the SCs, STs and women, where all of them unanimously applauded. This is called Janmabhoomi. Why have a Janmabhoomi programme run by the bureaucracy when you have got a Panchayati Raj programme that is to be run by the panchayats. It is a complete lack of sincerity in implementing not only the Constitution of India but the Act passed by the A.P. Legislature.

And, I felt, when I first came across Janmabhoomi, which was in a hotel in Hyderabad, that this is not going to work, because when the ad came, what did you see, you saw a bullet train, you saw a skyscraper, you saw an aeroplane flying in the sky and this beautiful song was being sung, which I couldn't understand. It said that this Janmabhoomi is going to bring all this to you. You go to any village in A.P., and you ask them is your top priority a bullet train, they all ask you what is a bullet train. And you tell them about building a skyscraper, they will give you the answer that was given to me in my constituency, when I was trying to develop it as a tourist area. In Tryankybar, Tarangambadi, Sonia Gandhi had come to unveil the statue of Rajiv Gandhi, and I made a speech in which I said, you see that ground there, we are going to develop it into an airport and the planes will land directly, I said, from Delhi and Chennai. And somebody in the audience said, 'Just get the Porayar bus to run on time, that's enough'. I learnt Panchayati Raj at that time. So its not skyscrapers, bullet trains and aeroplanes in the sky what we are looking for, it is drinking water, electricity and teachers in the schools, doctor's in the PHC's and somebody to look after the cows in the veterinary centre, a culvert that is broken, to get it repaired, that is what the people of India are looking for. They are not asking for the moon, they are asking for the earth and we can't give them the earth. And why do we have to give it to them? Let them take the earth, by empowering them to take it from us.

I have only finished about 5 per cent of my lecture. I think I have taken too much of your time already, and therefore instead of continuing this talk, I will bring it deliberately to a conclusion, but keep myself open to any specific questions that you might have to ask about any other matter. Since you have been such a good audience and have been listening so attentively to what I have said, I request all of you to arm yourselves with greater information about this by reading this article in the 'Economic and Political Weekly' which is translated into Telugu for all of you. And also, get hold of the 37th Report of the Parliamentary Standing Committee on Urban and Rural Development, try to see whether at least the recommendations given in bold letters, you can put those together and translate it in Telugu and make those available. Then, we will see what is the progress, how far we have come and how much further we have to go. I would have given up in despair if we had not succeeded in anything; it is because we have succeeded up to a point, that I have not given up hope and I still see a bright future.

But, I recall, and this is where I end with what Rajiv Gandhi talked to me about, referring to a book on the Soviet Revolution in 1917 by John Reid which had the title 'Ten Days that Shook the World'. Rajiv said that ours is not a ten day revolution, its going to take an entire generation. So, I will admit defeat 15 years from now, if after 25 years we haven't succeeded, but, until then I live in hope. I am sure our villages will truly become the source of the prosperity of India, because, Bombay Stock Exchange Sensex going up is a complete irrelevancy. One little child getting a full belly, going to school and being able to find a doctor in case it falls ill, that is what I regard as prosperity, that is what I think Gandhiji meant, when he said, 'India lives in our villages.'

---

* Text of First Barat Ratna Rajiv Gandhi Memorial Lecture delivered by Mani Shankar Aiyar on 20th August, 2002 at Tirupati (A.P.), under aegis of Academy of Grassroots Studies and Research of India (AGRASRI), Triupati.

3

Panchayati Raj Institutions in India: Power to the People

SUBHASH C. KASHYAP

The philosophy, motivation and historical evolution of the Panchayati Raj Institutions as also the structural-functional parameters and nuts and bolts of the entire machinery in operation need to be studied in depth and widely debated, and not only in the academia or among professional seminarians but by the people at large.

The most fundamental tenet of democratic polity is that sovereign powers vest in the people. It is in the exercise of that power that they are supposed to frame a Constitution for themselves. That is why the preamble to our Constitution speaks of "We, the people of India hereby adopt, enact and given to ourselves this Constitution."

The transfer of power from the hands of the British masters took place on 15 August, 1947. The Constitution was adopted on 26 November, 1949. With its commencement on 26 January, 1950, the Sovereign Democratic Republic of India was born. On that day, if not earlier, power was supposed to have come to the people. But the very fact that scholars keep talking of decentralisation or transfer of power to the people is proof enough that all these years power has been in the illegitimate hands of some usurpers and even after more than fifty years of the Constitution and the Republic, it has still to reach the people where it really belongs. The ordinary Indian in his hut and hamlet has still to feel the dawn of independence, the glow of freedom or the transfer of power to his hands. Masters have changed but the colonial model of the rulers and the 'subjects' continues. In a genuine democracy, the ordinary people should be respected as the real masters and all the administrators, legislators, ministers and judges should regard themselves as their servants. Both the rulers and the ruled are citizens of the country with the former charged with responsibilities of serving their fellow citizens.

Unfortunately, in another sense also, we still think in terms of the 1919 Act and talk of the central government, central laws etc., even though the Constitution discarded these terms and ordained us to talk in terms of the Union and the People of India.

The 64th and 65th Amendment Bills inspired and initiated by Shri Rajiv Gandhi which later became the 73rd and 74th Amendments were the first major constitutional efforts with the stated objective of transferring power to the grassroots people. The basic question was, from whom was the power being taken to be given away to the new local tiers of governance. The facts are that the powers that were proposed to be transferred, were hitherto those vesting in State Governments. As we know, the 64th and 65th Amendment Bills were lost in Rajya Sabha by 3 votes.

P.V. Narasimha Rao as Prime Minister succeeded in seeing through Parliament the two Bills in somewhat diluted form. The 73rd and 74th Amendments laid down the framework and guidelines in regard to the obligation to holding regular elections, restricting the period of supersession, providing for reservation for SC/ST and women etc. It was perhaps very unfortunate that instead of relying on the Election Commission a parallel and separate state election machinery was provided. It should be possible to somehow integrate the two and avoid duplication and frittering away of national resources—both financial and man-power.

The 73rd and 74th Amendments left a great deal for implementation by State Governments through state laws to be passed by their legislatures. Whether as an institution or as an individual, no one ever surrenders power voluntarily. The result has been that most grudgingly and reluctantly and at the last minute, different states have passed law which are at considerable variance with each other and in varying degrees try to deny the substance of functional and more particularly financial powers to the directly elected representatives in the PRIs The local MPs and MLAs consider the new emerging leadership in the Panchayats and Nagarpalikas as their rivals in the power structure who threatens to take away a share of the cake.

Despite all the imperfections and loopholes needing to be plugged it must be agreed that the 73rd and 74th Amendments have the potential of bringing about revolutionary changes in the political power structure and system of governance. It would bring a change in the federal structure of Indian polity from a two-tier to a three or four-tier system and one may add that with 3.2 million elected rulers Indian democracy could become a unique model for the whole world.

If we are really serious about providing multi level governance and taking power to the doorsteps of the people at the grassroots, the Constitution should clearly provide for distribution of powers between the Union, the States and the local governments of Panchayats and Nagarpalikas by suitably amending Articles 245, 246 and other relevant articles and the Seventh Schedule. It would certainly do no violence to the basic structure or features of the Constitution or to the Parliamentary system. It has the potential to powerfully contribute to the needs of good governance and development.

The 73rd and 74th Amendments left the question of association of MPs and MLAs to be tackled at the level of states. Accepted at that time as a political compromise, this needs to be looked at afresh from the angle of constitutional propriety and clean and people friendly governance. If the aim of PRIs was to reduce the unhealthy role of MPs and MLAs as power brokers, the decision of some of the States to include them in PRIs with or without votes does not seem to be justified. MPs and MLAs would have to come to appreciate that their role is that of law makers and policy setters at the Union level for the whole of India and at the state level for the state as a whole. Local matters must be left to be handled at local levels by the representatives of the people elected to the local bodies. Also, executive functions have to be left to executive agencies at concerned levels. Schemes like the MP and MLA LADS—Local Area Development Schemes with some 3000 crores of public money involved are, an affront to the constitutional principles of distribution of powers between the Union and the States and separation of executive and legislative functions. Also, these schemes make the financially bankrupt PRIs look insignificant and powerless with each MP and MLA having large funds at his disposal for spending on local area schemes which are most legitimately the concern of PRIs under the 73rd and 74th Amendments. Even if largely suggestive and illustrative, the 11th and 12th schedules to the Constitution become irrelevant if Members of the Union Parliament and of State Legislatures exercise executive powers in matters of local development otherwise supposedly reserved for Panchayats and Nagarpalikas.

One can delve deep into the functional details of PRIs. Much can be said about the contradictions and infirmities in different state laws, the working of State Finance Commissions, State Election Commissioners, District and Metropolitan Planning Committees, etc. But, all the shortcomings notwithstanding, grassroots democracy unleashed by the 73rd and 74th Amendments has come to stay and as time passes, its financial and functional domains will get extended. It can only get more assertive and strengthened till sovereign power really comes to belong to the people and the Gandhian dream of building from below, of the bottom up rather than the top down approach can be fulfilled.

4

Institutions of Local Self-Government in India: A Distance Dream

L.C. JAIN

> "I have not pictured a poverty-stricken India containing ignorant millions. Establish village swaraj—make each village self-governing and self-contained as regards the essential needs of its inhabitants."
>
> —*Mahatma Gandhi*

Historical Basis of Self-Government

"I am not interested", said Gandhiji, "in freeing India merely from the English yoke. I am bent upon freeing India from any yoke whatever". What were these other yokes: deprivation, disparities, discrimination. The search for ways to rebuild an India free from these yokes proceeded along with the struggle against foreign rule.

Soon after Independence the Indian National Congress reiterated the "Congress Objectives" in a resolution of November, 1947: "The AICC welcomes the elimination of foreign rule in India and the establishment of a free and independent state and a government responsible to the people of the country. Political independence having been achieved, the Congress must address itself to the next great task, namely, the *establishment of real democracy* in the country and a society based on social justice and equality. This can only be realized, when democracy extends from the political to the social and the economic spheres." Further, it pinpointed that:

The smallest territorial unit (the village) should be able to exercise effective control over its corporate life by means of a popularly elected panchayat.

Constituent Assembly: Notwithstanding such commitment and clarity, and despite the fact that many stalwarts of the freedom struggle were also members of the AICC and the Constituent Assembly headed by Dr. Rajendra Prasad, the "popularly elected panchayat" failed to find a place in the draft Constitution. The draft came under sharp criticism in the Constituent Assembly. Congress leader Kamalpati Tripathi said, *The draft Constitution can hardly be called the child of the Indian Revolution.* In the whole Draft Constitution, "we see no trace of Congress ideals and Congress ideology... no trace of Gandhian social and political outlook ... *it is terribly Centre-ridden".*

The demand for a revision of the draft, however, could not be met as re-drafting, it was explained, might delay the finalisation of the Constitution. But the substance of the demand was sought to be met by addition of Article 40 among the Directive Principles of State Policy, which was adopted unanimously:

Article 40: The state shall take steps to organize village panchayats and endow them with such powers and authority as may be necessary to enable them to function as units of self-government.

While moving the above amendment, K. Santhanam put on record the intent of the Constituent Assembly in stirring terms:

What is attempted to do here is to give *a definite and unequivocal direction* that the State shall take steps to organize panchayats and shall endow them with necessary powers and authority to enable them to function as units of self-government.

That the entire structure of self-government, of independence in this country should be based on organized village community life is the common factor of all the amendments tabled and that factor has been made the principal basis of this amendment. I hope it will meet the unanimous acceptance.

However, the sad fact is that this "definite and unequivocal direction" was solidly ignored by the authorities in the first forty years (1950 to 1990) of the adoption of the Constitution. 50 years after Independence, there is not a single village out of 350,000 villages, which is self-governing. Is it surprising that we still have 300 million people who are poverty-stricken and as many who are ignorant–deprived of literacy; and there are starvation deaths in villages alongside with buffer stocks of 60 million tones—Gandhiji had advocated food self-sufficiency at village level as the primary task of village panchayats and had endorsed Vaikunthbhai Mehta's suggestion of a village level foodgrain bank to ensure that no single person goes hungry even for a day.

Rajiv Gandhi's Initiative in the 80's: At the political level Rajiv Gandhi as Prime Minister was disturbed at the lack of responsiveness of the administration and held wide consultations with administrators on how to give India a Responsive Administration. This churning led to realization on his part that Representative Government was fundamental to making the administration responsive. This process led to his sponsoring a Constitutional Amendment (64th) in late 1980's to put panchayats on a sure footing. This Amendment was however lost in Parliament—but on grounds other than opposition to the principle and purpose underlying the Amendment. The pieces were picked up by the next Parliament in early 1990's adding Amendments 73rd and 74th.

Scope and Substance of 73rd/74th Amendments

At long last, in 1992, the 73rd and 74th Amendments were brought to honour Article 40 of the Directive Principles to establish institutions of self-government from village upwards. The Amendments incorporated in two Chapters IX and IXA of the Constitution were supported by all Members of Parliament across parties barring one who dissented on technical grounds.

These Amendments indeed went further than Article 40, in their social sweep and significance. By providing for a definite minimum reservation for discriminated groups: Women, Scheduled Castes and Scheduled Tribes in the elected bodies (Panchayats/Nagarpalikas) and by requiring local area plans to include *social justice* along with economic development, the 73rd and 74th Amendments added explicit and dynamic social dimension to the pursuit of decentralization. Namely, to provide institutional under-pinning for systematic pursuit of several other sister Directive Principles besides Article 40, which too have hitherto remained mainly uncared for. In particular:

Article 38: State to secure a social order for the promotion of welfare of the people.
Article 41: Right to work, to education and public assistance.
Article 45: Provision for free and compulsory education for children.
Article 46: Promotion of educational and economic interests of Scheduled Castes, Scheduled Tribes and other weaker sections.
Article 47: Duty of the State to raise the level of nutrition and the standard of living and to improve public health.

Besides, the changes envisioned by these Amendments extended in their scope and sweep the entire system of governance. The mandate required active participation (*via* Gram Sabha/Ward Committees) of every single adult member of our one billion population. Thus, for the first time, an active role and responsibility were devolved on every adult citizen who was an eligible voter in the system of governance.

This historical perspective must since 1992 be borne in mind while assessing what has actually been done to implement the mandate of the 73rd and 74th Amendments. We must also remember that the Constitution is not self-enforcing. It relies on designated agents to promote its purposes and enforce its provisions. In the instant case the principal agents required to implement the above Amendments are: Parliament, Central Government, State Legislatures, State Governments, State Election Commissions, Gram Sabhas, Panchayat Raj Institutions, Nagarpalikas, National Finance Commission and the Planning Commission which though not a statutory body, occupies a critical place in the development domain—in planning, allocation of resources and periodic monitoring of progress and evaluation.

For enforcement the Constitution depends simultaneously on the degree of awareness and alertness of the people at large on the one hand and on the other faithfulness and firmness with which those who take the oath of office obey and advance its meaning and mandate.

Raising Awareness of Adult Population to Its Role and Responsibility

The dynamic responsibility placed on all the adult eligible voters via the Gram Sabhas and Ward Sabhas dictated the imperative of minimum Constitutional literacy imparted to all our electorate. It was self-evident that in the absence of informed mass support, the objectives of the Amendments could not progress satisfactorily and speedily. This was particularly necessary since the new system envisaged by the two Chapters IX and IXA had to be raised on a ground which was already heavily occupied by entrenched centralized approach and enormous powers vested in Ministries, Departments, Officials in Planning, financial and administrative spheres in the absence of popular panchayats.

Little has been done to promote mass awareness of the Constitution and the purpose of the Amendments. A 2001 study of degree of Constitutional Literacy by an independent body (CHRI) found that a majority of the people do not know the Constitution. And, as will be shown, the concerned authorities even if aware of the Constitution have not been sufficiently mindful of their duty to the Constitution.

Reforming Pre-existing Legislation in Conformity with the Amendments

Amendments of Existing Panchayat Acts: The enactment of 73rd and 74th Amendments foresaw that the states will have to amend existing panchayat legislation to bring them in conformity with the Constitutional Amendments. The State Legislatures were given one year to pass conformity Acts. Not all the new state legislations conform faithfully to the letter and spirit of the Constitutional Amendment—but even such provisions which they have incorporated are not being followed by the State Governments faithfully.

Modification of Previous Acts Relating to Subjects in 11th/12th Schedules: Another mandate of the 73rd Amendment was embodied in Article 243N, which required the States to review and alter all existing legislation relating to subjects assigned to panchayats and nagarpalikas as per Schedule Eleventh and Twelfth, to ensure that such pre-existing Acts did not impinge upon or thwart the autonomy of the local self-government institutions within one year.

Article 243N: Continuance of Existing Laws and Panchayats: "Notwithstanding anything in this Part, any provision of any law relating to Panchayats in force in a State immediately before the commencement of the Constitution (Seventy-Third Amendment) Act, 1992, which is inconsistent with the provisions of this Part, shall continue to be in force until amended or repealed by a competent legislature or other competent authority or until the expiration of one year from such commencement, whichever is earlier".

The fact is that Article 243N has not been heeded by any state. And, though a number of state enactments which became null and void after the expiration of one year from the commencement of the Seventy-Third Amendment in 1992, by virtue of their being inconsistent with the letter and spirit of the Amendment, continue to assail the autonomy of the panchayat raj institutions. A number of parallel bodies are functioning under these otherwise null and void enactments — some which pre-existed and some which have been set up contrary to law, after the Amendment came into force:

The parallel bodies in various states, may be broadly classified into those that were created in the Pre-73rd Constitutional Amendment period and those created in the Post-73rd Constitutional Amendment period. The first category (Pre-Constitutional Amendment period) include those bodies that were functional even before the 73rd Constitutional Amendment Act came into being, like the Joint Forest Management, Water User Groups etc.

The second category (Post-Amendment period) includes those bodies that were constituted after the 73rd Constitutional Amendment Act came into being, e.g. the Expert Committees in Kerala, Janmabhoomi in Andhra Pradesh, Vigilance Committee in Himachal Pradesh and the Gram Vikas Samiti in Haryana. These bodies are the creations of the respective state governments.

The following table provides a glimpse into the areas overlapped by the parallel bodies and the relationship of the parallel body with PRIs in the respective state.

No.	State	Parallel Body	Areas of overlap/ substitution	Institutional Linkage with P.R.Is.
1.	Uttar Pradesh	Water User Groups (WUG)/Site Implementation Committee (SIC)	• Formulating, developing and approving plans of the area covered by the WUG • Selection of beneficiaries (farmers) • Construction, maintenance and management of link and main drains • policy decisions like decision on rates of water charges	Village Pradhan may be the ex-officio chairperson of the SIC.
2.	Haryana	Gram Vikas Samiti	Supervision of construction of work out of the funds released by H.R.D.F. Board, decentralised planning or any other state government scheme	The samiti consist of 4 members of gram panchayat—Chairperson Sarpanch Elected Members — one panch each from SC community, BC community and a woman panch.
3.	Kerala	Expert Committee	Preparation of panchayat development plans	Technical advisory body to the panchayats regarding the plans prepared by the panchayat.
4.	Andhra Pradesh	Janmabhoomi	Planning and implementation of development programmes at the local level.	Sarpanch and the concerned ward member finds representation in the Habitation Level Committee of Janmabhoomi.

(*Contd*)

No.	State	Parallel Body	Areas of overlap/ substitution	Institutional Linkage with P.R.Is.
5.	Gujarat	Joint Forest Management	• Cultivation, collection and sale of minor forest produce • Conservation and maintenance of common property resources	• A representative of village panchayat will serve as one of the members of the mandal or committee. • Village panchayat itself may become a mandal or committee for the purpose of J.F.M.
6.	Rajasthan	Watershed	Minor Irrigation	Panchayats can become Project Implementing Agency (P.I.A.) for watershed projects on priority basis.
7.	Himachal Pradesh	Vigilance Committee	Supervision of gram panchayat works/ schemes costing upto Rs. 50,000/-	Supervisory body within gram panchayat of the works, schemes and other activities of Gram Panchayat.

Source: PRIA (2001); Parallel Bodies and Panchayat Raj.

Thus laws which have become null and void are being kept alive to thwart, if not sabotage the working of the Constitution Amendments.

The Central Government has also failed in its duty to the Constitution. It does not appear to have challenged the continuation of these null and void Acts—administratively or in the Courts. In fact, it is knowingly aiding and abetting in this defiance of the Constitution by providing substantial funds to parallel structures of the type cited above.

A refreshing example however is an analytical and cogent discussion by S.M. Vijayanand, Member, 2nd State Finance Committee, Kerala in a discussion paper: Issues Related to Administrative Decentralisation and Administering of Decentralisation—Lessons from the Kerala Experience, June 2001:

There are several structures particularly at the district level consisting of officials and non-officials, generally nominated, discharging functions which have been transferred to the local governments—like DRDAs, FFDAs, various societies under Health Department, etc. These were constituted at a time when there were no democratic bodies at the local level. But now they have lost their relevance. Normally they have two components—a professional component and a political decision-making component. The latter one has to give way when democratically elected bodies emerge or else they can end up as parallel power centers. Ideally the professional wings should serve the local governments. Kerala has already abolished DRDAs and is in the process of restructuring FFDAs/BFDAs A similar restructuring of various Committees would be required.

Implementation

The pillars of the 73rd and 74th Amendments on which the "institutions of self-government" were to be erected and assured of certainty, continuity and strength supported by key statutory instruments: (1) State Election Commission and (2) State Finance Commission:

1. Time bound and regular elections to panchayats and nagarpalikas.

2. Devolution of functions, powers and resources such as to enable these elected bodies to function as an institution of self-government.
3. Constitution of District Planning Committees to harmonise and consolidate area plans for *economic development and social justice,* which are mandated to be prepared by village panchayats.

Concluding Remarks

When India took control over its own destiny in 1947, there was the promise of the freedom movement that political power will not be concentrated in few hands but will be widely shared with the people. This promise has been observed more in the breach. It is yet to be redeemed. Given the entrenched Centre-ridden mindsets, the future prospects are dim.

The main reason behind such a disturbing view is that those who are governing India have steadily liberated themselves from the history and dreams of the freedom movement. What is worse there seem to be a number of persons in the government at all levels who in the fashion of Winston Churchill are not convinced that people are fit for self-government. Hence, all their genius and ingenuity is employed to constantly invent ways to frustrate rather than further the Constitution.

One notable exception in this bleak scenario are the latest "Guidelines" of the Ministry of Finance as a follow up of the excellent and Constitutionally correct Report of the Eleventh Finance Commission. They set a pre-condition that states will receive their share out of the special allocation by the Finance Commission, only if they certify that they have implemented the basic provisions of the 73rd/74th Amendments. These guidelines represent rare, positive and committed vote in favour of 73rd and 74th Amendments. One prays they prevail and sustain.

5

Federation of Panchayati Women in India: Beginning of a Social Transformation

V. MOHINI GIRI

The 73rd Constitutional Amendment introduced by Shri Rajiv Gandhi is a major step forward in strengthening and revitalising of Panchayats, the third-tier of governance. The important provisions of the 73rd Amendment are regular elections at village, intermediate and district levels, reservation of one-third seats for women and reservation for SC's and ST's including for the office of the chairpersons, Constitution of Finance Commission, powers to raise resources.

What is sought to be achieved by the 73rd Amendment is to make Panchayati Raj Institutions instruments through which people could fully participate in the development process and it would promote genuine devolution of powers, functions and resources to local bodies the state level.

A significant feature of the 73rd Amendment to my mind is the provision for one-third representation to women in the elected bodies as well as reserving one-third of the offices of chairpersons for them. This provision has had far reaching consequences in India's social and political life. In a traditional society like ours, women, particularly in rural areas, are often prevented by cultural barriers from interacting or participating with menfolk and outsiders in matters of common interest. Further, there is ample testimony to the male bias in our society.

Traditionally, rural women are confined to child bearing, child rearing and household duties and work outside only to the extent assigned to them. Their participation in public life is minimal. As a result, women suffer from an innate sense of bondage and dependence. They have a low self-esteem and starts with the premise of that they cannot do too many things which the menfolk can do and further they are not designed to do several things which lie exclusively within the domain of men. This myth-foolish myth has only been perpetrated by a Patriarchal society to ensure the exclusive dominance of the patriarchs. The 73rd Amendment has for the first time in our country paved the way for rural women's participation in social, political and economic fields. In order that the rural women prepare themselves for this role it is essential that they are first convinced about their separate individual identity. They have to be made aware of their immense potential and capability. They must be inspired and activated to have their own aspirations, ambitions and social role. The quality of leadership amongst rural women has to be encouraged and allowed to grow so that women can develop confidence in decision- making, can identify their own problems, priorities and preferences and use their own wisdom, knowledge and judgement to suggest ways and means to resolve them.

Governance is a very broad concept while democracy has many shades. As somebody puts it, democracy is like a hat which has almost entirely lost its original shape in the process of it having been worn by many. It has to be acknowledged that a working definition of democracy has to be that of participatory system which provides adequate, unhindered, universal opportunity for all the promotion of an equitable and sustainable social and economic order. For achieving optimum results in a democracy, there has to be a partnership accord between women and governance, ensuring as also safeguarding individual liberty and dignity and common interests. In almost all cases, the failure of Government. In the words of Subhash C. Kashyap, it was mentioned that "governance has become a casualty of Government" with Government themselves more concerned with survival rather than attending to the needs of the people.

Panchayati Raj thus gives a great deal of importance where people themselves articulate for the first time. Because of women in Panchayati Raj women come to the centre stage thus bringing about peoples participation. Women's participation in the political process is the giant leap that will take us towards a truly gender bias free society. Once involved in political decision-making, her face is to be reckoned with both within society and the family. The sense of achievement in actually helping to make things change is the greatest fillip to self-esteem. And as I always say—you respect yourself and the world respects you.

Since democracy thrives through democratic institutions, it is not an isolated and insulated phenomena. The effectiveness or usefulness of democracy would depend upon the structures supporting it. Panchayati Raj can really be effective if the quality of that democracy means that everyone, and especially the poor and the marginalised like backward social groups and women, have access to decision-making levels through in built appropriate strategies so that their voices are heard and heeded. Further, as is the present case in our national government, democracy based on the principle of "consent" is more beneficial. The success of democracy, insofar as it concerns women would definitely be tested on the question of sensibility, sensitivity and suitability to answer to the needs of feminist concerns, though not divorced from society, nation and international interest.

Prof. Sushila Kaushik conducted a study on Stock Taking of Participation of Women in Panchayati Raj in 6 states in India under the aegis of the National Commission for Women. This study aimed to examine the patriarchal and myopic, critique of women's functioning in Panchayati Raj (rural local self-government), and to find out the problems faced by them in the course of their work and the ways in which they cope up and seek to overcome the same.

The working of panchayati raj and the participation of women in the same, has to be understood at the local level and in the local context. The present study, hence, deals with the experiences of panchayat women in six states of India—Haryana, Madhya Pradesh, Orissa, Rajasthan, Tamil Nadu and Uttar Pradesh.

Most of them faced opposition from political parties. The patriarchal view of men and even women considered that women were not capable and they were not fit for politics. Some women candidates also found illiteracy and lack of economic resources to be handicaps. Quite a few women also found social environment to be unfriendly and the purdah system disabling them. Domestic work, child care duties, lack of mobility partly due to social reasons, were also the main handicaps.

Many women were also subjected to votes of no confidence in Uttar Pradesh as their resignations will either enable the Sarpanch (often a male) to succeed or lead to a suspension of the panchayat and a new election. It will either way lead to a dereservation of the post. It is now believed that this sort of vote of no-confidence motion is being brought up repeatedly against women chairpersons who feel victimised.

Since independence, India's people have viewed their democracy with a sense of pride, and an appreciation that democratic governance is the key to a strong nation, a viable economy and a sense of social stability. A recent public opinion survey conducted in India revealed that two-thirds of Indians have confidence in the political system, a figure which is as low as 25 per cent in other parts of South Asia. A remarkable 93 per cent of those polled asserted that they vote in elections, displaying a high regard for the democratic system and its potential.

However having said that it is time that today we recognise the various loopholes that exist in the Panchayat Raj Act and take immediate steps to have these loopholes addressed. Naturally if you evolve a federation of Women Panchayats which I hope will spread throughout the length and breadth of the country, this federation will be a platform to advocate, lobby and bring about changes for grassroot empowerment.

A dedicated band of federation of working Panchayati women who are newly entering local political structures to ensure that they have the necessary training and resources to fully participate in local affairs. It is hoped that this federation would be prepared to work in partnership with India's women leaders as they create their vision and plans for a new future for their communities and for their country.

By ensuring the inclusion of women in local government, the 73rd and 74th Amendments are bringing Indian politics a step closer to a full reflection of the needs and wants of all of Indian's people, both women and men. The amendments represent an opportunity to focus on the priorities of development that women state as essential to themselves, their families and their communities. Furthermore, this represents the possibility of re-thinking leadership itself, so that it embodies the qualities of women in power, who value honesty, openness, patience, collective support, and accountability to the people they represent.

In order to participate in the Panchayati Raj Institutions, and in society at large, the Indian woman must first step forth from the enshrouding conditions that characterize her life. Her successful participation in the Panchayats is unquestionably linked to a process by which Indian society begins to break down the walks of tradition and custom that limit women's mobility and restrain their actions as key players in society.

Various societal supports, when created, can make room for women to act powerfully within society and thereby within its local political structure. To my mind district level federation would help the women in following areas:

Support within the Family

- Her husband and family encourage her participation in the Panchayats.
- Her husband and family assist her in household chores and family responsibilities, so that she has more time to engage in critical tasks as a Panchayat representative.
- Her husband and family accept the fact that she will be interacting with other men, and help her to overcome her shyness and reservation about doing so.
- Her husband and family understand the importance of her mobility, and allow her to determine her own movement outside of the home.

Support with the Community

- Local training programmes and workshops are created to empower women which treat gender issues and build their confidence, as well as analyze the particulars of Panchayat operation.
- Local training programmes and workshops are developed to enlighten men, by building their cooperative skills and treat gender issues.
- Day care programmes are made available so that children can be cared for while the woman is at work.
- Women's organization are created and strengthened so that women can exchange information and discuss ways to address their common problem.
- Women who have already served a term as panchayat leaders act as her mentors.

Support by Society at Large

- Government, NGOs and Civil Society institutions support her work by setting out funds for the Panchayats and making them easily accessible to women members.
- Government, NGOs and Civil Society institutions establish training broachers, satellite programmes, trips to seat of government and other special programs to facilitate her work.
- Political parties make the participation of women in Panchayati Raj an important plank in their platform, and support Panchayats in their interface with government.
- Media creates a supportive environment for women members by letting society know about their accomplishments, and by influencing public opinion in support of women's reservation and rights.

Political empowerment and consequent decision-making roles of women ensures harmony in society and paves the way for undisturbed economic and social progress, and more vitally the woman is able to view herself not just as a wife or a mother but as a vital factor in solving social issues. Her self-esteem is much higher a crucial factor in the development of equality. I want to recount a story of a woman elected to the Panchayat. She was asked to mediate a dispute between a Brahmin and different caste and she herself belonged to Brahmin community. She mediated the dispute successfully but when she came home her father-in-law was furious that she had given the judgement in favour of the other caste. That a rural woman's answer lit a great hope in me. She said "When I am in my official elected role I am not your daughter-in-law so do not interfere in my work outside the home. When I am at home, then I am your daughter-in-law." In the event of existence of such a federation women will remain confident and can interact with each other.

Recently we heard of small gram panchayat in Okha, Gujarat launching its own website. Such a federation would facilitate this kind of an achievement once again.

There is no doubt that women have traversed a long way in an uphill journey towards progress. However, they still have miles to go to achieve complete gender equality with social justice. Mere laws cannot ensure social transformation.

In the last five decades since India attained its independence, there has been a marked improvement in the quality of lives of many Indian women. There is a new awareness of women as a Vibrant entity, who can no longer be ignored or marginalised. What is most significant is that the Indian Women's movement has made the political leadership aware that there is a desperate need for reform. This consciousness marks the beginning of a change. A spark has been ignited by Rajiv Gandhi and during the coming decades, it will become a cleansing fire.

Thus, today this convention is of great importance which could not only realise Mahatma's dreams but enable women from all corners to interact with each other on a common platform. Let me tell you that Gandhiji also said that it would not be easy and I quote: "Self-government depends entirely upon our own internal strength, upon our ability to fight against the heaviest odd. Indeed, self-government which does not require that continuous striving tc attain it and sustain it is not worth the name."

6

Panchayati Raj Institutions in India: Real Powers and Responsibilities

C.B. MUTHAMMA

The Seventy-third Amendment to the Constitution, dealing with Panchayati Raj was a landmark measure which has the potential to transform this country by mobilising the people's power. It envisages, in effect, the handing over of power to the people to govern themselves. The word "Panchayat" in the amendment relates to the "Village, intermediate and district" levels. The "Powers authority and responsibilities of Panchayat" envisages that, subject to the provisions of the Constitution, the legislature of a state may, by law endow the Panchayats with such powers and authority as may be necessary to enable them to function as "institutions of self-government".

The statement of objects and reasons to the amendment points out that "Article 40 of the Constitution which enshrines one of the Directive Principles of State Policy lays down that the state shall take steps to organise village panchayats and endow them with such powers and authority as may be necessary to enable them to function as units of self-government. In the light of the experience of the last forty years and in view of the short-coming which have been observed, it is considered that there is an imperative need to enshrine in the constitution certain basic and essential features of Panchayati Raj Institutions to impart certainty, continuity and strength to them. Accordingly, it is proposed to add a new part relating to panchayats in the constitution..."

This new part, incorporated as Part IX in the Constitution, covers the subject extensively. In addition to spelling out that the Panchayat should be enabled to "function as institutions of self-government", it addresses the question of financing the panchayats. Several sources of funding are spelt out—viz. Powers for the Panchayats to raise taxes, funding by the State Government, and grants-in-aid from the consolidated funds of India. The 74th Amendment also deals with the question of financing of the Panchayat bodies.

The two amendments were published in a Gazette of India Extraordinary in April 1993—nearly a decade age. In the years that followed, how effective have the amendments and the new Part IX of the Constitution been?

It will be recalled that when the amendments were introduced there were some misgivings among state governments that their powers would be curtailed by the provisions. There were objections here and there that this was an attempt by the Union Government to go over the heads of the state governments to the people, and to interfere in what should normally be within the authority of the state government. From time to time reports have appeared in the press that this or that state government has not held elections to the Panchayats in their territories. Even in the case of the states that have established Panchayati Raj Institutions, these have run into a variety of difficulties. Given below are some illustrative cases, reported in the press.

Karnataka, which is a state that prides itself on having taken an early initiative to establish Panchayati Raj Institutions has cases which illustrate the problems. A few years ago, the state authorised the construction of a hotel in the Nagarhole game sanctuary. There was strong, widespread opposition in the district of Kodagu, in a matter that primarily affected the district and its population. It was clearly a case of the state government not only rejecting the views of the public but asserting its authority against the district in a matter in which the district should have had a say. If the Panchayati Raj provisions meant anything, they should certainly have pre-empted colonial-style authoritarianism, when what was required was to give a say to the people of the district. In the event a person from the district took the matter to the Karnataka high court which struck down the state government's decision.

Some months ago, a team of social scientists from a University in the state undertook a study of the working of the Panchayats in a selected district of the state. They discovered that in a case where the President of the panchayat was a woman from a backward class, she was prevented from functioning. To begin with, she was illiterate and needed to have the minutes of meetings read out to her, but she received no co-operation in this. In addition to it, the meetings were held in the local temple and the upper class members of the panchayats prevented her from entering the temple, so that, she was, in effect, prevented from attending the meetings. She was obviously a member of the panchayat under the women's and backward classes reservations provided for under the constitutional amendment. The team of academics found various other problems of this kind, so that the reservations provided were only nominally fulfilled and it actual fact nullified.

About a year ago there was a case reported about a village in Mandya district of Karnataka, where the people, after approaching the government year after year for various developmental projects, with no response from the government, resorted to a novel solution. At the last panchayat elections the villagers decided to auction the posts in the panchayat. Those who won the auctions were elected. The authorities concerned were obviously aware of what was happening, but there were no complaints of electoral malpractices, therefore nothing was done. The villagers thus had the funds for the works they needed to carry out.

A few years earlier, perhaps in 1998, a case was reported of children from a tribal village walking for three days through field and forest to get to the official dealing with tribal affairs, to tell him that the school provided in their area was non-functional. They reported that none of the staff, including the principal, ever came to school except once a month to sign registers to enable them to receive their salaries. The only person who came, they said, was the peon, who beat them up. Upon subsequent enquiry it was found that the staff also pocketed the funds allotted for mid-day meals for the children, who were not even aware that there was such a provision. This was not a question of inadequate funds, since the expenses for the entire exercise were being incurred. It was simply a question of the power lying with the state government, not with the village authorities. If the latter could have managed the school, including having the authority not only to pay the staff but to hire and fire them, the staff were most unlikely to have energed on their duties. But being the employees of a distant state government which was either unable or unwilling to actually supervise the functioning of the school meant that the staff was free of all control.

There have been comparable news reports from other states. Recently there was a newspaper recall of an earlier report from 1998 in the paper regarding another tribal school called Raite located about sixty-six kilometers from Nasik. The children of the school trekked the entire distance to meet the Tribal Development Commissioner to air their grievances. Their village was sixteen kilometers away from the nearest metalled road, and the dirt track that linked them was unpassable in the monsoons. There was no primary health centre or hospital. The so-called school hostel was a make-shift shed were children had got bitten by snakes and one child has died. The authorities had taken note of the problems only after the children's marathon trek backed by the press report.

The villagers obviously know what they need. But inspite of constitutional provisions, they do not have the funds or the scope for ensuring for themselves even basic necessities.

From time to time the press reports cases such as a village boycotting elections as the nearest polling booth was eight kilometers away, and there was not only no bus service but not even a proper road.

There cases might not necessarily reflect the overall situation. But they do point out to the fact that the state governments which have a crucial, in fact decisive role in the implementation of the Panchayati Raj provisions are not always willing to part either with the funds or the power, to the district and village authorities. But there are also local problems in implementation as discovered by the team of academics in Karnataka who took at the actual working of Panchayati Raj Institutions in one selected district in Karnataka.

In some cases, as in the case of the Nagarhole game park, an educated local citizenry is able to confront the state government. But even they are unable to cope wholly with recalcitrant district or municipal authorities in matters like clearance of rubbish, public hygiene etc. Local politics defeat attempts at ensuring good administration.

The experience of the study team of the Karnataka academics points to a possible way of ameliorating the situation. Perhaps the

Central and State Governments could constitute standing bodies from the civil society, including academics, journalists, professionals etc., to ensure that both the state and panchayat authorities do in fact conform to requirements. They could also be a point of appeal where the local citizenry, like the tribal children cited above, need help. Funds could be augmented from the developmental funds allotted to MPs and MLA's. The civil society groups, aided by NGO's, could, on the one hand, ensure provision of basic amenities such as schools, hospitals and roads in village and district areas, and on the other, acting as advisers, consultants and experts to the panchayats on developmental measures. Such bodies would have a beneficial effect where local politics present an obstacle to good administration, and on the other hand act as a life-line to distant and neglected village or communities who are in practice cut off from the mainstream. Such civil society/NGO monitoring groups could be a meaningful and live link between the Union and State Governments and the populace. They could be the instrument simultaneously of effective devolution of power and also of implementing national policies. In fact policies like compulsory universal literacy could be achieved faster if the implementation is left to district and village authorities, with the civil society groups monitoring both the full implementation by local authorities and the funding from various sources including the state governments. Problems like the Narmada Bachao Andolan, and less publicised smaller problems elsewhere of local interests being bulldozed by state and/or union authorities need not arise if our democracy can include institutions and procedures for the participation of affected populations in the decision-making process. In the Narmada case, the tribals of Madhya Pradesh make all the sacrifices, not only of land but of livelihood and cultural and spiritual milieu, whereas the benefits go entirely to other people elsewhere, backed by organised political forces. The aggrieved people have no say in the process; the decision is foisted on them in true colonial style, regardless of the totally adverse effect on that section of the population. If democracy and progress and self-government are the objectives, these methods are not justified. The so-called compensation also has been unilaterally decided and is stated not to have been fully implemented. Here again, participation by civil society, not just the Union and State

Governments, could, jointly with the populace concerned, perhaps have evolved a better solution.

It requires an alert and articulate public to see the fundamental flaws in the implementation of the Panchayati Raj provisions of self-government, or indeed the many other shortcomings in the implementation of the provisions of our constitution, which is truly democratic and people-oriented.

7

District as a Focus of Change: A Critical Element of Decentralisation

K.C. SIVARAMAKRISHNAN

It is almost a decade since the 73rd and the 74th Constitutional Amendments came into force. Even to the most casual observer, it will be apparent that the progress of decentralization in the country has been uneven and haphazard at best. At worst, new ways are being discovered in some of the states how to give powers to the panchayats and municipalities with one hand and take them away with another.

There is a major flaw in the perception of many people that the Panchayati Raj and Nagarpalika Amendments to the Constitution are initiatives of administrative and financial decentralization. The real purpose and intent of the constitutional changes was 'political'. This is not to use the term politics in a pejorative sense.

The late Shri Rajiv Gandhi was clear in his mind that the polity of this country could be preserved only if the doors of public participation were opened several times more. While introducing the Constitution 64th Amendment Bill on Panchayati Raj in Lok Sabha on 15th May, 1989, Rajiv Gandhi observed "the single greatest event in the evolution of democracy in India, the enactment of the Constitution, established democracy in Parliament and in the State legislatures. Putting together both houses of Parliament and all the State legislatures, we have only about 6000 persons representing a population of nearly 800 million. The number of persons holding elective office has been far too small in relation to the size of the electorate. As a consequence there is a vast chasm which separates the general body of the electorate from a small number of elected representatives. This gap has been occupied by power brokers, the middlemen and the vested interests. The super structure is strong (of democracy) but the foundation has been weak".

Today elections to panchayats and municipalities have been held in almost all the states of the country. In several states they have been held twice. The representatives from rural local bodies are as many as 30 lakhs. From urban areas the number is much less but it is significant and is about 60,000. It is to be emphasized that in the eyes of the Constitution, these elected representatives from panchayats and municipalities are on par with the MLAs and the MPs. The Panchayat Ghar and the Town Hall are sanctified as platforms of democracy as much as an Assembly or the Parliament. The Constitution does not envisage any hierarchy or class distinction among the elected representatives.

Yet, the political reality is different. MPs do perceive themselves as a somewhat superior group because of the large constituencies they represent. This arithmetic, however, gets diluted at the state level because there is not that much difference between the constituency of an MLA and the constituency of a person elected to the zilla parishad. In smaller states the distinction gets even more blurred. Obviously in such a situation the sharing of powers and responsibilities or in other words allocations of functional domain becomes an important question of turf. This has emerged as a major problem particularly at the district level.

The initial years of Rajiv Gandhi's Prime Ministership were characterized by his avid desire to learn as much, as quickly as possible. The series of meetings and workshops with the District Magistrates across the country in which Rajiv Gandhi personally participated was an important part of this learning process. Separately, he had also spent much time trying to understand the need and feasibility of disaggregated or decentralized planning in contrast to Yojana Bhavan as a highly centralized planning entity for the whole country. The District Planning Committee was envisaged as a possible solution. It should be noted that the District Planning Committee did not figure in the 64th Amendment Bill relating to Panchayati Raj. When the Bill was introduced in May 1989, the thinking on this item had not crystalized. Three months later, in August 1989, the 65th Amendment Bill on Nagarpalika was introduced. Recognizing that rural-urban divide was an artificial creation of colonialism, Rajiv Gandhi stated while introducing the Bill "the district is a composite of its panchayat and its nagarpalikas. Democracy and devolution must restore the interaction of rural and urban settlements so that the district as a whole prospers. With higher agricultural productivity greater incomes and larger employment and reciprocally urban prosperity being accelerated by linkages with the rural economy integrated development of the district, as a whole was essential. It is, therefore, proposed that a Joint Committee of the Nagarpalika and Panchayats be established to undertake this task", thus was borne the DPC. However, it was short lived. After both the bills failed to muster support in the Rajya Sabha and when they were revived by the V.P. Singh and Narasimha Rao governments, the district planning concept did not find a place in these revived versions. It was the Joint Parliament Committee which re-introduced the concept once again. Eventually the DPC became a part of the Constitution under Article 243 ZD, but the DPC has been a non-starter in many cases. Part of the problem is that the DPC is a stand alone committee though it is composed of the elected representatives of Nagarpalikas and Panchayats. In a few states like West Bengal, Kerala and Rajasthan the Chairman of the Zilla Parishad is also the chairman of the DPC and there are some effective functional links between the two. Unfortunately this is not the case in other states. As a result the DPC is either practically non-existent in states like U.P. or treated as an extension of the District Collector as in the case of M.P.

A major reason for the situation is that the Zilla Parishad has been wrongly categorized as a district level panchayat. It is neither a rural parishad nor an urban parishad. Its composition should therefore reflect the rural and urban composition of the district itself. The latest census indicates that out of 593 districts 165 districts have urbanization levels above the national average of 27.7 per cent. This is the direction for the future.

The district will be the platform where the urban-rural continuum becomes an economic planning as well as political-reality. To meet the challenge of socio-economic planning and development at the district level, we have to go back to the intent and purpose of the Constitutional initiative as expressed by Rajiv Gandhi. Addressing the District Magistrates during the workshop series on responsive administration Rajiv Gandhi had urged them in June 1988 to consider "how best to marry the institutions of Panchayati Raj with the requirements on district planning. Panchayati Raj without district planning might be somewhat a hollow shell, even as district planning without Panchayati Raj would be unrepresentative. Democratic district planning requires expertise. Your task here is to see how, without sacrificing technical excellence, district planning based on representative political institutions will reflect the peoples priorities and aspirations."

This task remains to this day largely unaddressed.

8

Role of NGO's and Administrator's in Grassroots Governance of India

M. GOPALAKRISHNAN

India has always lived in its villages i.e., three in four of its countrymen live there and are steeped in /poverty. Experienced administrators and committed Non-Governmental Organizations (NGOs) have began to come together to improve the lot of rural masses, particularly since the sixties of the last century. The Constitution of India has helped a little bit through its three-tier Government, to achieve the goals of planning. The initial "Trickle-down" effect by which our planners set much store has disappointed everyone by its inefficacy. So they changed tack and we now have efforts at full scale development programmes as well as real political and financial decentralization since 1993.

Government of India observed 1999-2000 as the "Year of Gram Sabha", the village council of governance. Many were initiated to empower gram sabhas beginning with the Constitution (73rd Amendment) Act, 1992 which, *inter alia,* provided for reservation for women in Gram Panchayats. Samities and Zilla Parishads. Direct devolution of finances from Central Government to those local bodies have also been planned for which the States have been asked to initiate legislative measures. Article 243G of the Constitution of India (COI) provides for the States/UTs to endow Panchayats by law with necessary powers to function as institutions of Self-Government and to make economic development plans.

In addition, Article 243H of the COI empowered State Legislature to enact Laws to authorize Panchayats.

(*i*) To levy, collect and appropriate some taxes, duties, taxes and fees.
(*ii*) To assign to the Panchayats some taxes etc., levied and collected by State Government.
(*iii*) To give grants-in-aid to the same bodies from the Consolidated Fund of the States.
(*iv*) To enable Panchayat to credit and spend money from above sources through creating funds constituted for the above purposes.

Article 243-I of COI provides for constitution, for a State, a State Finance Commission (SFC) to review Panchayat finances and suggest principles for devolution of funds to these bodies and to recommend to Governor suitably in the matter.

The 73rd COI Amendment Act, 1992 is a milestone in all these historical developments. It introduced.

(*i*) a three-tier system of Panchayat Raj (PR) for all States having a population of over 20 lakhs.
(*ii*) Panchayat-elections once in 5 years regularly.
(*iii*) Reservation of Seats for SC, ST and Women candidates to contest.
(*iv*) State Finance Commissions (SFCs) to be appointed.
(*v*) Constitution of District Planning Committees (DPCs) to make development plans for a district.
(*vi*) The empowerment of PR bodies for discharging their functions.

Now all these may sound very impressive. The questions being asked now are:

1. How to develop experienced village leaders who can handle the business of running Local Government?
2. How to equip them with necessary administrative infrastructure and administrative staff?
3. How to make them all function effectively and carry out their duties and responsibilities? To many it sounds like a tall order.

When India gained Independence in 1947 the same questions were asked. The following decades saw the grounding of many institutions along administrative financial and economic lines. Today we have no need at National or State levels to ask such questions as "How".

But when we talk of grassroots democracy some fundamental questions are being asked. Among them are:

1. Can any NGOs be encouraged and assigned Government grants to develop local cadres of village leaders to fulfil their new role?
2. Do any new/old type institutions need to be set up in rural India.
3. How to develop local talent to question and guide rural Government?
4. Can any National/State/Regional level institutions for Training and Research (including appropriate technology) be set up?
5. Schemes benefiting individuals and rural areas are all the time being ushered in by GOI as well as State Governments who should select beneficiaries—Central, State or Local Governments?
6. How to make transparent the functioning of these PR Bodies by developing the right (and access) to information so that there is a critical evaluation of these bodies.

After all, what are the goals of all these developments? Briefly they can be stated as follows:

1. To bring Governing closer to people in areas affecting them immediately.
2. To educate people to become better participants in local Government (and through that process) State and Central Governments.
3. To enable people to evaluate critically the performance of the representative who participate in Government.
4. How far are there each devolutions of powers (for self-rule and self-determinism) to the people at large?

All this requires, as stated earlier, educated masses, wise people who are already gifted with them tremendous common sense and new reading and writing abilities.

Sometime earlier I talked about Central and State Government. Schemes for benefiting individuals and institutions for research institutions in particular. The GOI has identified NGOs for this purpose. Most of these send proposals to the GOIs and State Governments For funding so as to enable the bodies.

(*i*) to educate the people in formal and informal ways.
(*ii*) to enable people to acquire skills to use the funds given to them.
(*iii*) to develop critical evaluatory skills to judge performance of the people in the functioning of schemes. There are number of such schemes in operation all over India:
  (*i*) Jawahar Gram Samridhi Yojana (started in 1999) which restructured the earlier National Rural Employment Programme (NREP) and Rural Landless Employment Guarantee Programme—RLEGP.
  (*ii*) Rural Roads being set up and improved.
  (*iii*) Rural Housing—Indira Awas Yojana set up in 1985 under which over 6 million houses are built.

For better rural housing capabilities, the setting up of Rural building centers with ability for technology transfer, skill upgradation and use of environment—friendly and Cost-effectives of this scheme cannot be overemphasized. Self-help 'groups' to be assisted to enable the rural potential to be built upon to enable them to become successful producers of valuable goods/services.

One can go on and on with enumeration of such schemes started during the last 4 decades. Many have picked up well. But the need for a greater and more dynamic role of NGOs is being felt all the time. They are catalysts of a high order.

To recapitulate, these organization (NGOs) have a vital role to play in both individual-benefiting and area-beneficial schemes like better forest use and development, waste and development, rainwater conservation and community use of resources. Thousands of crores of rupees are being spent annually. How do we ensure proper use? That is the big question.

9

Planning for Development at Grassroots in India: Tamil Nadu Experience

G. PALANITHURAI

Introduction

"Planning" in India is believed by everyone to be an exercise that can be done only by top level bureaucrats and technocrats with the direction of the policy-makers for the development of the whole country. The concept of planning as an exercise and process which can be done at the lowest level in the hierarchy of governing structure with the involvement of the people has also been posited to the policy-makers ever since India adopted planning as a legitimate government exercise but it did not gain any support (Raj, 1984). Committees were constituted to probe more into the details of the process and as a result reports were submitted (K.V. Sundaram, 1977). In the beginning of 1970s the dominant thought of keeping planning at the top become flexible to some extent as such planning had not yielded the expected results to mitigate the problems of the poor and initiatives at the provincial level that too at the sectoral level were allowed. It went still further in the 1980s with the initiative for planning being undertaken at the district level. The 1990s marked a historic departure from the conventional arrangements to achieve development so as to match globalization of economy and decentralization of powers and planning at grassroots was made mandatory to achieve development and social justice with the participation of the people (K.C. Sivarama Krishnan, 2000). Though globalization gained currency and its operation is in full swing decentralization did not get that much of attention as the stakeholders of decentralization are weak. To make decentralization work an array of support structures have to be created. Against this background, even for planning at grassroots one has to support the grassroots institutions. Though there were sporadic experiences in decentralized planning in the past, implementable strategies and devices could not be gained from all those experiments and experiences (T.M. Thomas Issac with Richard W. Franke, 2000, 21-29). The new initiatives, following the 73rd and the 74th Amendments to the Constitution of India, have to take into cognisance the fact that the top down planning has not addressed the felt needs of the people, has removed people away from governance and participation in development. Development as an activity to be done exclusively by officials resulted in large scale corruption in rural development activities. This too has to be recognized while considering the new option. People were made beneficiaries, the self-respect of the people was jeopardized and people were not as development participants (N. Narayansamy, M.P. Boraiyan and M.A. Jeyaraju, 2000). It is so not only in India but also in many of the developing countries. Bridging the gap between the people and the government is a difficult task in third world countries. (Commonwealth Foundation, 1999). In this context, planning at the grassroots, initiated through the 73rd and the 74th Amendments to the Constitution of India, has to remove all the above stated obstacles and barriers in the process of development.

The Problem

Though provision has been made in the Constitution for planning initiatives at the grassroots, to what extent steps are being taken at the state level and the Panchayat level to plan for development at the grassroots is a question to be probed. Further at what level initiatives gain momentum and how this can be sustained is yet another question to be clarified.

Objectives and Methodology

This study has the following objectives:

(*a*) to study the efforts of the State Government in strengthening the planning process at the grassroots;
(*b*) to what extent planning is initiated from below by the Panchayats with the participation of people;
(*c*) how the planning process is initiated from the grassroots by the Panchayats and with whose support?; and
(*d*) what are the implications of the intervention of the government and other agencies in the planning process at the grassroots.

The above stated objectives could be studied through documentary analysis and process analysis. The government's position on micro-level planning could be evaluated from the steps taken by the Government. A process analysis can be made on the initiatives of planning at the grassroots by the Panchayat Institutions with the support of development organizations.

Context

To analyze decentralized planning, there are two approaches so far developed. One is historical in nature and the other one is contextual or critical analysis. Through the historical approach, eversince the concept of planning gained currency in India, discussions and deliberations had been conducted as to what alternative strategies have to be evolved to overcome the difficulties of centralized planning (James Manor, 1999). But all the discussions and deliberations were held against the backdrop of centralized planning. The issues and problems were looked at from the perspective of the centre and not from the perspective of the periphery. Macro-economic activities through centralized planning did not mitigate the micro-level problems particularly these relating to the basic needs (G. Palanithurai, 2003). Hence, the policy-makers were compelled to think of planning units at different levels, namely the district and the block. Yet there was no conscious and deliberate decision to establish planning units below the State level. Even to establish a planning unit at the State level, it took nearly about two decades after independence. Such a kind of rigid centralization had been practiced in Indian politics and administration (Jayati Ghosh, 1998).

But the decentralized planning enunciated at present is totally different and it makes a heal breakthrough as it has been incorporated in the Constitution itself. It is not an isolated event that took place in Indian planning. It is a corollary of a worldwide event which pushes the economy to cross the boundaries of the nations and into every segment of the society. Both in economy and polity an overhauling took place by which the paradigm of governance, administration and development has been totally altered (Ajit M. Banarjee and K.A. Chidambaram, 1996; Sofi Ali and Anita Rao, 2000; Olle Tornquist, 1999). A new paradigm has been developed by which new opportunities, which are uncommon, can be harnessed by enhancing the capacity of the stakeholders (International Commission on Peace and Food, 1990). Through this paradigm power is given to the people to determine their destiny (The World Bank, 2003). People have been projected as the major stakeholders and they have to decide their course of action in the process of development (Robert Chambers, 1983). In the present context the concept "government" has been redefined. It is not a provider but a facilitator. The government takes a back seat and the community or the user group takes the front to take development initiatives. Thus the concept of government is no more relevant and it is only "governance" which is relevant at present (Rajesh Tandon and Ranjita Mohanty, 2002).

How for the development of the community, activities have to be initiated through a new system of governance created at different levels below the State with the introduction of the Amendments to the Constitution of India. Governance structures have been created at the village level, the block level and the district level, including towns, municipalities and corporations. To activate the people to participate in the development process, powers have been devolved to different levels and the planning mechanism had been incorporated in to the Constitution itself. By doing so the trend of development activities has been altered from "supply driven" to "demand driven" mode (G. Palanithurai, 2000).

The major provisions and basic principles have to be conformed to through an Act at the provincial level. Hence all the States have conformed to the bases of the Constitutional Amendments in State Acts. Tamil Nadu also has passed conformity Acts. Enacting a legislation is not a big task in a democracy since it is a representative democracy-based on the principle of majority in Parliament and Legislative Assemblies. To pass a legislation the members of the decision-making body have to be managed through the established procedure. The difficult task lies in operationalizing the provisions of the Act which has to take place in the society among the people. In India there are a large number of key provisions in the Constitution which are still no operated effectively because of social conflict, social discrimination and illiteracy. Hence, the focus should be on the operational part of the legislation. In the Tamil Nadu Panchayat Act due recognition was not given to the District Planning Committee and its responsibilities. The District Planning Committee and its functioning have to be seen and analyzed against the larger backdrop of devolution of powers in Tamil Nadu, because devolution of powers and planning at micro-level will alter the existing mode of governance (G. Palanithurai, 2003). To perform the above task the State Government and its leadership should have sufficient will, because this initiative to devolve powers, functions, finance and functionaries will cripple the existing exploitative and corrupt nexus between the ruling elite and the inert bureaucracy. It will mobilize the people for deepening democracy. People's perception has also to be changed as they regard themselves as beneficiaries instead of development participants having lost their self-confidence and self-respect. Further people have to be conscientized and capacitated. The whole exercise has to be done with the backing of the Central Government.

Perception

To undertake the gigantic and uphill task, normally any leader will pursue a normal course of action. In the Indian context, this new exercise of democratic decentralization starts only from the State Government not from the Central Government. Normally the term is used in development literature to refer to the transfer of authority to plan, make decisions and manage public functions from the national level to any organization or agency at the sub-national level and down below. Decentralization in India refers to a situation in which lower-ranking units below the State level acquire all powers and responsibilities from the State Government and also sole control over the determination of their goals and targets.

Tamil Nadu's ethnic political culture demanded adequate powers to the State Government since independence. Now these political parties, which are coming to power alternatively, view decentralization as a threat to the power of the State Government. These political parties, namely both the Dravida Munnetra Kazhagam and the All India Anna Dravida Munnetra Kazhagam, forcefully opposed the creation of the three-tier Panchayat Raj System as it would emerge as a countering political force. Hence, they have developed a strategy to keep the Panchayat system a weak instrument while appearing to conform to the major provisions of the 73rd Amendment to the Constitution of India (G. Palanithurai, 1999).

The Panchayat was created through the conformity legislation enacted during the period of the All India Anna Dravida Munnetra Kazhagam. The Act has many retrograde provisions (G. Palanithurai, 1998). The Act has not given any real power to Panchayats. The new Panchayati Raj was operationalized only during the period of the Dravida Munnetra Kazhagam. All the powers given to the Panchayati Institutions are supervisory in nature and not of the decision-making kind. The powers given to Panchayats, however meager, have not been given through Act but through Government orders. The ruling parties at the State level somehow or other have managed to keep the local bodies in their party fold as the ruling parties have to emerged victorious in the local body elections also. As a result most of the local body leaders never raise their voice against the State Government for more power, finance and functionaries to local bodies. Only the lowest units in the system, namely the Gram Panchayats, which are freed from political contest raise their voice against the State Government and demand powers to local bodies. The District Planning Committee was created and it was under placed the Chairmanship of the District Collector. After a prolonged fight he was replaced by the District Panchayat Chairperson. Elections to District Planning Committee were conducted and now it is in position but no activity is undertaken.

Virtually planning at muiti-level exists only in concept and theory but not in practice. But the State Planning Commission had prepared a report, guidelines and a training module for multilevel planning (State Planning Commission, 1997). Both leaders and officials had been trained (G. Palanithurai, 2000). The elected representatives elected to the District Planning Committee have taken cognizance of the mandatory functions of the District Planning Committee. But there is no concerted effort to build up this process of planning from below and, as a result, the rural development activities are carried out still in the supply driven mode and people are not involved in the development activities. More than that the felt needs of the people projected through the Gram Sabha are not met, but a variety of activities are being carried out through sectoral departments (G. Palanithurai, 2003).

In order to break the deadlock an exercise was initiated with the intervention of The Hunger Project by which ten Gram Panchayats in Sivagangai District and thirteen Gram Panchayats in Pudukkottai District have been set up as model Panchayats in terms of planning at micro-level with the participation of the people who are willing to involve themselves in the preparation of plan for the development of the communities in the Panchayat area. Why these Panchayats in these two districts? The leaders of these Panchayat showed interest in this exercise and volunteered while they were undergoing training. Further these Presidents are supported by the respective District Collectors who have assured that they will extend all possible support and coordination to this exercise.

Initiatives of the Government

By going through the document entitled "Report of the Working Group on Decentralized Planning and Panchayat Raj" prepared by the Planning Commission, 1997 one can infer the poor interest evinced by the Government of Tamil Nadu in all the past experiments. In the 73rd Amendment, while there was a discussion in the Parliament, the two major political parties, namely, the DMK and the AIADMK being in power in Tamil Nadu State alternatively, made a categorical statement that they had not imagined a structure for Panchayat Raj above the Block Panchayats. They wrote letters to the Government of India that the District Panchayat has to be abolished. With both these parties opposed to the district level structure what would have been the fate of the District Panchayat in Tamil Nadu? Further when the District Planning Committee was formed the District Collector was made the Chairperson of the District Planning Committee. After a prolonged fight the District Panchayat President was made the Chairperson of the District Planning Committee. To fulfill the Constitutional obligation, the District Planning Cell with a skeleton staff was created. It has to look after the day to day administration of the District Panchayats. Neither the State Government nor the District Planning Committee took any step with regard to the preparation of the District Development Plan. The State Planning Commission, though it took the initiative it did not have the backing of the State Government. As a result planning at the district level has not seen the light of day.

But organizations and activists engaged in public affairs, seeing the apathy of the State Government in taking the initiative for micro-level planning, because interested in taking the initiative. Except in West Bengal and Kerala, micro-level planning is the initiative of the development organizations. In this context in Tamil Nadu State The Hunger Project initiated the process of planning at Gram Panchayat level as Gram Sabha has got power to approve the plan document which becomes a legal and legitimate plan document. The Hunger Project has certain objectives namely ending hunger through micro plan mitigating malnutrition, empowering women and children through the micro plan, and working for social development through micro plan, all under women leadership. But The Hunger Project realized the fact that in the context of weak devolution of powers to the local bodies, micro level planning will be a meaningful exercise only when it is done with the partnership of the district administration as the sectoral departments are under the district administration. Since sectoral departments are not under the control of the Panchayat Raj system, for implementing the plans of the Panchayats, the cooperation of the sectoral departments is imperative. Against this background, working with the district administration becomes inevitable. Further, though the State Government is not interested in devolving powers, it is interested in achieving social development. This interest can be exploited to initiate micro-level planning. The Hunger Project in Tamil Nadu is taking a major lead in initiating micro-level planning at the Gram Panchayat level. Ten Gram Panchayats in Sivagangai District headed by women have planned and started working on the plan. Following

Sivagangai District, in Pudukkottai District, 13 Gram Panchayats have been selected and planning is over. Another 30 Gram Panchayats have been selected for this exercise in Tuticorin District and Dindigul District. Wherever, the district administration is taking initiative, the Hunger Project joins them as partner and initiates micro-level planning. Panchayats are selected for this planning on two conditions, namely, the Gram Panchayat leader should have honesty, commitment and capacity and the Gram Panchayat should enjoy the support of the communities without any social and political conflicts. Table 1 presents some details of the Panchayats selected for the pilot exercise in Sivagangai District.

PLANNING EXERCISE AT PHASE I

Table 1
Model Panchayats for Community Based Micro-Level Planning in Sivagangai District

Sl. No.	*Union*	*Panchayat*	*Name of the Panchayat President*
1.	Kallal	1. Eppangulam	Veera Kalaiarasi (SC)
		2. Nerpugapatti	A.Pushpam (BC)
		3. Kalipuli	S.Gandhimathi (SC)*
2.	Thirupathoor	4. Velangudi	A.Alphonsamary (BC)*
3.	Sigampunari	5. Vaduvanpatti	R.Rakku (SC)
		6. Sevalpatti	S.Poongothai (BC)*
		7. Kozhikudipatti	Nagajothi (BC)
4.	S. Pudur	8. Urathupatti	C.Chinnammal (SC)
		9. Manaloor	S.Gomathi (BC)
		10. Keelavayal	S.Sumathi (MBC)*

* The above Panchayats were included in this pilot exercise only at a later stage as per the suggestion of the District Collector.

A total of 10 Gram Panchayats headed by women were selected in four Unions of Sivagangai District, Tamil Nadu. Out of the 10 Panchayat leaders, 4 belonged to the SC.

Methodology of the Plan Preparation in the First Phase

Before commencing the actual work, an intensive training was organised for three days to build the capacity of the leaders including the men and women who were all committed to this exercise. The training programme was organised from the 27 to the 31 May, 2002 in Gandhigram Rural Institute as a fully residential programme. Experts were drawn from different institutions including the government to conduct the training programme (G. Palanithurai, 2002). All the six Gram Panchayat Presidents initially selected wanted to have a common workshop to sensitize the Panchayat Ward Members, community leaders, SHG leaders, members of the youth groups and opinion makers on the importance and the implications of grassroots planning. The lead NGO, Rural Welfare Trust, agreed to help the Panchayats to organise the workshop and do the needful for planning also. The Hunger Council of Tamil Nadu agreed to share some of the responsibilities. As a result on 17 August, 2002, a workshop was organised at Tirupathur for all the six Panchayats and around 210 members from all the Panchayats participated in the programme (G. Palanithurai, 2002). The whole exercise focused on planning at the Gram Panchayat level and the discussion was on the steps to be followed in the planning. It was agreed that the planning exercise would be completed before October 2002 and that the Panchayats and the NGO would take up the responsibility. Further, it was decided to identify what could be done by the leaders and the people of the respective Panchayats. What could not be done by the Panchayats would be done by the Hunger Project.

The next step was to collect basic data about the people and their conditions. This could be done by the Panchayats. Before starting the exercise the statutory seven committees had to be constituted so that the number of members in the orbit of governance would be increased. For the data collection a well developed schedule prepared by the State Planning Commission was used. After collecting the data from each village a PRA exercise was carried out with the help of the staff of the Kottayam based NGO, Centre for Rural Management (CRM) to assess the needs of the people and to prioritise the needs. This exercise was done extensively and the staff of the CRM prepared a plan. Simultaneously the representatives of the people in the Panchayats also prepared a plan based on the PRA exercise. Finally both the plans were synthesized and brought out in the form of a document. In the whole process the concept of development was critiqued, the role of the government was criticized and people expressed their willingness to participate in the whole process as the Panchayat leaders provided ample scope for people to participate in the planning exercise. When the document was ready for presentation in any forum for critical evaluation. The Hunger Council of Tamil Nadu organised a development seminar with a set of objectives, namely, of making this document legitimate, to sensitize the government on planning at the grassroots and to motivate other Panchayat Presidents to start this kind of exercise in their Panchayats also. On 26 and 27 October, 2002, the development seminar was organised in Gandhigram Rural Institute, inviting the State Minister for Local Bodies, secretaries, directors, planning officials, experts, representatives from the media, MLAs, community leaders, Panchayat leaders and women and youth groups from the six Gram Panchayats and women Gram Panchayat Presidents from all over Tamil Nadu numbering around six hundred.

The perspective plan document of the six Gram Panchayats contained a brief history of the Panchayats, details about the former Panchayat Presidents who held office during the pre-73rd Amendment era, basic data about agriculture, source of irrigation, veterinary facilities, land utilization, land ownership, landless families with social background, facilities available in schools, admission in schools, dropouts in schools, status of women and children, energy utilization, non-conventional energy sources, environmental conditions, skills available in the village, housing facilities etc. After projecting all these the document projected the needs and prioritized them. Further, it stated how these prioritized needs are to be met (Veerakalaiarasi, 2002; A. Pushpam, 2002; K. Rakku, 2002; V. Nagajothi, 2002; C. Chinnammal, 2002 and S. Gomathi, 2002).

Responsibilities were fixed on individuals and groups to take steps to meet the needs indicated in the plan document. Achievable indicators were fixed to monitor the activities of the Panchayats. It was stated unequivocally that the Panchayat would concentrate on 100 per cent school admission, ensure the normal weight of new born babies, institutional delivery, pre-natal and post-natal care, malnutrition, family welfare etc. Thus this plan document became a vision document. Responsibility was not fixed on the government alone. Activities were classified and accordingly responsibilities were fixed by which partners were identified for administering development and social justice.

Reactions and Responses to Plan Document

Officials from the State Planning Commission and the Project Office of the District Rural Development Agency of Sivagangai District first examined the document and offered their comments. They found certain deficiencies in the process of data collection. Apart from the basic data all other data were collected through PRA exercises and prioritization was also done through the same exercise. This was not approved of by the officials. The activities envisaged in the plan document could not be carried out under the available schemes of the government. The Panchayats had not identified the individual beneficiaries for the government schemes. While entering the activities in the plan document, the Panchayats had to indicate the source of funding to carry out all the activities. Further, they questioned the legitimacy of the plan document in the absence of a planning exercise at the Block level and the District level. On certain issues such as agriculture, veterinary care, non-conventional energy and environment, the people in the villages had not consulted the government departments while projecting activities in the plan document. These subjects were highly technical in nature, but the Panchayats had taken the opinion of the people in deciding upon the activities. On the whole it was an expression of cynicism. It is to be noted here that, in the inaugural function, the Minister for Panchayati Raj and Rural Development, Government of Tamil Nadu, showered encomium on the women leaders for their exercise and he said that despite the implementation of a variety of schemes and programmes of the Central and State Governments, people's felt needs could not be met and that this kind of micro-level plan would reverse the trend and the felt needs would be met and thereby wasteful expenditure could be avoided. He further said that this kind of exercise would trigger a movement for people's planning. He even appealed that in each district this kind of exercise should be initiated.

Despite the remark of the Minister, the officials recorded their negative remarks about the whole exercise. Following the reaction and response of the officials, some of the experts from the audience came forward to express their opinion. Prominent among them were B.S. Raghavan, retired Chief Secretary of West Bengal and adviser to the FAO, A.K. Venkatasubramanian, retired civil servant specializing in Public Distribution System, Dr. Rajagopalan of the

M.S. Swaminathan Foundation, Mr. Vallinayagam, retired Additional Director of Rural Development and Mr. N.S. Chidambaram, retired Additional Director of Rural Development. First all the experts appreciated the effort expended in taking up this cause and facing all the problems in collecting data and putting them in a plan proposal and getting the approval of the people in the Gram Sabha and the Panchayat Council. It is a plan of the people prepared by the people and not a plan prepared by officials. It is their vision. They have chalked out their activities on the basis of their felt needs. It is true that they have not chalked out activities to implement the schemes of the government and hence there will be a gap between the available schemes and the activities envisaged in the plan document of the Panchayats. The plan document is not a petition prepared by them to get sanction from the government. It is their plan and they seek to be partners in governance to administer development. They have indicated the possibilities to generate employment opportunity with the resources and skills available in their respective Panchayats. Further it is to be noted that social development issues have been projected in the plan document and it is indicated that they will take up the responsibility to achieve sustainable results in development in the social sector. While appreciating the efforts of the Gram Panchayat leaders, they addressed a few questions to the government officials and a few suggestions to the Gram Panchayat leaders.

In fifty years of democratic governance in India, no such document was prepared for village development by the Government. Even after the introduction of the 73rd Amendment and the constitution of the District Planning Committee, no systematic effort was made at the micro-level, despite planning officials working at the district level. Having failed miserably in discharging duties and responsibilities at the government level, it was unfair on the part of the officials to criticize the efforts made by the women leaders for their small technical lapses. Further, it was characteristic on the part of the officials to denigrate the people's efforts as unscientific. Since the officials have been oriented to act in the supply driven mode of development activities, they look at everything from the supply side and not from the demand side. While evaluating the proposal, officials had looked for proposals for the government schemes and programmes and that was why they were not in a position to suggest ways and means to meet the demands which could not be fulfilled by the Government schemes and programmes. The experts said that the officials could have offered their suggestions rather than criticizing the plan. Even the model plan prepared by the officials in some of the villages in Tamil Nadu did not include social development issues. The model plans prepared by the officials have not seen the light of day.

It is a unique exercise in fifty years of governance because every segment of the rural community has been involved in this exercise to make a declaration that their destinies are going to be decided by their efforts only. Now owners have been found for the rural development activities. They have realistically projected their needs as felt by the community without looking into the supply side of it. Hence it is the responsibility of the officials to help in identifying the institutions to be involved in the process of fulfilling the needs of the people. The existing schemes of the government could be utilized for many of the demands and for some of the demands a slight modification is necessary in implementing the existing government schemes for which the District Collector as Chairman of the DRDA and Inspector of Panchayats can make use of his discretionary powers. Demands which could not be met through government schemes could be taken to various financial institutions for financial support with a viable action proposal prepared by professionals for which the Panchayats have to seek the support of NGOs. It is fortunate that the Rural Welfare Trust is working with all these six Panchayats. The same organization can be involved in preparing such proposals and approaching CAPART, DST, NABARD and other agencies. For the social development issues targeted, achievable and quantifiable indicators have to be fixed. For instance school enrolment of students, birth weight of newly born babies, institutional delivery, reduction of school dropouts, providing safe drinking water supply to all families, ensuring sanitation facilities to all families, eradication of plastics and so on have been identified as activities and responsibilities have also been fixed in the case all the above said activities. The seven statutory committees in the villages have to be activated to involve themselves in all these activities. What the Gram Panchayats now require is partners to carry this task further.

After making these observations the experts again requested the officials directly dealing with planning at the grassroots to give their feedback again. The officials from the State Planning Commission and the District Rural Development Agency informed the audience and more specifically the Panchayat Presidents of the possibility of making use of many of the Central and State Government Schemes and programmes to meet many of the issues projected in the plan document. For other issues and demands the nodal agency, the NGO, Rural Welfare Trust, was to prepare and send proposals to NABARD, CAPART and other agencies. Achievable indicators have to be explicitly entrusted to the committees of the Panchayats and their activities have to be monitored every year. This was the assurance given to the Panchayats by the officials.

Finally the Panchayat Presidents concluded their presentation by assuring the officials that they would take up the responsibility to achieve many of the achievable indicators on social development. Further, they informed that they would meet all the sectoral departments to seek their help to fulfill all the demands of the people mentioned in the PRA meetings while preparing the plan for the Gram Panchayats. The women leaders, while expressing their gratitude to the officials, explained their struggle to make use of the power devolved to them.

The whole exercise and the presentation of the plan in the development seminar provoked the women leaders assembled in the seminar to think on the social issues highlighted by the women Presidents of the six Gram Panchayats. The women Presidents who assembled in the seminar from all over Tamil Nadu under the banner of the Tamil Nadu Federation of Women Leaders prepared a charter of activities and declared it a charter of activities for the next year. The charter is presented hereunder.

Declaration

We, the elected women representatives who are gathered here at Gandhigram Rural Institute on this 27th day of October 2002, declare that we will address the following issues in the next one year:

1. All the eligible children (girls and boys) will be enrolled in schools.
2. We will strive to remove malnourishment amongst children in the age group of 0-5 years. As elected

representatives we shall ensure that no underweight babies are born in our villages. The mothers will be given proper nourishment before and after delivery.

3. Better anti-natal and post-natal care will be provided for all the women in our Panchayats.
4. Any injustice against women in our Panchayats will be dealt with firmly. As a collective we will fight against domestic violence and also any other form of violence against any women in our Panchayats.
5. We will ensure that child labour is abolished in our Panchayats.
6. We will ensure equitable access to and distribution of Panchayat resources among all the people in the Panchayats and guarantee at least the provision of the basic minimum requirements for the poorest. The PDS system will be improved with our intervention.
7. Problems faced by the women Panchayat leaders and women in general will be addressed collectively by making alliance with supportive institutions and organizations.
8. The newly implemented sanitary complexes meant for women will be effectively managed by women's groups with the support of the Panchayats.
9. Our Panchayats will not suffer from lack of drinking water. Everyone will be entitled to safe drinking water.
10. We will ensure that Gram Sabhas take place regularly and more and more people take part in these meetings. We will ensure that a minimum of 50 per cent of the total women in the Panchayat attend the meetings and that their issues are properly heard.
11. We commit ourselves to the implementation of the 15-point programme prepared by the Tamil Nadu Government and request the State Government to devolve necessary powers to the Panchayats and local bodies for the same.

Following the presentation of reports and the declaration of the charter of activities for women Panchayat Presidents, the Pudukkottai District Project Officer, DRDA, representing the Pudukkottai District administration, pleaded that this kind of exercise be undertaken in the whole of Pudukkottai District for which he sought the help of NGOs and Gandhigram Rural Institute. Women leaders from Pudukkottai District who attended the development seminar expressed their willingness to undertake this kind of exercise in their Panchayats. Thus the micro-plan exercise done in six Gram Panchayats and the presentation of all the six plans in the development seminar in the presence of the Minister for Panchayati Raj and Rural Development, Government of Tamil Nadu, officials of the State Government, experts in Micro-Level Planning and six hundred Gram Panchayat Women Presidents created an awareness among the minister, the officials and the local body leaders on the importance of micro-level planning and, as a result, the State Planning Commission started the exercise of giving training to the local body leaders on planning exercises to be done at the grassroots.

Analysis of I Phase Efforts

Primarily, though it is a constitutional mandate that the planning exercise has to be initiated at the grassroots, beyond the State Governments and the Central Government producing documents on decentralized planning, nothing has been done on the ground in the 9th and the 10th Plans. These six Panchayats, under the leadership of women, have sensitized the minister and the higher officials to the implications of micro-level planning.

Secondly, while carrying out this exercise, it could be seen at what level devolution of powers has taken place in the state as the Panchayats faced problems in getting the support of the sectoral departments. Empirically this proved the extent to which powers have been devolved to the Panchayats.

Thirdly, in the process of interacting with the officials and hearing views of the officials on the plan proposals of the Panchayats, the official attitude to this new dispensation and the exercise has been exposed and they have been sensitized to the legal and social implications of micro-level planning.

Fourthly, the other women Presidents have gained confidence that this kind of exercise could be done in their Panchayats also as they heard the methodology adopted in the six Gram Panchayats for planning at the micro-level.

Fifthly, social development issues came to the limelight because of the micro-plans of the six Gram Panchayats. These six Gram Panchayat leaders gained this insight while they were in self-help groups and thereby they quickly grasped the social development issues and fixed achievable indicators for the Panchayats. This kind of exercise motivated the other Panchayat leaders to take up this issue. As a result the women Panchayat leaders published a charter of activities to be undertaken by the Panchayats in the social development sector.

Sixthly, in the recent past people have been mobilized by various agencies for participation in the implementation of various schemes and programmes brought from above. But the position "we govern you receive" has not altered. By undertaking the planning exercise by the people, people's demands and priorities have been prominently projected in the plan document and thereby the old position "we govern you participate" has been replaced by "you govern and you participate."

Seventhly, the six Panchayat Presidents have started negotiations with officials, representatives of the people like MLAs and MPs and NGOs for fulfilling the requirements of the plan. They have developed skills of negotiation.

Eighthly, the hidden potential of the leadership has been exhibited through this process. Class, caste and political organizations have their own roles in the activities of the rural society. While mobilizing all the groups cutting across these differences, the women leaders have exhibited a high decree of democratic leadership. Even the traditional Panchayat leaders have extended their fullest cooperation to the efforts of these Panchayat Presidents.

Ninthly, the conventional mode of looking at issues and demands from the supply mode has been done away with and instead issues are being looked at from the perspective of the people and thereby a sense of ownership has been cultivated among the people for the development of the community.

Tenthly, so far the Panchayats negotiated for schemes and programmes of the government. Now the trend has been reversed and they ask for the government's participation in their schemes and programmes. Petitioners have changed their role to that of negotiators because of this new exercise.

Eleventhly, the Panchayats have started mobilizing partners for their development activities. They have gathered many organizations to their support in implementing their schemes.

Twelfthly, the leaders have built a vision document through this exercise. They have gained rich input on vision building from the training undergone elsewhere by the Presidents. While doing so they are critiquing the very concept of development. They move around the skills and the resources available at their disposal.

Though they are women and, that too, three of them are of the Backward Class and another three are Dalits, their leadership is recognized, appreciated and supported by even traditional Panchayat leaders. The women leaders, by their performance, have won the recognition of the community. Since initiatives are taken jointly by the leaders, the administration becomes transparent and it reduces corruption to the maximum extent. The planning exercise has made the people volunteers in the development initiative.

Summing up of I Phase

Planning at the grassroots for administering development and social justice has long range implications in the paradigm of development. It alters the entire process of development. The roles of the government and the community have been reversed. All the loopholes in the development process in the existing paradigm have been exposed and people have developed a new perspective to look at issues and now plans of activities are chalked out on the basis of their demands and needs as prioritized by the people and not on the basis of the available schemes and programmes of the government. The concept of "we govern you receive" has gone and the new concept "you govern and you participate" has been ushered in. Social development issues have drawn the attention of the people because of this exercise and achievable indicators have been fixed for social development issues and people have taken up the responsibility of achieving the target. People have developed a sense of ownership as this plan document carries the demands of the people as schemes and programmes. Now the government finds itself in a tight spot as to whether this is to be allowed or not. There is no other option except to allow and continue the new practice. Over and above, at the earliest, the entire state has to take the initiative to plan for development from the Gram Panchayat to the

District Planning Committee. The new paradigm will gain momentum and it will ultimately end in a movement for decentralized governance for development and social justice.

Exercise in II Phase

Based on the exercise undertaken in Sivagangai District micro-level planning was started in Pudukkottai District. Pudukkottai District offered three advantages for undertaking this exercise. They were: the District Collector is pro-Panchayat and he believes in the potentialities of the Panchayats and the community; the link between Panchayats and the communities is strong; and, the capacity of the leaders is very high as periodical orientations apart from training were given to the Panchayat leaders. As the District Collector invited the Hunger Project, it was decided to work with the Panchayats. The district administration provided office space for the Hunger Project in the District Panchayat Office. Thirteen Gram Panchayats were selected from all the 13 Blocks. The main criteria adopted in the selection process is that the Panchayat leader should have commitment and honesty, the link between the leader and the community should be so strong, and there should not be any communal and political conflict between and among the collectivities. By adopting the criteria the following Gram Panchayats were selected in a meeting held in the Collectorate with the participation of the Hunger Project staff, the District Collector, the Project Officer, DRDA, of Pudukkottai District. Table 2 presents the list of the selected Panchayats.

Planning Methodology in II Phase

After getting consent from the Panchayat leaders, the President was asked to constitute the statutory Panchayat Committees along with the Panchayat Planning Committee. In all the Committees it should be mandatory that women and dalit representatives should find a place. Panchayat President, Vice-Presidents, Panchayat clerk, Committee members, Traditional Panchayat leaders, SHG leaders, Youth leaders and Retired officials of the Panchayat areas were drawn for training. A three-day training in planning at the village level was offered. It was a residential

Table 2
Model Panchayats for Community Based Micro-Level Planning in Pudukkottai District

Sl. No.	Name of the Panchayat	Panchayat Union	Name of the Panchayat President
1.	Merpanaikadu	Aranthangi	Ms. Bhavani Ilango
2.	Poovalur	Avudayarkoil	Mr. Sarvana Perumal
3.	Melathur	Thiruvarankulam	Mr. Saravanan
4.	Edaiyathimangalam	Manamelkudi	Mr. Arumugam
5.	Elaikadaividuthi	Karambakudi	J. Manjula
6.	Melaputhuvayal	Kunandarkoil	Ms. Dhanalakshmi
7.	Parambur	Annavasal	Mr. Abdulwaheed
8.	Nerinjikudi	Ponnamaravathy	Mr. P. Ramnu
9.	Punalkulam	Gandarvakottai	Mr. Shanmugam
10.	Mookampatti	Pudukkottai	Ms. V. Mangalam
11.	Meenaveli	Viralimalai	Mr. Alagiri
12.	Virachilai	Tirumayam	Ms. Devi
13.	K.Rayavaram	Arimalam	Ms. Rani Sathappan

Out of the 13 Gram Panchayat Presidents 6 are men and 7 are women.

training programme and it was conducted in Gandhigram Rural Institute. In the training exercise emphasis was laid on participation of people, especially women and dalits, and social development issues. Following the training in each Gram Panchayat a sensitization exercise was conducted to prepare the people for evolving a perspective plan for socio-economic development of the Gram Panchayat area. To change the mindset of the people, this exercise continued till the draft plan was approved in the Gram Sabha. Sensitization was also done on social development issues. When the training was over, responsibilities were fixed as to who and how the needed data have to be collected from both primary and secondary sources. After collecting the data, a neat profile of the village was developed which was termed a development report. After consolidation of the report a Participatory Rural Appraisal for every Panchayat was to be conducted to prioritize the works that were to be undertaken in the Panchayat.

After prioritizing the activities, the Hunger Project staff, with the help of the Panchayat leader and the clerk identified the vulnerable families and gave numbers to the families. A list of the disabled was made for constant monitoring. Schools, anganwadi, primary health centre service would be assessed by the staff of the Hunger Project. Thus social development activities because the primary concern of the Panchayat. A manual, listing the activities related to social development to be carried out in the Panchayat area by the Panchayats in partnership with other agencies was supplied to all the Panchayat leaders (activity chart). Malnourished children, pregnant women affected by anemia and poor women affected by diseases would be identified and all the lists would be attached to the plan document. Finally responsibilities were fixed as to how these prioritized activities were going to be carried out and with whose partnerships. All the needs identified and prioritized through the PRA were to be matched with the schemes and programmes of the Central and State Governments that being operated through sectoral departments. For unmatched issues Panchayats were to seek the help of MLAs and MPs and to get substantial funds from their Local Area Development Fund. The whole plan document was placed before the Gram Sabha for evaluation, suggestion and approval. After getting the approval, with modifications if any, the plan document was to be printed.

The printed plan document would be circulated to all the sectoral departments. The District Collector as Inspector of Panchayats would give necessary instructions to the sectoral department heads to carry out activities in the Panchayats based on their needs. The Panchayats with the help of the Planning Committee and the representative of the Hunger Project should do the follow-up activities.

Lessons Learnt

It is not a State driven planning activity. It is initiated from below. Though it was initiated by the leader of the Panchayat in the process of mobilization, people have been made to participate in the process of preparation of the development plan. Panchayat leaders and the members of various committees have developed negotiating skills in the process of the preparation of the plan. They negotiate with the sectoral departments, MLAs and MPs. Further they negotiate with Union Councillors and District Ward Members to make use of the funds available in the Block and District Panchayats. Since there was no initiating from the State

Government and the Central Government for planning from below with the participation of people, these Gram Panchayat leaders took the initiative and followed the guidelines provided by the State Planning Commission for planning at the micro-level, especially at Gram Panchayat level. Because of these initiatives, even the State Planning Committee has started doing this exercise in 250 Gram Panchayats throughout Tamil Nadu. It is also not planning but preparing a development report.

While engaged in this exercise it could be visualized at what level devolution of powers has taken place in the State as the Panchayats faced problems in getting the support of the sectoral departments. Empirically this proved the extent to which powers have been devolved to the Panchayats. Further while interacting with officials in the process of plan preparation the attitude of the officials towards planning could be seen. Thanks to this exercise the officials are exposed and sensitized towards planning and social development. The grassroots leaders have exhibited an extraordinary commitment towards communities social development. The micro-level plan experience made the Panchayat leaders enhance their capacity and use the full potentiality of leadership. Panchayat Presidents and the people have prepared a plan. Now they have reversed the process of development activities from supply driven to demand driven mode. Realistically speaking the plan is a vision document and the activities listed in the plan document are only their wish list when there is no conducive atmosphere for micro-level planning.

Summing up of II Phase

The new dispensation of micro-level planning with the participation of the people to administer economic development and social justice envisioned in the Constitution through the 73rd and the 74th Amendments has far reaching implications in the development paradigm in the context of redefining the concept of the Government against the backdrop of democratic decentralization of powers and globalization of economy. This new initiative has reversed the process from supply driven to demand driven activities. The old practice of the government providing and the people receiving has been reversed. Now people plan and participate and the government just supports. The whole development exercise moves in a different mode which is totally different from that of the government. People's wishes and vision have been projected as a major set of activities and people have taken up responsibilities.

There is yet another striking feature in the micro-level planning process. In all such previous exercises only infrastructural facilities were projected as the major set of activities. But now people have focused more on social development activities because of the continuous sensitization and conscientization programme. This kind of people's initiatives in a few Panchayats has put the Government in a tight spot. As a result the State Planning Commission has taken efforts to prepare a development report in about 250 Gram Panchayat as a pilot project. Thus this new paradigm will gain momentum and it will ultimately end in a movement for decentralized governance for development and social justice.

Integrated Analysis

It has been tested in the process of planning at grassroots that planning is be possible even without much power and the cooperation of the government departments. By initiating the process the gap between the Panchayat leaders and the community is bridged. People are mobilized constantly and conscientised on social development activities. Ownership is being developed among the people for many of the development activities. In the process of interaction with Panchayat leaders and officials, Gram Sabha members have established a grip over the Panchayat administration. While the Panchayat Presidents are organizing meetings with various committee members the Panchayat administration becomes transparent and non-corrupt Planning initiative at the grassroots involves the women and thereby women's issues have been dealt with. Slowly Panchayat leaders, Ward Members and Committee Members are sensitized towards gender issues. Committee formation is a process by which women members and representatives from the Dalit community are inducted and their participation in the meetings has created sensitiveness among all towards the issues of Dalits. Panchayat leaders have started bargaining with other representatives of the people namely, MLA, MP, Ward Members of Block Panchayats and District Panchayats. The leaders have developed bargaining capacity to deal with officials. Panchayat leaders have developed a vision for the development of the community. Panchayat leaders and the people have realized the fact that for most of the social development activities money requirement is minimum and that to accomplish the same what is needed is commitment on the part of the Panchayat leaders and the community. The District Collector and his team of officials have shown much interest in Panchayat activities as they have faith in the Panchayat's potential. Along with Panchayats, the officials also claim credit in achieving the target of all development activities. Without the cooperation of the Panchayats and the community, officials cannot achieve the target successfully and hence they now bank on the Panchayats. Further the quality of the works carried out by the Panchayats with the participation of the people is good compared to the work of the contractors. Each and every Panchayat is having a plan document which is regarded as it pride.

By developing a plan document at the village level, indirectly a compulsion has been placed on the sectoral departments to work in the villages with their allocation of resources restricted to the activities indicated in the plan document of the respective Gram Panchayats.

Conclusion

In the given context, however poor devolution of powers, functions and finance in Tamil Nadu, planning at grassroots will compel the government to devolve the same. Administration becomes transparent and involvement of women and Dalits is remarkable in the activities of the communities. Both people and their leaders are sensitive towards the social development issues. Every Village Panchayat has a legitimate vision document which prevents the sectoral developments spending unilaterally. It bridges the gap between the people and the government. The entire State can replicate it.

REFERENCES

1. Ali Sofi and Rao Anita, Reinventing Public Administration for 21st Century, *The Indian Journal of Public Administration,* Vol. XLVI, No. 2 April-June 2000.
2. Banerjee, Ajit, M., and Chidambaram, K.A., (eds) *Renewing Governance: Issues and Options,* New Delhi: Tata McGraw Hill Publishing Company, 1996.
3. Chambers Robert, *Rural Development: Putting the Last First,* Harlow: Longman Scientific and Technical, 1983.

3(a). Chinnammal, C., *Perspective Plan for Development of Urathupatti,* Thirupathur: Grama Iyakkam, 2002.

4. Ghosh Jayati, *Development Strategy in India: A Political Economy Perspective* in Nationalism, Democracy and Development: State and Politics in India (Eds.), Sugata Bose and Ayesha Jalal, New Delhi: Oxford University Press, 1998, pp. 165-83.

4(a). Gomathy, S., *Perspective Plan for Development of Manalur,* Thirupathur: Grama Iyakkam, 2002.

5. International Commission on Peace and Food, *Developing Human Resourcefulness: Strategies to eradicate poverty in the 1990's,* Daft Working Paper, California: ICPE, 1989.
6. Issac Thomas, T.M., and W. Franke, Richard, *Local Democracy and Development,* New Delhi: Left Word, 2000, pp. 16-32.
7. Manor James, *The Political Economy of Democratic Decentralization,* Washington DC: The World Bank, 1999, p. l.

7(a). Nagajothi, Y., *Perspective Plan for Development of Kozhikudipatti,* Thirupathur: Grama Iyakkam, 2002.

8. Palanithurai, G., *Development Roles Reversed: People's Initiatives and Governments Participation,* (monograph), Gandhigram, Rajiv Gandhi Chair for Panchayati Raj Studies, 2003.
9. Palanithurai, G., *From Participation to Self-Governance: An Agenda for Restructuring Tamil Nadu Panchayat Act 1994,* Gandhigram: Department of Political Science and Development Administration, 1998.
10. Palanithurai, G., *Grassroots Democracy in Indian Society,* New Delhi: Concept Publishing Company, 2000.
11. Palanithurai, G., *New Panchayat Raj System at Work: An Evaluation,* New Delhi: Concept Publishing Company, 1999.
12. Palanithurai, G., *Panchayat Raj System in Tamil Nadu: With Original Act,* New Delhi: Concept Publishing Company, 2003.
13. Palanithurai, G., *Report of the Training Programme on Training of Trainers in Multi Level Planning Conducted for DRDA Officials,* Gandhigram: Rajiv Gandhi Chair for Panchayati Raj Studies, 2000.
14. Palanithurai, G., *Report of the Workshop on Panchayati Raj: Trials and Triumphs,* Gandhigram: The Hunger Project, 2003.

14(a). Palanithurai, G., *Report of the Training on Multi Level Planning,* Gandhigram: Tamil Nadu Council for Sustainable Livelihood, 2002.

14(b) Palanithurai, G., *Report of the Workshop on Multi Level Planning,* Gandhigram: Tamil Nadu Council for Sustainable Livelihood, 2002.

14(c). Pushpam, Y., *Perspective Plan for Development of P. Nerpuhapatti,* Thirupathur: Grama Iyakkam, 2002.

15. Raj, K.N., *Some Thoughts on Decentralization of Development Planning and Implications,* keynote paper presented at Seminar on Decentralized Planning and Implementation, 29 Nov. and 1 Dec., 1984, ISEC, Bangalore.

15(a). Rakku, K., *Perspective Plan for Development of Vadavanpatti,* Thirupathur: Grama Iyakkam, 2002.

16. Sivaramakrishnan, K.C., *Power to the People?: The Politics and Progress of Decentralization,* New Delhi: Konark Publishers Pvt. Ltd., 2000, pp. 95-96.

17. State Planning Commission, *Report of the Working Group on Decentralized Planning and Panchayati Raj,* Chennai: Government of Tamil Nadu, 1997.

18. Sundaram, K.V., *Decentralized Multi Level Planning,* New Delhi: Concept Publishing Company, 1997.

19. Tandon, Rajesh and Mohanty Ranjita, *Civil Society and Governance,* New Delhi: Sanskriti, 2002.

20. The World Bank, *World Development Report, 2004: Making Services Work for Poor People,* Washington DC: The World Bank, 2003.

21. Tornquist Olle, *Politics and Development: A Critical Introduction,* New Delhi: Sage Publications, 1999.

21 (a). Veerakalaiarasi, *Perspective Plan for Development of Veppankulam,* Thirupathur: Grama Iyakkam, 2002.

Gram Panchayat and Social Development

Activity Chart

INDICATORS

Sl. No.	*Activities*	*Responsibility*	*Outcome*	*Verification*
1.	100 per cent enrolment of eligible children	President, Vice-President, Ward Members, P.T.A., S.H.G. Members, Youth Clubs, N.G.O., Retired Officials, Education Committee	Level of literacy increased	School records
2.	Reduction of Dropouts	President, Vice-President, Ward Members, P.T.A., S.H.G. Members, Youth Clubs, N.G.O., Retired Officials	Increase in Educational standard	School records
3.	Ensuring protected Drinking Water Supply to School	President, Vice-President, Ward Members, School Teachers	Improvement of students health, reduction of ill health of students	Physical verification
4.	Providing toilets to school	President, Vice-President, Ward Members, School Teachers	Increase in health of children	Physical verification
5.	Utilizing the toilets by the school students	President, other members of the Panchayat Council, Teachers, P.T.A., Parents	Toilet Culture Developed	Physical verification
6.	Cutting the nails of the students every Monday in Balwadi and School	Youth club, S.H.G., Panchayat Ward Members, School Teachers	Health education, reduction of diseases, improvement of health	Physical verification

(*Contd.*)

Sl. No.	Activities	Responsibility	Outcome	Verification
7.	Planting of saplings in the school premises	President, teachers, agriculture departments	Environment awareness eco development	Physical verification
8.	Creating a school garden	President, teachers P.T.A., Youth clubs, Agriculture Department.	Increase in nutrition as the vegetables are given to noon mean centers	Physical verification
9.	Keeping the Balwadi clean and neat	Balwadi teacher. President, Vice-President, Ward Members	Health education, increase in status of health, culture of cleanliness is cultivated	Physical verification
10.	Providing a toilet in the Balwadi	President, Vice-President, Ward Members	Education, increase in health status	Physical verification
11.	Bringing a toilet culture among the kids	Balwadi teacher	Health education, increase in health status	Physical verification
12.	Adding vegetables to the noon meal by getting donations and getting the vegetables from the school garden	President, Vice-President, Balwadi teacher, School teachers	Nutritive food for students	Physical verification

(Contd.)

Sl. No.	*Activities*	*Responsibility*	*Outcome*	*Verification*
13.	Taking steps to prevent the practice of child labour	President, Vice-President, Ward Members, School teachers, P.T.A., N.G.O., S.H.G., Youth club	School enrolment, literacy, H.R.D.	Physical verification
14.	Cleaning over head tanks	O.H.T. operators, under the instruction of panchayat regularly	Health status, productivity	Verifying the records
15.	Creating awareness among the people about the consequence of alcohol and stop brewing and selling the same in the panchayat premises	President, Vice-President, Ward Member, Health Committee, S.H.G., Youth Club, N.G.O.	Economic status of poor, status of women and children, health of individuals and reduction of social problems	Physical verification
16.	Creating Awareness among the people about family welfare	P.H.C. Staff, President, Vice-President, Ward Members, Health Committee, S.H.G., Youth	Livelihood security ensured	Verifying the records small family
17.	Identify the vulnerable families and ensure food security to them and constantly monitor them with the help of government schemes	President, Vice-President, Ward Members, S.H.Gs.	Income generation, reduction of poverty, status of women	Physical verification
18.	Building the skill of the women through training	Presidents, Vice-President, Ward Members, Training Institution, Social Welfare Department at the District Women Development Corporation	Income generation, reduction of poverty, status of women	Physical verification

(Contd.)

Sl. No.	Activities	Responsibility	Outcome	Verification
19.	Establish link between the skilled persons and banking sector for the establishment of business venture by the women	President, Vice-President, Ward Members, Planning Committee Members, N.G.O., Banks, S.H.G.	Development of rural economy, and increase of status of women	Panchayat profile
20.	Building the skills of the youth through training	President, Vice-President, Ward Members, Training institutions, N.Y.K.	Human Resource Development, Economic Development	N.Y.K. Report
21.	Establish link between the skilled persons and Banking sector for the establishment of business venture by the youth	President, Vice-President, Ward Member, Planning Committee Members, N.G.Os., Banks, N.Y.Ks.	Development of Rural Economy	Panchayat Profile
22.	Ensuring proper functioning of P.D.S.	President, Vice-President, Ward Members and S.H.G., officials of Civil Supply	Food Security	Verifying the B.P.L. List
23.	Prevent open defecation in the villages by creating awareness and constructing toilets in each and every house	President, Vice-President, Ward Members, S.H.G., Youth Club, N.G.O., Project Staff, T.R.S.P., Retired Employees	Improvement in Health, Sanitation Environment	Physical verification

(Contd.)

Sl. No.	Activities	Responsibility	Outcome	Verification
24.	Creating awareness about R.C.H. by printing a card and giving it to every family	President, Vice-President, Ward Members, Health Committee, N.G.O., Staff of P.H.C.	Improvement in women and children, health, economic status	P.H.C. records
25.	Ensure the delivery of services from sub-centre and P.H.C. to the people through the schemes available for pre-natal and post-natal care	P.H.C. Staff, President, Vice-President, Ward Members, S.H.G., N.G.O., Health Committee	Increase in health status and economic status	Veryfying the P.H.C. records
26.	Creating awareness about growing medicinal plants and make it a business by involving S.H.G. and youth clubs	President, Vice-President, Ward Members, S.H.G., Planning Committee, Youth Club, N.G.O., NABARD Bank Staff.	Income generation for women-improvement of rural economy	Physical verification
27.	Creating awareness among the importance of water management	President, Vice-President, Ward Members, Community leaders, Planning Committee Members, N.G.O.	Rational Utilization of Water	Physical verification
28.	Creating a common burial ground in to grave yard in the villages	President, Vice-President, Ward Members, S.H.G., Youth club	Social justice	Physical verification
29.	Taking steps to manage the solid waste and earn money from it for panchayats	President, Vice-President, Ward Members, Planning Committee, N.G.O., S.H.G.	Environment development, income generation, better agricultural practices	Panchayat Records

(Contd.)

Sl. No.	Activities	Responsibility	Outcome	Verification
30.	Organise workshop for pregnant women to disseminate the needed information akin to A.N.C. and P.N.C.	P.H.C. Staff., S.H.G., President and Vice-President	Increase of health awareness, health status, economic status, Reduction of infant mortality and new born babies are in exact weight	Verifying with P.H.C. records
31.	Conducting medical camps for poor and school children	President, Vice-President, Ward Members, N.G.Os., S.H.G., nearby Rotary and Lions Club	Improved health status	Verifying with P.H.C. records
32.	Make the S.H.G. and Youth clubs to take up Panchayat works instead of employing contractor	President, Vice-President, Ward Members, S.H.G. Youth club, N.G.O.	Employment opportunity, quality of work, reduction of expenditure, local needs	Panchayat records
33.	Regularly conducting Gram Sabha meetings	President, Vice-President, Ward Members	Peoples participation, Good Governance	Panchayat Records
34.	Ensuring 60 per cent attendance in Gram Sabha meeting.	President, Vice-President, Ward Members, all eligible members, S.H.G. members, N.G.Os. working in the Panchayats	Transparency, accountability of panchayats	Panchayat Records

(Contd.)

Sl. No.	Activities	Responsibility	Outcome	Verification
35.	Ensuring Women / Dalit participation 50 per cent of attendance	President, Vice-President, Ward Members, S.H.G., N.G.O.	Social justice, status of weaker section	Panchayat Records
36.	Information disseminations • Income/Expenditure display • Report on schemes implemented display • List of schemes proposed to be implemented • List of beneficiaries	President and Panchayat Clerk	Transparency, accountability credibility of Panchayat, Better participation	Seeing the Display Board of Panchayat
37.	Participatory decision-making • Opportunities for discussion to all communities • Equal status to all in seating • Developing consensus	President, Ward Members, community leaders/ retired government officials, school teachers, Planning Committee Members, Dalit Leaders, N.G.Os. and other association members	Achieving communal harmony evolution of social capital	Verifying the records of Panchayats
38.	Develop a system of communication to give information about Gram Sabha meeting	President, Clerk, Ward Member, S.H.G., Youth Clubs, N.G.Os.	Transparency, accountability	Physical verification

(Contd.)

Sl. No.	Activities	Responsibility	Outcome	Verification
39.	Provision of water supply to Dalit hamlets	President and the concerned Ward Members, Committee for water supply	Receiving the services continuously	Physical verification
40.	Removal of untouchability by • Preventive the two tumbler system • Participating in temple festival	President, Ward Members, S.H.G., Youth Clubs, Community Leaders	Social justice, Communal harmony	Physical verification
41.	Training to Dalit Youths in skill development and availing THADCO schemes	President, Youth Clubs, N.G.Os., Education Institutions	Economic development, social justice	Physical verification
42.	Identification of all C.P.R. verifying the status of encroachment details	Panchayat President, Vice-President, Ward Members, Government Officials, Police, Department	Environment development social justice, income generation	Verifying Panchayat Records
43.	Removal of encroachments	Panchayat President, Vice-President, Revenue & Police Department	Productive use of resources, equity, income generation for Panchayats	Verifying Panchayat Records

(Contd.)

Sl. No.	*Activities*	*Responsibility*	*Outcome*	*Verification*
44.	Utilizing the Common Properties and developing the same	Panchayat president, Ward Members, N.G.O., S.H.G., Youth groups	Environment development, income generation	Verifying Panchayat Records
45.	100 per cent house tax collection	President, Clerk, Vice-President, Ward Members, S.H.G., Youth	Financial status of Panchayat more government funds	Verifying Panchayat Records
46.	Panchayat functioning as a system	President, Clerk, Vice-President, Ward Members	Accountable	Verifying Panchayat Records
47.	Records maintenance/ transparency	President and Clerk	Good Governance	Verifying Panchayat Records
48.	Preparing a perspective plan through village planning forum	President, Ward Members, Planning Committee, School Leaders, N.G.O., Youth, S.H.G.	Planned development better use of resources	Verifying Panchayat Records
49.	Formation of Statutory Committees	President	Efficiency of Panchayats accountability	Verifying Panchayat Records

(Contd.)

Sl. No.	Activities	Responsibility	Outcome	Verification
50.	Old age, Physically and mentally disabled, destitute, orphan and other vulnerable sections	President, Ward Members, S.H.G., N.G.O., Government, and Planning Committee	Social security, social harmony	Verifying Panchayat Records

The above projected activities could be carried out easily if the Panchayat meets some key assumption. They are:

Key Assumptions

- Harmony prevails in Panchayat.
- Panchayat is perceived as development space.
- Community supports the Panchayats.
- Panchayat leader has got commitment.
- Panchayat leader has vision.
- Panchayat leader has got skill and capacity.
- Panchayat is not leader centric.
- Panchayat is people and system centric.

10

The Panchayats and the Administrators: Need for New Culture for Development at the Grassroots

GEORGE MATHEW

"I toured hundred of villages. I spoke to countless people. There in their hearths and homes I experienced the cruelty of an unresponsive administration, the oppression of an administration without a heart, the callous lack of compassion that most of our people find at the hands of much of our administration."

These were the words of Prime Minister Rajiv Gandhi when he addressed the Lok Sabha participating in the debate on the 64th Amendment to the Constitution Bill on 13 October, 1989. This was the first bill ever aimed at strengthening the Panchayati Raj by giving Constitutional status to it. Those who advocated decentralisation of powers to the people at the village community level believed that the administrators and the officials will become real 'servants of the people' when the Constitution is amended and powers are transferred to the local self-government bodies.

Let me quote Rajiv Gandhi again,

> I then looked at the administrators themselves? most of them dedicated young men and women, of extraordinarily high intelligence, deeply concerned about the people placed in their charge and yet, apparently incapable of converting their enthusiasm and personal compassion into a responsive administration. I sought an answer to the riddle, a solution to this conundrum.

At that time, I must confess, we were in quest of managerial solutions to an unresponsive administration. We were looking to a simplification of procedures, grievance redressal machinery, single-window clearances, computerisation and courtesy as the answers to the problem. As we went along, we discovered that a managerial solution would not do. What was needed was a systematic solution.

We learnt that a grassroots administration without political authority was like a meal without salt. We learnt that however well-intentioned our district bureaucracy might be, without effective elected authority the gap between the people and the bureaucracy could not be closed. We learnt that the vacuum created by the absence of local level political authority had spawned the power brokers who occupy the gap between the people and their representatives in distant Vidhan Sabhas and the ever more remote Parliament. We learnt that corruption could only be ended by giving power to the panchayats and making panchayats responsible to the people. We learnt that inefficiency could only be ended by entrusting the people at the grassroot level with the responsibility for their own development. We learnt that callousness could only be ended by empowering the people to send their own representatives to institutions of local self-government, by empowering the people to reject those who betray their mandate.

The amendments we present are the distilled essence of the views of thousands of elected local body representatives, hundreds of district magistrates, scores of senior government servants and dozens of ministers and chief ministers.

The Panchayati Raj and Nagarpalika Bills are not only instruments for bringing democracy and devolution of every *chaupal* (square) and every *chabutra* (pillar) to every *angan* (verandah) and every dalan, they are also a charter for ending bureaucratic oppression, technocratic tyranny, crass inefficiency, bribery, jobbery, nepotism, corruption and the mission other malfeasance that afflict the poor of our villages, towns and cities. The bills are not the warrant for ending the reign of the power brokers, of the intermediaries.

But what has happened in the last ten years? Has the administration become more responsive? Has the gap between the people and the bureaucracy closed? Has the bureaucratic oppression ended? Even the optimists would say that the situation has hardly changed. Instead of the Panchayati Raj which we envisioned it is still the Collector raj or at the lowest level it is Patwari raj or Gram Sevak raj.

My field work in some of the states revealed that the letter from the Collector is what the CEO of the panchayat follows, not the directives of the elected bodies based on constitutional mandate or state laws. The other side of the story is that the elected members or Village Presidents fall flat at the feat of BDOs and Collectors.

In Maharashtra, considered to be a progressive state, I participated recently in a meeting of the residents of the village Tirth, 30 kms from Osmanabad town. More than 50 villagers along with the Sarpanch, Upa-Sarpanch and the former Sarpanch had gathered for the meeting. I enquired about the budget of the Gram Panchayat. The Sarpanch said he did not know anything about it, only the Gram Sevak would tell us. All documents of the village and village activities are with the Gram Sevak. The Sarpanch doesn't even have a copy of the income-expenditure statement of the panchayat. He takes away the key of the almirah. Ordinarily a Gram Sevak in Maharashtra has about six Gram Panchayats to look after and everything in a village centres around the Gram Sevak and not the elected representatives, even after ten years of the enactment of the Constitutional amendments. Nothing in the village can happen without him. Not even a spare key of the almirah is with the Sarpanch or the Upa-Sarpanch for, they cannot be trusted.

What is happening in Maharashtra regarding officials and panchayats is true of almost all the States except perhaps very few.

What is the basic cause for the continuation of the official hold over the elected bodies at the district and below? No measure is taken by the State Government to give finance, functions and functionaries to the panchayats because no State Government has the political will to do it. If a State Government takes an interest then the bureaucracy sees to it that the initiative is killed in the beginning itself. The officials are unwilling to work the elected panchayat members. They cannot give up their interest in the money flowing for rural development. If all the 29 subjects are brought under the Panchayat elected representatives or the standing committees what is left for them? If the villagers keep a watch over the works being done in their local areas, how could the officials take their share of the cake? These village level, block level and district level officials have become so corrupt that they put all kinds of road blocks in the way of making the panchayats really 'institutions of self-government.'

Isn't it shocking that even today the Gram Sevaks are not answerable to the elected panchayat but to BDO only. The BDO is not answerable to Block Panchayat but to the Collector only. The Collector is not answerable to the District Panchayat but to the Chief Secretary of the State only. Take the case of Tirth village again.

In 1997, the then Gram Sevak collected Rs. 7000 as tax and spent Rs. 1000 to whitewash/paint the GP office on the occasion of the Governor's visit. Incidentally the Gram Sevak in Maharashtra can withdraw the tax money from the Bank with his own single signature. In this case the Gram Sevak refused to show the accounts and when a complaint was made by the Sarpanch he was merely transferred. The new Gram Sevak withdrew Rs. 1600 from the Bank. Neither the account nor a report about its utilization was given. When the matter came into the open, he was transferred. Any punishment? No. Because when the Gram Sevak had gone under another Block Development Officer and how could the BDO under whom he first served punish him? Interestingly, the Gram Sevaks cultivate their own clientele in their Gram Panchayats as well. They go to the houses, discuss the funds availability under different centrally sponsored schemes, and fix a percentage for ensuring the sanction of their individual applications. Thus, he creates a support base among the "well to do" in the Gram Panchayat to become popular in the area. The Gram Panchayat and its elected members are inconsequential. For the officials, democracy and election in villages are a mere formality prescribed in the Constitution.

I took the Tirth case as an exception in the State and wanted to knowhow things were in other villages. I travelled to Wakharwadi, Tugaon, Wadgaon and Yadshi Gram Panchayats in the 60 kms radius of Osmanabad town and also Chincholi and Ramvadi villages in Latur district. Everyone I met had more or less the same story to tell—there is no power for the elected members or Sarpanches or Presidents at the Taluka and District levels. A social worker in one of these meetings stated that she saw in a nearby district the Zilla Parishad President not getting even a seat before the CEO of the district and that he had to stand all the time to explain certain matters before the officer.

The District Rural Development Agency (DRDA) is the biggest money-spinner in a district. But who is controlling this DRDA? The *palak mantri* (minister in charge of the district) and the CEO The minister presides over the *Sarvochya Sabha* (general body) and the CEO is heading the finance and administration as chairman of the Working Committee.

Examples can be multiplied. Unless and until the officials are shown their place our democracy at the grassroots will not work. We have to create a new culture for it. An important step for making the officials responsive to the elected bodies will be to create a Panchayat cadre at the District and below. The mindset of the present officials is such that it is not easy to change. The constitution amendments or government orders have very little impact on their behaviour or attitude.

In order to achieve all the ideals which Rajiv Gandhi stated in his speech, the Constitutional Amendment is only the first step. Several serious actions have to be taken up to protect the people's democratic aspirations and their institutions from the insensitive, corrupt bureaucracy. Creation of a new generation of officials committed to the ideals of grassroots democracy of the new generation of panchayats will be the other major step.

11

Capacity Building for Effective Local Self-Governance: The Indian Experience

RAJESH TANDON

Capacity is a multi-dimensional and complex attribute. Some of these attributes may be awareness, knowledge, skill, self-confidence and actions. Building these attributes has become a need and integral part in the functioning of any system of governance. This article traces the trend in Capacity Building, its conceptual understanding, its present demand and supply in strengthening the Local Self-Governance.

Context

Nearly 88 countries of the world have begun to promote some form of decentralised local government in the past 5-10 years. Despite enormous variation across the countries and regions, two common elements of this decentralised local government are:

1. Some form of regular election to local level bodies with elected representative council for a village or town;
2. Specific administrative and financial devolution to these elected local bodies for undertaking and managing programmes of local development.

In South Asia, this trend began in the early 1990s. In India, the 73rd and 74th Constitutional Amendments brought in 1993 provided the Constitutional framework for constituting such local bodies. The provision in these amendments have some far reaching implications with respect to the governance of local areas in rural and urban centres. By providing 1/3rd reservation for women and proportionate reservation for other socially excluded and deprived sections (tribals, dalits, etc.), the Constitutional framework for local bodies in India has an enormous affirmative action potential.

The experience of functioning of these local bodies in the past 6-7 years in India makes it clear that effective local self-governance is still a distant dream and requires enormous interventions to realise its potential.

However, the complexity of the situation demands a broader understanding of the methodologies for capacity building. This paper presents our perspectives on the same, based on our experience during the last 5 years.

Meaning of Capacity Building

Capacity can be defined as the totality of inputs needed by an actor to realise its purposes. Applied to local bodies, this will ensure that such institutions are able to function effectively as institutions of local self-governance in the perspective elaborated above. Capacity of such institutions can also be seen in three distinct though inter-related aspects:

(a) Intellectual Capacity

This implies capacity to think, reflect and analyse reality independently and in pursuit of self-defined purposes of local self-governance.

(b) Institutional Capacity

This implies procedures, systems, structure, staffing, decision-making, transparency and accountability, planning, implementation and monitoring. It also includes mechanisms for building linkages with others.

(c) Material Capacity

This includes material resources, physical assets, funds, ability, systems and procedures to mobilise revenues; and access and control over physical and natural resources and infrastructure; systems and procedures required for adequate management of funds and such infrastructure.

Viewed in the above sense, capacity of a development actor or a local body means an examination of its purposes at a given period of its life cycle. The capacity building needs change over time.

One of the consequences of the above is an acknowledgement of diversity and temporal dynamism in the requirements of capacity for any development actor. What then is Capacity Building? Invariably, training of individuals is seen as the sine-qua-non of capacity building through some pre-determined package of inputs. However, capacity building comprises of a variety of other approaches and processes such as, organisational strengthening, institutional learning, field exposure and projects, horizontal sharing and solidarity are some of the other illustrations of practical, on-the-job and experiential learning processes to capacity building.

Viewed in this sense, capacity building is a long-term process of strengthening an actor (or a local body) based on systematic learning of new knowledge, skills and attitudes. Like all learning, the actor herself must see the value of and take responsibility for that learning. This capacity building cannot be imposed from outside. Preparation of the actor (or a local body) to identify its particular capacity needs and motivation to take responsibility for learning those is a major part of capacity building intervention in such a framework.

This does not imply that external interventions have no role in capacity building. There are many:

- Preparation of the actor (or a local body) in terms of external stimulation and intervention.
- Providing opportunities for systematic learning and facilitating such learning.
- Accessing and making available resources for capacity enhancement.

- Supporting on-going and sustained capacity enhancement over a long-term.

In this framework, capacity building efforts address needs for enhancing capacity at the level of individual and organised collectives. In the framework presented above, different elements and processes of capacity building for local self-governance in the Indian context are elaborated and illustrated.

System of Local Governance

Through Constitutional Amendments, the system of local self-governance established in India has the following broad features:

1. There are 3-tiers of elected bodies in rural areas—Gram Panchayat (GP) at the village level; Panchayat Samiti (PS), at the block level and Zilla Parishad (ZP) at the district level.
2. The village assembly of all adult voters is identified as Gram Sabha.
3. At all tiers of elected representatives, l/3rd of all seats is reserved for women. Like-wise, reservation for socially oppressed (dalits and tribals) has also been mandated.
4. Regular elections every 5 years have been constitutionally mandated.
5. The Constitution lists a number of development areas for which the three-tiers of the local bodies have responsibility.
6. Finance Commissions have been constitutionally required to allocate budgetary resources and the power for mobilising revenue to local bodies.

In a vast country like India, this democratic decentralisation has enormous challenge. In rural areas, nearly a quarter million local bodies exist. Nearly three million elected representatives are there in these local bodies, of which nearly one million are women.

Capacity Building for Local Governance

PRIA's focus of interventions to strengthen local self-governance has targeted the lowest tier of this structure. Therefore, the interventions aimed at capacity building have largely been of two varieties: demand and supply. Fig. 1 provides a schematic overview of the system of local governance and its demand-supply linkages.

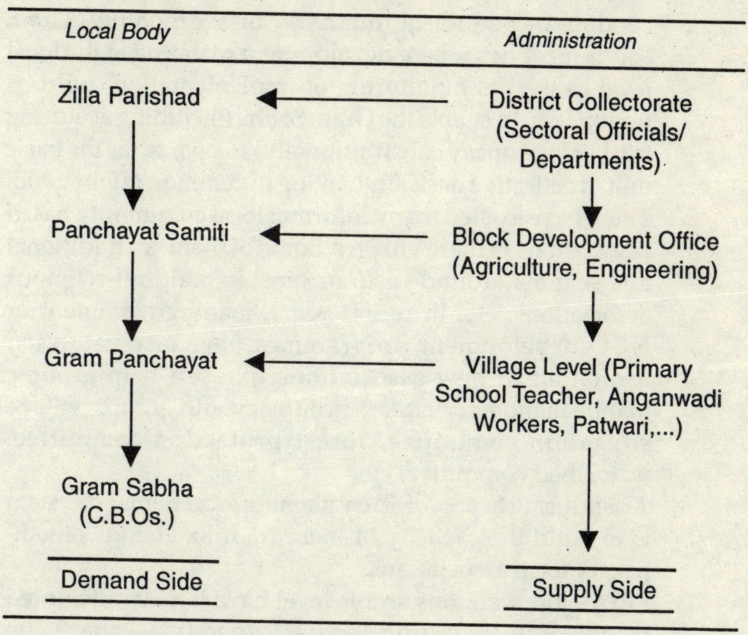

Fig. 1: Tiers of Local Body and Administration.

A. Strengthening Demand

Effective functioning of local self-governance requires active, engaged and organised citizenry. In the practical context of today's reality, families and communities have been increasingly divided around caste, religion, ethnicity and gender. Therefore, the most significant intervention needed is to strengthen Gram Sabha as contemporary civil society formation in each hamlet and village.

1. Capacity enhancement interventions at this level would entail an appreciation of the collective identity of Gram Sabha. Such an intellectual preparation requires inculcating a perspective of collective citizenship as the basis of civil society. PRIA's efforts at mobilising

individuals and families in a hamlet or a village to work together to address common problems at the village level has been inspired by this approach.

2. A strong Gram Sabha also requires institutional mechanism to function effectively. It requires effective conduct of periodical (quarterly or six monthly) Gram Sabha meetings where development planning at the local level as well as monitoring of implementation could be undertaken to enable the Gram Sabha (including acquiring further legitimacy constitutionally) to operate as the basic unit of collective decision-making in common public good.
3. There have existed many informal local community based associations in these villages. Some of them are traditional associations around caste or kinship, cultural-religious associations, etc. In recent years, many government or NGO development programmes have also catalysed formation of new associations like self-help-groups, mahila mandals (women's groups), youth groups, village education committee, forest protection committee, watershed committee, etc.

   A significant aspect of strengthening local demand system is to build the capacity of these traditional and contemporary local associations.

   PRIA's interventions at this level have largely attempted to enhance their intellectual capacity to share the perspective of local governance. This enables these traditional and contemporary local associations to work in synergy with the Gram Panchayat and the Gram Sabha.
4. The elected representatives of Gram Panchayat (numbering between 7-11 members), represent a small hamlet or village. In addition, there is a Sarpanch—elected as Chief of Gram Panchayat directly by all members of Gram Sabha. In some ways, this body is the first and most direct representative body of local self-governance. However, Gram Panchayat as a vehicle for exercising representative leadership with transparency and accountability to Gram Sabha is a distant ideal.
   (*a*) To understand the autonomous and basic democratic nature of Gram Panchayat as a collective decision-making body, most significant interventions have

focused on preparing this collective identity. Such interventions have aimed at developing a common perspective and intellectual appreciation of the Gram Panchayat.

(*b*) The second set of interventions aimed at Gram Panchayat is their institutional mechanism to function as transparent and accountable local body. This includes mechanisms for conducting meetings, preparing minutes, sharing information with Gram Sabha, securing participation and contribution of Gram Sabha, developing participatory micro plans, procedures and systems, effective implementation and monitoring of these plans, securing and mobilising resources and maintaining transparent systems of financial management, etc.

(*c*) The capacity building intervention at this level also needs to address the question of enhancing the material base of Gram Panchayat to make them financially autonomous and sustainable entities. Capacity enhancement interventions in this area particularly focus on mobilising local resources from the village.

5. Perhaps, the most significant interventions in capacity enhancement at this level need to focus on building individual leadership of each of the elected representatives. This is particularly relevant for women, dalits and tribals. Political participation in public space is being experienced by these newly elected leaders for the first time in their life. Thus, enhancing their leadership roles requires capacity enhancement in several ways:

(*a*) Access to authentic information about the system of local governance, their roles and responsibilities and financial resources available to them are the first and foremost requirement. Capacity building for these literate and semi-literate constituencies such as women, dalits and tribals, requires methodological innovations in audio-visuals, folk forms, etc., to be carried out in different settings.

(*b*) Most of these elected women have not left their house or hamlet ever before. Therefore, opportunities for homogenous groups of women, dalits and tribal to share their experiences, express solidarity and provide mutual support need to be created. It is in this context that exposure visits for groups of elected representatives, joint camps and big sammelans (Conferences) have been utilised as innovative approaches to building self-confidence for the elected leadership.

(*c*) Exercising new leadership also requires learning new skills. These skills include how to conduct a meeting, how to prepare minutes, how to prepare village plans, how to manage funds, etc. Learning these skills through training, practical demonstration and hand-holding needs to be promoted.

Therefore, capacity enhancement interventions aimed at individual strengthening and empower-ment of new leaders is a fundamental challenge in local governance.

6. Given different tiers of local bodies, vertical linkages across them need to be strengthened.
7. One of the most significant areas of strengthening is to enable horizontal linkages between different tiers of local bodies and commensurate tiers of local administration. These include primary school teachers, village level workers, Anganwadi workers, multi-purpose health workers, forest guards, police hawaldars (constables), etc.

According to constitutional provision, all the above mentioned government functionaries should be accountable to Gram Panchayat. However, this is not a reality anywhere in India so far. Gram Panchayat needs to learn how to assert their rights and supervision over the concerned government functionaries and relevant government development programmes and resources. Structured learning opportunities heed to be created separately for Gram Panchayat, as well as jointly with concerned government officials and their supervisors.

8. Another area of horizontal networking is building relationships and support mechanisms with other elected representatives in neighbouring villages, blocks and districts. Support towards building such horizontal

networks as bottom-up pressure groups and mutual support mechanisms are a major challenge of capacity building in local governance.

B. Strengthening Supply

Another aspect of building capacity is to influence and enhance the supply side in local governance.

1. Orientation and attitudinal change for government functionaries at all levels is a major challenge in working with responsive and accountable bureaucracy. A primary vehicle for bringing this about is through civil service training institutions at the district, state and national levels. This may imply improving pedagogy and quality of facilitators in such government civil service training institutions.
2. The second area of capacity enhancement for government functionaries has to do with specific skills that they may need to work with Panchayati Raj Institutions. For example, in the system of top-down development interventions, lowest level government officials have no skill in planning and monitoring since all of that has been centralised. They need to learn skills in promoting micro plans (including budgeting) as well as social audit and community monitoring of implementation of these plans.
3. Sensitisation and attitudinal changes are also a major arena of capacity enhancement for political leadership at all levels. Barring a few individuals, the political culture in most political parties and among active and elected politicians is one of the disregard for the activities and motivations of ordinary people to take responsibility for village level development. Carefully selected communication strategies, meetings, dialogues and workshops could be utilised for such capacity enhancement interventions.
4. Another aspect of supply side is intermediary development NGOs. Most of them have a package of development programmes, which they implement in various villages. Orientation and sensitisation of these

intermediary NGOs to work through Panchayats and the Gram Sabha is a necessary challenge of capacity enhancement. PRIA and its partners' interventions have reached out to more than 500 such NGOs in the country. Yet, there are many more who are neither convinced about the significance of local government nor willing to change their approaches and programmes to respond to them.

5. Capacity enhancement interventions are most urgently needed to sensitise and re-orient donors. Despite general discussions, concrete shifts in donor policies, resources and programmes towards strengthening institutions of local governance is yet to take place.
6. Finally, there is a vast arena of public education for society at large so that different individuals and institutions such as the media, academic institutions, youth groups, human rights organisations and others who need to be sensitised and oriented to the challenges faced by local bodies in building their capacities to accomplish their constitutionally mandated purposes.

To ensure the match between strengthening the demand side and responsiveness of supply side is a challenge in the present context. This is particularly so when demand generates heightened levels of expectations, which are not adequately responded to by the supply side.

Conclusion

The above narrative describes the challenges facing effective development for effective local self-governance. Bulk of this capacity focuses on promoting participation in local public institutions. Obstacles to such participation are cultural, systemic, institutional and human. Thus, inclusion of the marginalised is a primary challenge of capacity enhancement interventions.

Local governance can be made more transparent and accountable to local community only if civil society assertions are coherent and persistent. The interface between strong civil society and effective local governance can be secured more organically if capacity building interventions are properly designed and implemented.

Changing attitudes and beliefs is at the very heart of democratic functioning. This implies a culture of dialogue, consultation and consensus building. These values and processes need to be nurtured through sustained capacity enhancement interventions.

Intensive documentation of these interventions is a necessary first step. Sharing of innovations and experiments and best practices is an important part of this effort.

REFERENCES

1. Enter the New Millennium, 1999, PRIA.
2. Future Capacity building of Southern NGOs, 1998, *IFCB, Funding Conference in Brussels.*
3. Capacity Building in Civil Society, 1997, Paper presented by Dr. Rajesh Tandon at *Support Organisation Meeting in Harare.*
4. Future Capacity building of Southern NGOs, *1998, IFCB, Funding Conference in Brussels.*
5. *The Challenges in Capacity Building: Support Organisation in South Asia,* 1999, Dhaka, Bangladesh.
6. Entre the New Millennium, 1999, PRIA.

The earlier version of the paper was presented on behalf of International Forum of Capacity Building (IFCB) for the Interaction Forum meeting during April 17-18, 2000 at Washington D.C.

12

Strengthening Rural Democracy in India: A Case Study of Rajasthan

N.S. GEHLOT

The State Legislative Assembly passed the Rajasthan Panchayati Raj Act on April 23, 1994, in accordance with the 73rd Constitutional Amendment, while giving 29 subjects to be governed by these grassroots bodies. The state had the rich experience of the functioning of these bodies prior to the passage of the above cited amendment by Parliament. Need not to mention, Rajasthan was the first state of the country which laid foundation of the process of decentralisation and panchayat raj system in 1959. As per the Act, 1994, the state has successfully conducted the two elections of the three-tier system since 1994, one by the BJP—led government headed by Sri B.S. Shekhawat in February, 1995 and the other by the present Congress headed by Ashok Gehlot in the year of 1999. Both the regimes have shown the faith in the process of decentralisation and democratisation of these grassroot bodies. They have accorded importance to women empowerment as well as reservations to the weaker sections of society, along with the autonomy of these bodies. The Act has defined the functions and powers of these bodies, but it is silent about the executive powers of Panchayat Raj Institutions in regard to recruitment, appointment of staff and the control under them. As per the census of 1991, the process of delimitation of those bodies were undertaken by the Government in 1994. Consequently, the number of Village Panchayats, Panchayat Samithies and Zilla Parishad increased to 9,187,237 and 31, respectively. There were 9,185 panchayats. Thus the entire rural Rajasthan was brought under the umbrella of Panchayati Raj system. It is being strengthened.

Rajasthan had 27,000 Women Panchayats for the first time. Of the 9,173 panchayats, 3058 panchayats were women sarpanchas. The state had 237 Panchayat Samithies. The elections for the three-tier Panchayati Raj Institutions were held in phases. The elections were held on party lines as there is no restrictions in the Act on the basis of the understanding among the political parties. The elections of the *pradhans* were held on political lines in the state. The sarpanchas will not become members of the Panchayat Samithies and the *pradhans* will not become members of the Zilla Parishads. The MLAs and MPs cannot contest panchayat elections.

Rajasthan is the first state to introduce the two children restriction on the candidates contesting the panchayat elections. However, relief has been granted to the candidates having twins. Where the couple have only one child on the date of the commencement of the Act and thereafter, any number of children born out of a single subsequent delivery shall be deemed to be one entity. Those convicted of an offence punishable under the Rajasthan prevention of Mrityu Bhoj Act, 1990 will be disqualified from seeking the panchayat elections. However, there is no disqualification for those encouraging child marriages. The Government, however, on the eve of the civil elections in Rajasthan, waived the condition till November, 1995.

The State Government has drawn up many special thrust on employment and training for women with the purpose of securing equal rights and empowering the rural women. These include the Anganwadi Plan, the support to Training and Employment Programme (STEP), the Employment-cum-Income Generation-cum-Production Units NORAD and the Indira Mahila Yojana (IMY), Programmes of Education, etc. The aim of these schemes is to change the social attitude to facilitate equal participation of men and women and pave the way for harmonious social growth to create a conducive environment for the advancement of women in Rajasthan. The state has also taken steps towards/setting, up commissioner for women's right in accordance with the goals of National Policy for the Empowerment of Women and the advancement of gender equality. The State's budget 1995-96 contained special clause for it. On the other hand, the Government of Rajasthan has strictly enforced the two children condition for the elected members, and numerous elected candidates both men and women have been disqualified on account of the violation of the clause of the Act. Its purpose is to restrict the growing rate of population in Rajasthan.

On being challenged Section 19 of the Rajasthan PR Act, 1994, and Section 26 of the Rajasthan Municipalities Act, 1994 providing for disqualification of elected representatives for routing the two children norm, the Rajasthan High Court on August 30,1997 held the norm laid down in the legislation constitutionally valid. According to the Division Bench of the High Court, the provision is in the national interest. This is one of the pioneering steps to check the growing rate of population in the state. This norm can be followed by other states also for their elected members.

EDUCATION: THE BASIS OF STATE'S GROWTH

The present Government's attempt has been to expand the basic education network. For it, education is the foremost condition for development, which can only help in checking the growing population and ensuring economic prosperity. The Government has launched many such measures and projects to enlighten the people about their rights and duties. They are: *Shiksha Apke Dwar, Lok Jumbish Shiksha, Shiksha Karmi*, DPER etc. The experiment of opening Rajiv Gandhi Swaran Jayanti Pathshalas on the Madhya Pradesh pattern in strengthening the education sector in the state has earned popularity. Over 12,000 buildings for such *pathshalas* (Schools) have been constructed under Famine Relief Programme. Under this school system, educated youth of villages are employed for imparting education. For this purpose, it may be recalled, the *Shiksha Darpan* survey was carried out in 2000 to identify the urban and rural children who had not been enrolled in these schools. Over 23 lakh such children have been identified who were deprived of basic education. Today, hectic efforts have been made to enroll over 12.35 lakh children, and about 10.65 lakh children are yet to be enrolled in schools. Most of these children belong to SCs, STs, minorities and other backward classes. This programme today is carried out under *Shiksha Apke Dwar* campaign. If it is successfully implemented by officials, government employees and school teachers, it would bring the state in the category of the developed state of the country.

Likewise, the State Government has given top priority to strengthening the road network in the state. In this direction, a sum of Rs. 600 crore has been sanctioned on upgrading 24,000 km roads in the state. The Government is serious to see that the Pradhan Mantri Gram Sadak Yojana is fully implemented to connect all villages of over 1,000 population. The cooperation of Panchayats is currently sought to ensure that the target of expansion of basic amenities including roads, power, education, medical health and drinking water in the rural areas of the state is achieved by March end of 2003, or before the next assembly elections. The ruling party has in its mind the fall out of anti-incumbency factor, which finished the BJP's base in the 1998 elections.

Notably, Chief Secretary Inderjit Khanna in a many meetings of top brass has directed officials concerned to lay special emphasis on completing the basic amenities in the rural areas as per the schedule. Stress is being given for the effective implementation of all those programmes as cited above. Congress President Mrs. Sonia Gandhi, too, has asked all the Congress Chief Ministers to implement the Party's poll manifesto in totality in their respective states in the Gauhati session of the party. She has taken the three meetings with the CM of Rajasthan to see that the dalits, minorities, women and backward classes are properly cared of through the development programmes. The State Government has taken many steps to strengthen the working of Panchayati Raj bodies in the rural areas.

About Rajiv Pathshalas

When the Chief Minister took over the reigns of the state, he directed the officials to follow the manifesto of the Congress Party like 'Bible' and accordingly he shaped the policies and projects to achieve the mission. The CM is determined to raise the literacy rate by providing education at the door step. His slogan *Pani Bachao, Bijli Bachao, Sabko Padhao* (save water, save electricity and teach all) has earned popularity and the World Bank has even appreciated the slogan. But so far as the employment sector is concerned, it has not been able to generate many jobs. Instead of providing jobs, the state has surged to 12 lakhs employees. The only consolation for the educated youth is the Rajiv Gandhi Pathshalas. These *pathshalas* impart primary education and appointment of the teachers are done through Gram Sabha—the lowest tier of the rural administration.

Each Gram Panchayat has a woman teacher and by appointing 32,000 such teachers, eight lakh children who were deprived of basic education are now likely to get education. The teachers of Rajiv Gandhi Pathshala get an honorarium of Rs. 1300 per month. The then Opposition leader Bhairon Singh Shekhawat blamed the government for opening an avenue for the Congress cadre and paying them Rs. 1300 per month through the Rajiv Gandhi Pathshala Scheme.

The Gehlot Government is finding it tough to implement the recommendations of the Fifth Pay Commission to abolish 10 per cent of posts in various government departments on an annual basis. It is so because the State Government has signed an MoU with the Union Government to this effect. However, the State Government feels that large scale abolition of posts will not be practical and it would cause a setback electorally. The Government is unable to abolish posts in the health, education and police departments though a sub-committee of the cabinet had suggested that 6,000 posts should be abolished. Against the recommendations of the sub-committee, only 3,000 posts have been abolished. The present work force of government employees are six lakhs and those working in the Panchayat Raj is about a lakh. The state is finding it difficult to disburse salary every month.

Rooting Out Corruption

As regards rooting out of corruption in the state, the State Government has appointed a Chief Vigilance Commissioner (CVC) to weed out corruption at high places. The State's Anti-corruption Bureau has booked a number of cases against high officials including some Collectors. As first CVC, Sri R.K. Naiyar received over one thousand complaints against officials, but no action was taken. There is a growing trend corruption at the Panchayati Raj level too. The sad thing is that the role and powers of the CVC has not been properly outlined and Sarpanchas are taken out of the purview of the CVC. The Personnel department has not given the CVC powers to book State Government employees. At present there is a Lokayukta institution headed by Justice M.C. Jain, but it has proved to be a toothless body.

Land Allotment Campaign

According to official figure, the State Government claims to have allotted land to 57,000 families through the camps known as 'Prashashan Gao ke Sang', 'Prashashan Shaharo Ke Sang'. According to the Government, over 57,000 families of different categories have been allotted the land worth Rs. 200 crore during camps organised under land allotment and regularisation campaigns in different parts of the state. Under the campaign, over 27,000 families of general categories have benefitted from the allotment and regularisation of 42,414 acres of land worth Rs. 72.22 crore it is claimed that in these camps, nine thousand acres of land, costing 28,92 crore has been allotted to 7,716 families of scheduled castes and 23,509 acres of land, costing Rs. 72.22 crore to 22,247 families of scheduled tribes. Over 50,000 families have been allotted agricultural land under the land allotment and regularisation campaign in the state. It includes 7,165 families of Ajmer Division, 1,455 families of Bikaner, 6,966 families of Jaipur, 1,041 families of Jodhpur, 10,128 families of Kota and 24,305 families of Udaipur. As many as 6,507 scheduled castes families, 21,344 scheduled tribe families and 22,210 families of general categories have been benefitted under the campaign.

Similarly, land of 6,898 families has been regularised, including 1,209 families of scheduled castes, 903 families of scheduled tribes and 4,786 families of general category. (*The Times of India*, New Delhi, Edition., 9th July, 2002, p. 3).

Implementation of Family Planning Rule

Rajasthan is the pioneer state to adopt the family planning concept at the Panchayat Raj level and as per the provision of 39 (2) of the Act, the born of a third child of any elected member is a crime. Rajasthan is the first state to adopt this rule. Accordingly, the state officials have been very much serious about the implementation of this provision. A number of elected members from *Pradhans* towards have been disqualified in 2001-02, after a thorough investigation by Divisional Commissioners, though in most of cases, local level feuds have been the cause of complaints by villagers. Third child has practically proved to be a curse for these elected members at the grassroot levels.

The administration has instructed all officials to ensure effective implementation of 'Shiksha Aapke Dwar' campaign and mid-day meal programme in all districts. Most of the primary schools have been involved in this mission. The rural administration bears the responsibility of enrolling children under the 'Shiksha Aapke Dwar' campaign, so as to achieve cent-percent target of literacy. As regards arrangement of the mid-day meal programme rural officials have been asked to ensure that wheat should not be rotten. Tehsildars, have been made in-charge of this programme.

The present Government has taken up the Anti-poverty project at District/Panchayat level to benefit those families who are below poverty line. It is meant to eradicate poverty. This programme is being carried out with the assistance of the World Bank. The CM has very much serious about the proper implementation of the school children nutrition programme (mid-day food) and to effect the CM has written a letter to the Centre on July 13, 2002 to ensure the supply of a good quality of wheat being provided by the FCI for these poor and dalit children. This is meant to avoid any health hazards to children. This state administration has received numerous complaints about the poor quality of wheat. Even many parents have directed their children not to consume the mid-day food (Gughari).

In Rajasthan, the polity is gradually changing. The ruling party has started giving importance to 'good governance'. The Chief Minister emphasised all efforts to project the right image of his Government so that it can return to power next year. The party has picked up cudgels in advance to keep the anti-incumbency factor away. The grit and determination has been shown 15 months before the party faces the next assembly elections falling due in 2003.

Among other priorities, the ruling Congress in Rajasthan has been giving to priority to supply of potable water in the far flung areas of Rajasthan, and the CM has sanctioned to increase the capacity of the Rajiv Gandhi Lift Canal to benefit more villages. For this purpose Rs. 108 crore has been sanctioned. The CM is concerned of the constant lowering of the underground water level in the state. To fight the current curse of famine seems to be a serious challenge for the State Government both administratively and electorally. The second top priority of the CM is power sector reforms. The power production has been improved/increased due to power reforms.

The CM has laid the foundation stone at many places to erect more grid substations, in order to ensure adequate supply of electricity in the rural belt. The Congress Party has launched many other campaigns to bring respite to the common people. For example, over 66 lakh rural population had been benefitted under the 'Prashashan Gao ke Sang,' campaign and 12 lakh urban population under the *Prashashan Sehron ke Sang*. Under these campaigns many land regularisation and allotment of land has been carried out. This approach has yielded positive results. Now the Government has initiated to open 'cyber kiosks' in many villages.

With a view to bring about improvement in the nutrition and health level of children and women, the state administration has initiated 66 child development projects under the ICDS III project of the state. They commenced in the year 1999 and shall be continued till 2004. Under this programme, over 9, 648 new anganwadi centers would be opened. At present, 9,240 such centers are already functioning and the centre has earmarked over Rs. 190.68 crore for this purpose. Like-wise, the CM plans to spend Rs. 120 crore for nutrition programme to benefit school children in the state.

Concluding Observations

The pattern of decentralisation of administrative machinery has reduced the role of the bureaucracy and local autonomy and accountability have been strengthened. But the apprehensions are expressed that the devolution of this power under the new act may create a sense of deep frustration among bureaucrats, who are now expected to work under the elected representatives in panchayats, and they may handle the new assignment half heartedly, against the spirit of democratic decentralisation. The danger at this moment is that if the euphoria is generated about the 'power to the people concept', the bureaucracy may be seen as friend to the PR system. This is possible only if it ensures the freedom to these bodies in terms of their powers entrusted under the Constitution Amendment Act, 1992. The question is—how to motivate the bureaucracy to make the PRIs successful? It is proposed that periodic conferences/seminars or meetings of various heads of departments and elected members local bodies may be convened to highlight the roles to be played by the civil servants in making the scheme a success. These conferences/

meetings should be addressed by the Chief Minister and the role of bureaucracy *vis-a-vis* the elected members should be clarified in the era of globalisation and liberalisation. A motivated bureaucracy is a necessary condition for the success of the nascent democratic polity at the lowest level or PR system.

The slogan 'power to the people' shall have to be linked with the past mischievous and demagogic experiences in which the real powers are yet to be transferred to these people. It may be recalled that our colonial hangover system of district administration remains intact and it is responsible for the failure of our PR system. It may negate the potentiality of the reforms even today. Therefore, there will be need to ensure under the new changes in the act that the measure does not suffer in the course of implementation. The State Government will have to provide adequate funds to empower these grassroots bodies to raise them. Care will have to be taken to ensure that the new decentralized system does not become the prey of our societal structure, back wardness, illiteracy and the culture of poverty, coupled with caste, communalism and the other group rivalries in the majority of the villages.

It is heartening that the ruling Congress Party is sensitive to the power to the people concept, or the functioning rural democracy in Rajasthan. It is gradually reducing the powers of the bureaucracy to ensure the concept of autonomy, transparency and accountability of these bodies. There is no doubt that the middle classes and peasants as well as women have been enlightened by programmes and policies carried out by the State Government. However, the State leadership is supposed to take into account the following aspects:

(*a*) The grassroots bodies should not be allowed to suffer from the paucity of funds.

(*b*) The interference of the party in power in the state should be minimal and the role of the Collector and his jurisdiction should be finalised in respect of the running the self-government. He is still the symbol of imperial rule on a republic base. The trend of politicisation of the local administration through the bureaucratic staff should be discouraged as the state had the experience of it before the enactment of 73rd/74th Amendments Act. The need of an hour is to have a proper coordination, both vertical and horizontal between the popular and bureaucratic elements. There is also a need for change in the psychology of the government servants. The voice of elected members must have primacy over the bureaucratic element, and for this a proper training should be provided to the administrative personnel.

(*c*) The proliferation of caste-cum-trends at the grassroots level must be prevented in order to boost up egalitarian trends contribution towards the socialistic pattern in our rural economy. Care has to be taken that new economic order of the country with the market oriented forces does not become a source of exploitation of poor/rural masses of the state through the dominant caste superiority or rampant factionalism. Real rural leadership should be allowed to merge in palace of forged linkages between caste and politics.

(*d*) The practice of child labour is still widespread and our children are employed in local factories, small industries and farm fields. The mission of curbing child labour can be achieved by rapid growth and expansion of primary and secondary education at the grass-root levels.

(*e*) Social mobilisation is vital for the removal of poverty and the success of poverty alleviation programmes hinges crucially on social mobilization, which will in turn lead to greater efficiency in the use of resources. But it has been seen that no state has so far set up any machinery under the new legislation enacted through the 73rd Constitutional Amendment relating to Panchayati Raj. Our concern is that social mobilisation *vis-a-vis* poverty alleviation pro-grammes should be linked with the grassroots level planning process and the efforts should be made by our Planning Commission to involve Non-Governmental Organisation (NGOs) for the success of the programmes and plans. A top bottom approach without adequate participation has been mainly responsible for the failure of such programmes. In this process, the district should be the basis to deal with the issues like illiteracy, land degradation, continued population growth, gender inequalities, food security, application of technologies, maintenance of rural health etc.

13

Decentralised Governance at Grassroots Level: Experience of Panchayati Raj in Madhya Pradesh

YATINDRA SINGH SISODIA

Village communities have been in existence in India for over centuries and panchayats have been an intimate part of the Indian culture. Panchayati system is one of the unique democratic institutions evolved in India by country's own genius and ethos (Kashyap, 2002). After independence efforts were made to create and strengthen the institutions of local self-governance but all in vein as the issue of people's participation at grassroots level was not taken into serious consideration. 50 plus years of independence witnessed the multi-dimensional approach of various governments at Centre and State for planned development of vast rural India. Despite plethora of schemes and massive investment in rural sector, the rural scenario remained under-developed with no infrastructure and basic amenities like—road, water, electricity, school, hospital and opportunities for employment.

The idea that produced the 73rd Amendment Act was not a response to pressure from the grassroots but to an increasing recognition that the institutional initiatives of the preceding decades had not delivered, that the extent of rural poverty was still much too large and thus the existing structure of government needed to be reformed. It is interesting to note that this idea evolved from the Centre and the State Governments. It was a political drive to see PRIs. as a solution to the governmental crises that India was experiencing (World Bank, 2000). The Institution of

Panchayati Raj in its rejuvenated form seeks to achieve the objectives of democratic decentralization to accelerate socio-economic development and usher in equity and social justice. The enactments of the 73rd Constitutional Amendment Act and the subsequent state-wise Panchayat Raj Acts in India have brought to frontline the significance of grassroots democratic processes. This change in the Indian political system is the result of a growing conviction that the big government cannot achieve growth and development in a society without people's direct participation and initiative. This experience has brought the lesson that the success of the new panchayat raj system largely depends on the congruence of perception and commitment of people, their leaders and the officials, about the role to be played by them in the new system. Contextually and theoretically too, the new panchayat raj system has been created as a model of self-governance (Sisodia, 2002 a). The objectives of decentralisation are to execute and implement schemes and programmes to meet the local needs, to mobilise people, to channelise their energies towards socio-economic reconstruction and to involve them in all the activities of the communities through the new institutions. Its objectives include also to reduce the size of work of the higher level government and leaving the responsibility to the people to decide their destiny as per the new dispensation.

Madhya Pradesh is the first state in India, which had not only prepared its state legislation in accordance with 73rd Amendment Act but also conducted election in May-June, 1994. Madhya Pradesh Government has been doing remarkable work for the strengthening of panchayat raj system since its inception. The term of five years of this system was over in June, 1999 and elections for the second term of the panchayats were held in January-February, 2000. Looking in to the relevance of new system, an attempt is made to evaluate the ground reality and potentiality of the panchayat raj system in Madhya Pradesh. The paper is dealing with the issues of gram sabha, reservation, women representatives, working of panchayats, panchayats and bureaucracy, devolution of powers and finance in separate sub-headings.

Gram Sabha

The legislative empowerment of the gram sabha in India is a political development of utmost importance, because it marks the clearest break from the most dominant political orthodoxy of this century (Mander, 1999). This recent faith in gram sabha is based on the belief that the objective conditions of the poor are directly involved in the process of formulation and implementation of decisions affecting their lives.

It is important to recognise that this faith in the gram sabha is based on several extremely important but largely untested assumptions. It is assumed firstly that even in a village society with deep schisms of caste, class and gender, an organic community still exists and that given appropriate legal and institutional spaces, it can act cogently and responsibly as a community. The second assumption is that the collective of the gram sabha would be a more reliable vehicle of good governance than a relatively unencumbered bureaucracy or local elected representatives.

The experience of panchayati raj in Madhya Pradesh indicates that the State Act has been amended from time to time to make it more effective in establishing panchayati raj system as genuine structure of grassroots democracy since 73rd Amendment Act came into effect. Original Act had a provision of a Gram Sabha every year with a quorum of 10 per cent of members. By the first Amendment to the Act in 1994 themselves the meetings were increased to at least one in every three months.

It is evident from the experience of panchayat raj that the level of participation of people at grassroots level was very low and gram sabhas were almost a formal institution with no role in various assigned works related to rural development. This situation has explored a solid ground for the introduction of Gram Swaraj on 26 January, 2001. The State Government transferred nearly all of the powers previously exercised by gram panchayats to gram sabha. It has thus gone from representative democracy at the grassroots to direct democracy. More than 60 countries worldwide have experimented with some sort of democratic decentralisation over the last 15 years or so. But evidence currently available indicates that none has gone for direct democracy at the local level to the extent that Madhya Pradesh has now done (Manor, 2001).

Gram Sabha or people's forum has always been an integral part of the concept of a gram panchayat. Rajni Kothari visualises gram sabha as 'watchdogs' coming between the politician-bureaucratic nexus (Kothari, 1998). It is unfortunate that both grassroots leadership and grassroots bureaucracy both could not strengthen the Gram Sabha. The institution of Gram Sabha is dysfunctional due to the lack of leverage of local leaders to initiate meaningful participation in the sabha and their incapability to persuade people to support local initiatives (Fernandes, 1999). It has been evident that meetings called were mostly without prior and adequate notice. In most places, only a formality was observed; proxy meetings, at time were convened and proceedings were written even without the knowledge of those who attended. Meeting, if arranged, either proved to be abortive or unsuccessful because of thin attendance with the panchayat or discussion (Mander, 1999). It is certain that unless we have a vibrant gram sabha, we cannot have empowered and accountable panchayats (Nambiar, 2001).

Legislation by itself is not adequate for correcting a wrong. The experience of the last eight years has revealed a general indifference towards the functions of Gram Sabha and its meetings. The significance of Gram Sabha has not as yet rubbed upon the villagers. Their eyes are still focused on the Gram Panchayat as the hub of all activity. Not only this, even panchayat officials and the local elite have evinced little interest in the functioning of the Gram Sabha. Although there is a provision in the Act to remove a Sarpanch who does not convene a Gram Sabha meeting as stipulated by the Act, no such removal has taken place till now.

Gram Sabhas are to be made effective, active and creative so that the expected result could be accessible to the rural society. It is foremost responsibility of the panchayat raj representatives to convey to the people the real nature, function and the real spirit of Gram Sabha. Meeting of Gram Sabha can be a good platform for the solution of various day-to-day problems pertaining to the village society. This platform can also be used for the initiation of community work. Most of the basic rural problems, which have hardly any cost effect, can be solved through motivation among the villagers and the Gram Sabha is the right forum to discuss all such issues.

The vibrancy and efficacy of Gram Sabha will remain dismal if it does not posses the capacity to perform assigned roles and responsibility. This question becomes more pertinent in a socio-cultural milieu where human resource development is low and society is deeply fragmented and hierarchical. And therefore it is urgently needed that marginalised sections of society which have been out from the process of decision-making have to be taken in mainstream through sensitization and capacity building. The need is to address the issue of awareness generation among masses. Training camps, awareness campaigns and audio-visual mediums can be of critical importance for the sensitisation and capacity building.

Reservation

The state legislation has made provision for the reservation of Scheduled Castes, Scheduled Tribes and Other Backward Castes. All these groups had negligible presence in the rural politics before this statutory provision. It is definitely a very important step through which largest political recruitment has become possible.

The Scheduled Castes have been provided reservation in proportion to their population. A basic difference between the SC and the ST is that while the latter reside in specific habitats, the former livealong with the people of the general category. As a result, they face more difficulties because of social deprivations. The emergent SC leadership is confronted with greater discrimination and receives much less cooperation from the administration and the other groups. Acute poverty, illiteracy and predominant position of rural elite have further incapacitated them in discharging their duties effectively. Panchayats, which are 'institutions of self-governance', cannot function in a society that is ridden with caste, feudalism and poverty. Therefore, PRIs should be made effective instruments of social transformation through a vibrant democratic political process at the local level (Mathew, 1996).

The state of Madhya Pradesh has the highest number of tribals in the entire country. They have also been given reservation in proportion to their population. When one examines the degree of their participation in the panchayati raj system, it emerges that much needs to be done to equip them for facing the new task. Many reasons can be pointed out for this situation: illiteracy, poverty, lack of awareness, socio-cultural deprivations, lack of experience and training etc. The new Act, provided respectable space to the tribal people in the working of the panchayati raj system, such legislation could not make the tribal communities the sole masters of their socio-political destinies in their homelands. The need was always felt that the institutional structures within the Scheduled Areas were to be in consonance with the tribal needs, ethos and tribal institutions with which these people were familiar for ages (Purohit, 2002). Accepting the felt needs Union Government passed an amendment known as *Panchayat (Extension to the Scheduled Areas), 1996* and accordingly the State Government has also made an Amendment in the state legislation in 1997. However, a gradual process of change can be discerned. The tribal leadership is getting increasingly involved in understanding the system and coming to grips with it (Sisodia, 2002b).

OBC hold a position different from that of the SCs and the STs. Even before reservation they had representation in the Panchayats as well as in other Institution. Their social position in the traditional social set up was also more respectable. The same can be said about their economic standing. As a result of these factors they have made use of the new panchayat raj system more effectively. The administration also has shown greater cooperation towards the OBC leadership.

It is, therefore, essential that while the position of the OBCs needs further consolidation that of the SCs and the STs should be ameliorated a great deal. In this endeavour through legislation is important, much more important is attitudinal change on part of the administration and also of the society at large. The weaker sections need more training and experience in the exercise of their powers. Equally important are concrete measures to remove illiteracy and poverty from amongst them.

Only political recruitment of all the sections of society will never attain the desired goal. The basic idea behind the reservation was to provide an opportunity to the depressed classes to come forward and be a part of the total development process. In spite of all bottlenecks, gradually the changes are taking place. It happens so in a new system where representatives are not familiar with the working of the system. Even than slowly and steadily changes are visible. Taking lessons from the working of the panchayats, the leadership is getting skilled. At the same time the other person of the society are sharing several experiences as well. This process of decentralised governance will provide opportunity to rural people, particularly the persons of backward classes, to involve in development activities and several other works for the betterment of their life. The common man of the society will gradually become aware about day-to-day functioning and that way the coming generations will be well acquainted with the processes of development. This will certainly enthuse younger people to participate in the political process in the larger interests of the community.

Women Representatives

From the point of view of women representation it is a landmark decision that 33 per cent of the seats are reserved for women. Women are being considered as a backward class because of their negligible representation in political process. As a result of this statutory provision for reservation for women, situations have dramatically changed. It is generally believed of the rural women that their responsibilities are confined merely up to kitchen and farms. This prolonged myth is changed as a result of big number of women joining the panchayat elections.

To ensure adequate and effective participation of women in the panchayati raj system, the Madhya Pradesh Panchayati Raj Act, 1993 reserves one-third of the seats for women in all the three-tiers. Most of these women representatives have entered in the political process for the first time. However, many of them in general and the OBC category belonged to families, which had traditional political base. Yet the situation of women leadership and its working is not very encouraging. The reasons of their poor performance are more or less because of their overall backwardness. Other important bottlenecks among women representatives are interference of male members of their families *viz.*, of the husband, brother, father, son etc. However, in many cases now such interference is gradually declining. The reasons behind involvement of male members are very clear: first, rural women do not have the required exposure; secondly, lack of experience of working in panchayati; thirdly, there is a non-co-operative attitude of other panchayati raj representatives and government officials.

If an evaluation of their functioning is done it becomes clear that with the passage of time the women leadership became more assertive and independent as well as aware of the systemic processes. However, to strengthen this segment it is necessary to do away with illiteracy, socio-economic deprivations and many other complexes. It is equally important that to equip these women properly sufficient training programmes should be organised for them. There should also be a change in the attitude of their men folk and the administration. If women's empowerment has to be successful then the existing feudal patriarchal structure in most parts of the country has to be dismantled. Moreover, women's empowerment through the panchayats requires a sustained campaign and vigorous efforts for creating awareness about their rights and duties (Datta, 1997).

It cannot, however, be denied that as a result of reservation for women their participation in the political process has been ensured and they are playing a constructive role in development and welfare activities now. This will lead to positive changes in the entire social system.

These problems are, of course, initial hurdles. With the passage of time and gaining of experience, it is believed; women leadership will become more mature and effective. Regular training of this class, co-operative attitude of males and government officials will definitely provide strength to the leadership to work with perfection.

Working of Panchayats

The Panchayati Raj Institutions have been made the units of self-governance and they have been empowered to perform various powers and duties. However, certain issues are very important in respect to the working of panchayats.

The Panchayati Raj Institutions have been established as units of self-governance. There are many dimensions to the functions performed by the panchayats. The meetings have pre-determined agenda. For discussion new subjects can be taken up with the permission of the chair. Personal issues, which are directly related to some members, are often debated at length. On many occasions themes, which pertain to comprehensive rural development, are overlooked due to involvement of vested interests. In decisions taken by the panchayats the acceptance or approval of people's representatives or those in power is a must. This process of decision-making fails to fix correct priorities. Although elected on a non-party basis, the functionaries are influenced by political affiliations in debates and in the decision-making process. It would be more meaningful if party politics brings about greater politicisation and participation rather than socio-political fragmentation. The influence of factors such as caste, class, community, religion cannot be wholly denied as these do have a role to play. However, occasions have not been few where panchayats have in fact played a cementing role.

As the panchayats have been saddled with a plethora of activities, a lot of paper work obviously becomes necessary. While these records are maintained properly at the Janpad Panchayat and the Zilla Panchayat levels, the situation is not so rosy at the Gram Panchayat level due to inexperience of the panchayati raj representatives and lack of staff support. There is also an increasing need to inform the people about the meetings of panchayats, their decisions and policies. The panchayat functionaries are also not too keen about ensuring transparency and informing people about their activities. Efforts should therefore be made to make the people more vigilant.

The Panchayati Raj Institutions have been given the responsibility of implementing different governmental schemes. For this the panchayats select the beneficiaries and also examine as well as control the objectives of such schemes. The beneficiaries are selected through the Gram Sabha. The Gram Sabha has to try to select people on economic basis so that the genuinely needy person should get the benefits on a priority basis.

Thus, the functioning of the different panchayat bodies, though it is improving, still needs further streamlining. It has, however, to be understood that it is still their infancy period. Things will definitely get better with more training, experience and increasing awareness about powers and duties. Their efficiency and effectiveness will surely infuse greater confidence among the people at large in their activities. Active participation of the members, co-operative response of the community and a spirit of selfless dedication to panchayat work are necessary for the successful working of Panchayati Raj Institutions.

Panchayats and Bureaucracy

In the period prior to the implementation of the Madhya Pradesh Panchayat Raj Act, 1993, the control of bureaucracy over rural development was complete. However, now all the responsibilities relating to rural development have been handed over to the panchayats. This has necessitated fundamental changes at the bureaucratic or technocratic level also.

There is thus a widespread feeling of fear, mistrust and insecurity among the panchayat representatives regarding their staff. A clear-cut need exists for greater understanding between the two sets of functionaries to remove misperceptions and apprehensions regarding each other. The bureaucracy has to understand its position and responsibilities in a democratic system. A system has to be developed where accountability informs the upper echelons of administration and our understanding shows that authority resides with the lower levels.

The panchayats at all the three levels must be provided with a separate and autonomous cadre, which should be de-linked from the State. Responsibilities relating to recruitment, promotion, transfer etc., should be handled by the panchayats themselves or through some relevant agency. Posting at local levels should be permitted on permanent basis. This would solve the problem of transfer and official will have wide knowledge of his area. Misuse of power should be checked through a system of checks and balances. There is also a need of simplification of procedures so that usual and routine matters do not cause confusion, delay and deadlocks. A Panchayat Manual should be prepared as an authentic and ultimate source of eliminating all confusion or possible misunderstanding. Multiple and periodically recurring orientation programmes should be organised for both the groups.

Devolution of Powers

The Constitution of India vide Schedule 11 has laid down 29 subjects related to social justice and economic development. These have been devolved upon the panchayats for planning and implementation. This Schedule finds a place in the Madhya Pradesh legislation as Schedule 4 and it is on the basis of this Schedule that important powers of all departments have been handed over to panchayats. Importantly, these departments are: social welfare, agriculture, mineral resources, food and civil supplies, games and youth welfare, rural development, village industries, livestock, dairy and poultry development, revenue, public health and engineering, forest, school education, labour etc. All these departments have vested different types of powers and responsibilities to the three-tiers of panchayat. However, most panchayat representatives do not possess adequate knowledge about the functions and responsibilities entrusted to them by the various departments. As a result, their role as regards a number of such departments is negligible. Such devolution, therefore, would be fruitful only when the representatives are made aware of their role and encouraged to perform such roles.

The elected representatives have been provided with many administrative powers, which relate to recruitment, supervision and control. However, many of them have no experience of such jobs and find it difficult to handle them judiciously. As a result in the exercise of these powers the importance of administrative officials and influential people has increased. For proper use of these functions the panchayat representatives should be given proper training.

Members of Parliament and State legislators are *ex-officio* members of different tiers of the panchayat raj. They take part in the meetings. Though denied by the Act, in practice they exercise undue influence in the functioning of these bodies due to their political clout and access to centres of power. Even the panchayat representatives become subservient to them to seek favours from them. The MPs and MLAs have often shown disinterestedness in successful functioning of the panchayati raj institutions as in their perception this would limit their own area of influence. The feeling is growing that if direct elections are held to all positions in the PRIs the influence of representatives would get augmented. It has also been suggested that the development fund available to MPs and MLAs should be spent in consultation with the panchayati raj functionaries. Separate development funds should be provided to the panchayat representatives enabling them to spend it in accordance with the felt needs of the people. To streamline the division of functions between the three-tiers, a suggestion has been made to establish State Commission to distribute the 29 subjects judiciously and also provide a 'local list' in the Constitution along with the Union, State and Concurrent lists.

Finance

Finance is the first and foremost necessity of any institution for its successful working. It is important to make panchayati raj institutions financially sound and self-sufficient. Panchayats of Madhya Pradesh have two resources—funds from government and local tax collection. It is observed that majority of the panchayats depend on funding from State Government but do not levy local taxes for political reasons. The State Government allocates the money to the three-tiers meant for rural development. These bodies are provided finances to implement government schemes.

The State Government has been attentive to the need of financial efficacy of the panchayati raj institutions. These have been empowered by the Act to levy many new taxes i.e., market fee, property tax, land tax, private toilet tax etc. The Government also constituted a State Finance Commission and many of its recommendations were accepted with regard to distribution of financial powers to the panchayats. Yet the panchayati raj institutions cannot be regarded as financially self-reliant. Their dependence on the State Government for grants is not conducive to their successful functioning. Not many panchayats have utilised the powers given to them to levy local taxes. The functionaries have expressed the view that most of the people living in rural areas are poor and it would be improper to levy more taxes on them. Moreover, such new taxes would make them politically unpopular among the people. As such the taxes should be levied only on those who are able to pay. The rural leadership should also realise the significance of tax collection, as these constitute the major source of their income. They have to establish examples of devoted and transparent work so that people do not mistrust them when new taxes are levied. Greater participation of the people in the whole process should be ensured.

Despite all these efforts one would not be in a position to state that the panchayats are financially self-sufficient. Dependence of panchayats on State Government for funds is not good for the health of the new system. The leadership will have to come forward to meet the financial needs locally. Various provisions are available to generate resources. This way alone the scheme of decentralisation will bear fruits.

Conclusion

The establishment of panchayati raj system in Madhya Pradesh is indifference to the provision of the 73rd Constitution Amendment Act. The State Act has been amended from time to time to make it more effective in establishing PRIs as genuine structure of grassroots democracy. Through a system of reservation, participation of the weaker sections has also been ensured. The three-tiers have been empowered significantly to enable them to discharge their duties properly and fulfill the expectations of the people. However, much needs to be done as yet. Gram Sabhas are yet to perform their role in the panchayat raj system. Reservation has provided an opportunity to all backward classes to come out and play significant role but the process of political socialisation is slow among these classes. Women representation in panchayats is a matter of some satisfaction but their performance is poor as compared to other classes of the society. As far as the working of panchayats is concerned, the level of awareness about attending meetings and active participation at Gram Panchayat level is very low as compared to Janpad Panchayat and Zilla Panchayat levels. The bureaucracy has to be made more responsive to the needs of the PRIs. Greater financial autonomy must be provided to the panchayats. Better coordination has to be established among the three-tiers of panchayat. Greater clarity of roles and tier-wise division of functions is essential. Of no less importance is optimal direct participation of people in the developmental process. To generate this what is of crucial significance is the principle of accountability and continual social auditing of the performance and transparency in the form of right to information pertaining to administrative activities. The panchayats should be given the power to form organisations like neighbourhood groups to stimulate and direct people's participation in administration and development. Concrete efforts should also be made to reduce governmental interference in the day-to-day functioning of local self-government bodies and the process of their dissolution needs to be made more politics proof. Such measures will go a long way in establishing the panchayats as *Village Republics.* The panchayati raj system has provided opportunities for wider political recruitment to all sections of the society, which should lead to achieve the goals of social justice and economic development in the years to come.

REFERENCES

1. Prabhat Datta, Political Empowerment of Rural Women in India, *Administrative Change,* Vol. 24, No. 2, January-June, 1997.
2. A. Fernandes, *Reconnecting the Sabha to Gram,* Paper Presented at the National Conference on Gram Sabha, National Institute of Rural Development, Hyderabad, July 28-29, 1999.
3. Subhash C. Kashyap, *Blueprint of Political Reform,* New Delhi, Shipra Publications, 2002.
4. Rajni Kothari, *State Against Democracy: In Search of Human Governance,* New Delhi, Ajanta Publications, 1998.
5. Harsh Mander, Towards Direct Democracy: The Legal Empowerment of Gram Sabha, *Kurushetra,* Vol. 48, No. 1, October, 1999.
6. James Manor, Madhya Pradesh Experiments with Direct Democracy, *Economic and Political Weekly,* March 3, 2001.
7. George Mathew and Ramesh C. Nayak, *Panchayat at Work: What it Means for Oppressed?* ISS Occasional Paper Series-19, New Delhi, Institute of Social Sciences, 1996.
8. Malini Nambiar, Making the Gram Sabha Work, *Economic and Political Weekly,* August 18, 2001.
9. B.R. Purohit, Panchayat Raj System in Scheduled Areas of Madhya Pradesh in G. Palanithurai (Ed.), *Dynamics of New Panchayati Raj System in India,* Vol. I., New Delhi, Concept Publishing Company, 2002.
10. Yatindra Singh Sisodia, Panchayat Raj System in Madhya Pradesh: An Appraisal, in G. Palanithurai (Ed.), *Dynamics of New Panchayati Raj System in India,* Vol. II, New Delhi, Concept Publishing Company, 2002.
11. Yatindra Singh Sisodia, Decentralised Governance in Madhya Pradesh: Experiences of the Gram Sabha in Scheduled Areas, *Economic and Political Weekly,* October 5, 2002.
12. World Bank, *Overview of Rural Decentralisation in India,* Volume III, Washington D.C., 2000, p. 24.

14

Gram Sabha: Its Problems and Prospects after 73rd Constitutional Amendment

Y. BHASKAR RAO

"Gram Sabha" is a formally constituted body under the law, which comprises all those on the voter's list of the habitations comprising the village as formally defined. Since the 'village' is defined with reference to the need of spatial planning and civic administration, it is usually a conglomeration of a number of natural villages, each of which may be a community 'Gram Sabha' in common parlance comprises village community. However, in practical terms, each word of Gram Panchayat should constitute a Gram Sabha. Then all these word level Gram Sabha should constitute the Gram Panchayat level Gram Sabha. Draft Report of the sub-group on Empowerment of Gram Sabha.

Background

The concept of Gram Sabha is built upon the assumption that there should be a forum for the periodic expression of the voice of people in a spirit of intimate democracy and it is most appropriate at the village level where governance is the most palpable. This is a radical perspective as opposed to the powerful rationalist approach to decentralisation that dominates the discourse on decentralization. Civic engagement and social capital formation are mutually correlated and both these are seen essential for sustainable governance (Putnam, 1995). Theoretically, the Gram Sabha provides a site where the space for the generation of both can be realised.

Gram Sabha (GS) is the centre of democratic power in the village and is the centre of activity. The basic philosophy in the concept of Gram Sabha is villagers as a collective body to discuss, decide holistically about the village issues, problems, problems of particular group's etc. *Gram Sabha based comprehensive planning to be the basis of self-governance.* Unfortunately many State Governments dictate the terms of Gram Sabha and limit the scope of Gram Sabha to identification of beneficiaries of few schemes or implementation of Employment Guarantee Schemes (EEGs).

The Diwakar Committee (Government of India, 1963), which made the all India study of Gram Sabha found the body in bad shape and advocated a more restricted role for it in the short-run and hoped that once real powers have been handed over to the Gram Panchayat, the Gram Sabha would grow organically and find its rightful place in the Panchayat set up, The Committee took, the view that it is premature and dangerous to strengthen the Gram Sabhas, which are amorphous at the expense of the Village Panchayat. Iqbal Narain (1962), one of the early commentators on Panchayat Raj, also held the view that the emergence of an effective Gram Sabha is a derivative of the maturing of the Panchayat Raj system and not a precondition for strengthening of the Panchayat system. He envisaged an exclusively consultative role for the Sabha.

Ensuring popular participation has been one of the central themes of the post-independence period and when popular participation was not forthcoming in the wake of the Community Development Programme launched in 1952, Balwant Rai Mehta Committee was set up to suggest ways and means of ensuring this. However, participatory democracy at the village level received little attention of the Committee since it was largely concerned about the representative base of panchayat raj, especially the middle tier where synchronisation with the Development Blocks took place. Maddick says: "The Mehta team took the Gram Panchayat for granted and directed all its energy to the problem of making the block administration more democratic" (1970, p. 74). The legal powers of the Gram Sabhas have not been actually put to use in the pre-amendment phase. "No Sarpanch has ever been recalled, no budget has ever been rejected. More serious than this, in the majority of the states, the Gram Sabha has failed to attract a sufficient number of the local adults to be termed a fully representative body" (p. 76). Committees of the Gram Sabha could be formed into which the defeated candidate also can be drawn in. Maddick added—"the existing public attitude to the Gram Sabha Panchayat. The growth of Gram Sabha as an active, articulate body, with a further subdivision of responsibilities for executive functions at the lowest level, would be detrimental to effective and efficient administration."

While the Ashoka Mehta Committee (1978) affirmed the role of Gram Sabha, it did not recommend invigoration of the body. It said, "The Grama Sabha has an important role in activating the democratic process at the grassroots level, in inculcating community spirit, in increasing political awareness, in strengthening development orientations, in educating the rural people in administrative and political processes and in enabling the weaker sections to progressively assert their point of view." Although all these studies and reports were skeptical about the role of Gram Sabha, the 73rd Amendment accorded the body a pre-eminent position which holds up the ideal of participatory democracy even though the empirical reality is far from this ideal.

The Institution of Gram Sabha has been in vogue in many states in India for long. Tamil Nadu and Kerala however did not have Gram Sabhas. With the passing of the 73rd Amendment to the Constitution, the body has become an integral part of Panchayat Raj, the third Stratum of government, in all the states of India. The record of Gram Sabha as an assembly of village adults has not been viable anywhere in the country, even in states like Uttar Pradesh where these bodies have been in existence since 1947. The extent to which powers have been devolved to the Panchayats will have a directed debarring on the extent of matters over which the Gram Sabha can exercise some control. With the declaration of 1999-2000 as the 'Year of the Gram Sabha' by the Union Ministry of Rural Development, the importance of the body in the new Panchayat set up has been publicly recognised and affirmed.

Importance of Gram Sabha

Gram Sabha is one of the most important three basic institutions of the new direct democracy at the village level. The other two are (Gram kosh) a village fund and (Gram shanti Seva)—a village peace corps. Therefore, it must be made successful. Gram Sabha is a village assembly of all adults, men and women, which would regulate and develop village life and function automatically. This was a structure based entirely on people's power (Lokshakti) expressing itself in the form of village power (Gramshakti). Thus the village would emerge as an organised unit to look after its internal administration, development, and agro-industrial economy. This was a model for democracy at the grassroots based on direct participation by the people. Democracy has been defined as "a government where everybody has a say." A democratic administration by a panchayat cannot be a good substitute for it.

Gram Sabha is an institutional approach to popular participation. It provides a base for the three-tier structure of the Panchayati Raj Institutions. It is regarded as the grassroots organization of democracy. To J.P. Narayana, the Sarvodaya thinker, Gram Sabha signifies village democracy. To him representative government from the village to Delhi was no good substitute for direct democracy. Gram Sabha could be set up on a defect basis. Speed was the essence of the strategy and people's participation would be the index of its success. The idea of Gram Sabha, by and large, has not struck roots in the minds of the people. It has so far reached the prominent persons in the village. The positive outlook of the prominent persons in the village on the Gram Sabha has to be tapped and activised to bring the common people in large numbers within the fold of the Gram Sabha. To enlist the people's active cooperation in the national campaign to secure the proper distribution of foodgrains and other necessities, it is necessary to organise Gram Sabhas in the villages and Ward Sabhas in towns and cities.

The Gram Sabha agenda should cover the budget and earlier audit reports along with their compliance. It should discuss the annual administrative report and the progress report of the development works. It should consider the proposed works programme of the village. Taxation proposals or increase in the existing rates also should be putforth for discussion though they need not be put to the vote. This would result in developing the feeling that the Gram Sabha was intimately linked with the vital decisions of the village community. As this feeling gathers, the faith in the institution also would grow. It has been suggested that low power transmitters should be installed and these should broadcast panchayat news, important decisions and interesting discussions of the panchayat meetings.

The 73rd Constitution Amendment: Gram Sabha

The necessity to give a practical shape to grassroots democracy became a reality with the introduction of 73rd Constitution Amendment. It sought to integrate the democratic processes at all levels by formalizing a mechanism wherein people at all levels would have an opportunity to participate openly in matters which concern their welfare and development. The amendment thus ushered in an era of decentralised governance to harness local wisdom in a democratic way. In order to provide the Gram Sabha a key place in the overall system of panchayati raj, specific outline has been provided in the 73rd Constitution Amendment through Article 243(B) which reads as follows:

"Gram Sabha" means a body consisting of persons registered in the electoral roles relating to a village comprised within the area of panchayat at the village level. Its role has been laid down in Article 243 (A) which states, "A Gram Sabha may exercise such powers and perform such functions at the village level as the legislature of a state may, be law, provide."

Palanithurai maintains that under the new panchayati raj system, the rural people would get a link upto the district level through the Gram Sabha. Further, he states that the Gram Sabha being the primary body would be face-to-face organ of direct democracy, not made up of representatives but comprising or all adult residents.

According to R.C. Choudhury and S.P. Jain, one of the most important aspects of devolution package was to empower the Gram Sabha so that it may act as a vibrant institution to provide the elements of transparency, responsive administration and accountability which were hitherto missing. Almost all the States Acts have provided for Gram Sabha but its functions and authority have not been spelt out in detail. Consequently, these institutions, by and large, continue to function in effectively. Though the meetings are generally held as prescribed, the purpose is hardly served in the absence of a well-defined and directed mandate. More often, there is a attendency to conduct the meetings in a formal manner and finalise the proceedings in haste. The prescribed quorum is also not given the due importance. The cases were cited where the meetings were conducted without any consideration to the requirement of the quorum. The absence of women folk in the meetings of the Gram Sabha was a common feature. The participation of the people belonging to the weaker sections was also minimal. Only such of the people from these groups participated in the meetings when they were to be identified as beneficiaries under a given scheme. The entire exercise thus becomes formal and incapable of yielding the expected results.

While most of the State Acts have outlined the institution of Gram Sabha in conformity with the 73rd Constitution Amendment, the scope, functions and the dispensation to this body vary from one to state to another. In general, it has been conceived as the primary body of panchayati raj system, intended to facilitate direct participation of the people in local activities. The Gram Sabha is thus a statutory body and an integral part of the panchayati raj system in all the States. It is established for a village or a group of villages and consists of all residents registered in the electoral rolls pertaining to the Gram Sabha area. It is established for a village or a group of villages and consists of all residents registered in the electoral rolls pertaining to the Gram Sabha area. It serves as an assembly of the village(s), acts as a watch dog of working of the gram panchayat, and facilitates people's participation in the decision-making process. The status of statutory provisions in respect of key aspects of the working of the institution of Gram Sabha is evident from the following description:

Membership of Gram Sabha

Different provisions in various Acts in respect of membership, while in Andhra Pradesh, Assam, Gujarat, Jammu and Kashmir, Madhya Pradesh, Maharashtra, Punjab, Uttar Pradesh and West Bengal. Gram Sabha is composed of all the voters on the electoral roll, while in Bihar, Karnataka, Orissa and Rajasthan all adults residing in the area of the Gram Sabha are considered to be its members. The membership of the Gram Sabha arise from state to state ranging from 250 to 5000. The area of a Gram Sabha is generally co-terminus with that of the village. However, more than one village have been grouped together to form a Gram Sabha.

Scheduled Areas and Gram Sabha

The Panchayat (Extension to the Scheduled Areas) Act, 1996,

endowing Panchayats with such powers and authority as may be necessary to enable them to function as institutions of self-government, a State Legislative shall ensure that the Panchayats at the appropriate level and the Gram Sabha enjoys certain powers under the Act as follows:

(*i*) the power to enforce prohibition or to regulator restrict the sale and consumption of any intoxicant;
(*ii*) the ownership of minor forest produce;
(*iii*) the power to prevent allenation of land in the Scheduled Areas and to take appropriate action to restore any unlawfully allenated land of a Scheduled Tribe;
(*iv*) the power to manage village markets by whatever name called;
(*v*) the power to exercise control over money lending to the Scheduled Tribes;
(*vi*) the power to exercise control over institutions and functionaries in all social sectors;
(*vii*) the power to control over local plans and resources for such plans including tribal sub-plans.

Focus of Gram Sabha Experience

Making Gram Sabha a deliberative body is ideally the best. But in practice, instead of giving a solution it would pose another problem. The administrative homogeneity would be disturbed at the village level. Similar deliberative powers would be claimed by the higher level institutions and the gravity of the problems would assume larger proportions. Present experience also does not justify extension of statutory powers to a Gram Sabha. It is feared, not without reasons, that extension of functions to the Gram Sabha would tend to irritate the destructive forces and thus defeat its own purpose.

Gram Sabha as a deliberative-cum-executive body is also not a desirable proposition for similar reasons. It is again an oversimplification for the issue. What is practicable and justifiable is to develop Gram Sabha as a consultative body, a forum of thought, an essential medium for rural education by activising people into an enduring partnership "a partnership in all virtues, in every walk of life and in all perfection." The immediate task is to make the institution of Gram Sabha a "live" institution and then allow it to grow to its potential. The growth would be gradual and "from within." This growth cannot be dissociated from the actualities of the rural life.

The president caste and class conscious society could with the affluent landlords commanding influence in the villages would make it difficult for local leaders to avoid /benami members from entering the three-tier system. If the yardstick of 'absolute power' that 'corrupts' is applicable with regard to the functioning of the panchayat institutions, it could be asked whether the system would succumb under pressure from rich and powerful vested interests. The question also arises whether politicians at the State and national level would allow the panchayats to enjoy the powers vested with them by the statute. People were anxious to enjoy the powers of self-governance at the grassroots level. Ultimately it was the awareness of the villagers and their monitoring of the panchayats that would prove the success or failure of the decentralisation experiment. As part of this experiment, the Gram Sabha which constitute the base of the Panchayati Raj system, should function as a vital institution and should be also to exert its influence on the Gram Panchayat, if the latter is to function institutionally and in a democratic manner. It is unfortunate that the Gram Sabhas have not been working effectively and its meeting have either been irregular or marked with disinterestedness of the participants. The Gram Sabhas—the grassroots of democracy as it called must work effectively if panchayati raj is to achieve any success.

The re-organisation of panchayats, after the 73rd Constitutional Amendment came into force in 1995, has completely changed the nature of local governance in India. The Amendment created the basis for establishment of formally democratic institutions for local governance. The most important change has been that all the members of the panchayat are elected from the village. Before 1995, a number of members in the panchayat used to be nominated by the State Government. An important feature of the post-1995 panchayats is also the reservation of seats for the socially marginalized sections and women.

The evidence on functioning of new institutions of local governance in different parts of India has indicated vast potential of using these institutions to generate local resources. The findings from the study villages broadly support this body of evidence. The Panchayats have undertaken several activities for village development. These activities can be strengthened by further devolution of resources and powers to these institutions. In particular, the panchayats have shown exemplary performance in several states in respect to implementation of rural development programmes. Effectiveness of these programmes has been found to be markedly better in States where panchayats were involved in these programmes.

The experience gained so far with the working of Panchayati Raj in the country is that although 29 subjects are transferred to PRIs uniformly throughout the country, the extent of devolution of powers and functions to PRIs vary from state to state. In fact, panchayats were given even other subjects apart from the mandatory 29 subjects in several states. And the role of each tier of PR has not been well defined as regards a powers and functions to be performed by them. Added to this, the Gram Sabha and the Gram Panchayat meetings area held as mere rituals. The devolution of powers, functions and finances has not taken place below the district level. And no additional staff of worth consideration was given to the panchayats.

The Panchayats failed to sufficiently mop up resources except showing lukewarm attitude while the Gram Sabha turned a Nelson's eye on this crucial problem. The poor resources of the panchayats throw them in a bad light and made them constrained to provide basic amenities and services to the people.

There seem to be no expertise at the grassroots level to prepare plans. To check corruption at all levels, there is need for transparency and the right to information. The active participation of women and weaker sections in the grassroots democratic institutions is rather discouraging. As a result of poverty alleviation programmes, the socio-economic conditions of the weaker sections have only marginally improved.

The attendance at the Gram Sabha meetings in several states is razor thin rather than encouraging. The women belonging to upper castes do not attend the Gram Sabha meetings in states like Uttar Pradesh, Madhya Pradesh and Rajasthan. By and large, the public do not show much concern or inclination for the Gram Sabha meetings. The women in Orissa and West Bengal find it difficult to attend the Gram Sabha meetings held in the neighbouring villages away from their neighbourhood. The role of fair sex in village development cannot be undermined as women are a formidable force to reckon with to implement prohibition and curb the spread of intoxicating drinks.

The poor turn out to the meetings of the Gram Sabha is also due to the fear of foregoing daily wages by the bread winners who keep themselves away from the meetings of the Gram Sabha *vis-a-vis* PR theatre. This tendency is more discernible in States like Goa where the ruralities are more interested in their bread winning spree of collecting peanuts, cashew-nuts and coconuts. Even other States like Andhra Pradesh and Haryana are no exception as the ruralites are actively engaged in agricultural operations and other wage labour. The lack of quorum and poor attendance at the meetings of the Gram Sabha are also attributed to the village factions. Although, the Gram Sabha is provided as a cushion and leverage to control power, the SCs, STs, and women failed to play an active role to share-power. With the result, the devolution of powers and responsibilities remained a distant dream.

The Gram Sabha as a village commune can control human resources and natural resources like land, water, forest and environment. To energise Gram Sabha it should be vested with the powers of referendum and recall of erring elected representatives of the Gram Panchayat. The process of responsibility and sharing of powers should start forthwith. The poverty in rural area can be removed through an effective Gram Sabha. The British legacy of trust the structure, trust the system, trust the official but not the people was followed in the country for several years. In sum, proper devolution of powers and delegation of powers/ authority to the people was followed in the country for several years. In sum, proper devolution of powers and delegation of powers/authority to the people is basically lacking in the past 50 years. In reality, no state gave any powers to the Gram Sabha in the country before 1973. And it was since 1978, things started moving in different directions.

The bulk rural masses are governed by the laws which they do not know. And the Gram Sabha is meant to enable them manage their own affairs. A benign was made for the Gram Sabha in Karnataka since 1987. Nevertheless the practice has been that the

Gram Panchayats used to convene the meetings of the Gram Sabha since 1959 in Karnataka. The Gram Sabha has to conduct social audit of the plans, works, schemes, programmes etc., of the Gram Panchayat but due to factions in villages in several states the Gram Sabha meetings often end up with violence. Quite often, there were many irritants against the selection of beneficiaries in Gram Sabha meetings.

Meetings of the Gram Sabha

A Gram Sabha should meet compulsorily for as many times in a year as provided in the Panchayati Raj Act of the respective states. A meeting of the Gram Sabha will be presided over by the Chairperson (pradhan/sarpanch) or in his absence vice-chairperson of the gram panchayat. The Secretary of the gram panchayat will act as Secretary of the gram sabha. He will prepare the resolutions and place them (the resolutions) before the gram panchayat meeting for follow up action.

For any meeting of the Gram Sabha, a prescribed number of members will form the quorum. But usually no quorum will be necessary for a meeting, adjourned for want of quorum. However, it will be the duty of the Panch/Sarpanch and members of the gram panchayat to ensure that larger number of residents attend the meetings of the gram sabha. The provision regarding the number of gram sabha meetings very from state to state. However, most of the acts provide for at least two meetings in a year. The frequency of the meeting of the gram sabha in different states ranges from one to four in a year, as may be seen from the following statement:

Sl. No.	Frequency of Meeting	States
1.	Annual	Madhya Pradesh, Chhatisgarh, Tripura and West Bengal
2.	Twice a year	Andhra Pradesh, Goa, Gujarat, Haryana, Himachal Pradesh, Karnataka, Kerala, Maharashtra, Manipur, Punjab, Orissa, Rajasthan, Sikkim, Uttar Pradesh and Uttaranchal
3.	Thrice a year	Tamil Nadu
4.	Four times a year	Assam, Bihar and Jharkhand

In some of the acts the sarpanch or pradhan have been empowered to call for an extraordinary or special meeting of the gram sabha. A meeting of the gram sabha can also be called on the basis of requisition in writing from not less than one-fifth of the number of members of the gram sabha. The period within which such a meeting is to be called is generally 21 days. In case of the failure on the part of the sarpanch to call such a meeting within the stipulated time, the prescribed authority has been empowered to call the meeting.

Quorum of the Gram Sabha

While some acts are silent on the question, others do contain some provisions. In Uttar Pradesh and Punjab, the quorum for Gram Sabha meetings is one-fifth of the total number of members, whereas in Madhya Pradesh and West Bengal, it is one-tenth. As regards the person who will preside over the meetings of the gram sabha there appears to be some uniformity in the provisions. The sarpanch of the panchayat or in his absence the up-sarpanch of the panchayat or in the absence of both any members of the Gram Sabha elected by the Gram Sabha will preside over the meeting. The only exception to this uniform pattern is found in Maharashtra and Gujarat acts where in the absence of sarpanch or up-sarpanch the members of the Gram Sabha shall elect one of the members of panchayat present to preside over the meeting.

Functions of the Gram Sabha

As in the case of constitution and the procedure to be followed by the Gram Sabhas, there is diversity of provisions with regard to the functions of the gram sabha. However, there are some common features in the acts of most of the States. A study of different panchayati raj acts across the states reveal that each of the states has accorded a specific status to the institution of gram sabha in terms of powers and functions. A synthesis of various powers and functions assigned in different states in panchayati raj system reveals the following broad areas of powers and functions:

1. Examine annual statement of accounts and audit report;

2. Discuss report on the administration of the preceding year;
3. Review programme of work for the year or any new programme;
4. Consider proposals for fresh taxation or for enhancement of existing taxes;
5. Select schemes, beneficiaries and locations;
6. Mobilise voluntary labour and contributions in kind and cash for the community welfare programmes;
7. Render assistance in the implementation of development schemes and rendering services in villages;
8. Undertake programme for adult education, family welfare within the village;
9. Promote unity and harmony among all sections of society;
10. Seek clarifications from the mukhia and members of the gram panchayat about any particular activity, scheme income and expenditure;
11. Consider last audit note and replies made thereto;
12. Consider the budget prepared by the gram panchayat and the future development programmes and the plans for the gram sabha area;
13. Consider and scrutinise the existing schemes and all kinds of activities of panchayats;
14. Maintain a complete register for all development works undertaken by gram panchayat or by any other government department;
15. Scrutinise the complete works and all kinds of activities of the gram panchayat; and
16. Seek clarification from sarpanch and panches of the gram panchayat to clarify the panchayat activity, income expenditure, scheme and other matters and sarpanch of the gram panchayat shall be responsible for it.

It is thus evident that a wide variety of functions have been accorded to the institution of gram sabha. A state-specific analysis reveals that there is no uniformity in assigning the functions. While some of the states have perceived the role of gram sabha in terms of activating participatory process and discussion for the preparation of development plan, etc., others have chosen to provide them specific responsibilities (statement).

Statement Showing Functions Assigned to Gram Sabha in Different States

Sl. No.	*Functions*	*State(s)*
1.	Examine annual statement of accounts and audit report	Andhra Pradesh. Bihar, Gujarat, Haryana, Karnataka, Madhya Pradesh, Punjab, Rajasthan, Sikkim. A & N Islands
2.	Discuss report on the administration of the 4 preceding year	Andhra Pradesh, Bihar, Gujarat, Karnataka, Madhya Pradesh, Rajasthan, A & N Islands
3.	Review programme of work for the year or any new programme	Andhra Pradesh, Bihar, Gujarat, Karnataka, Madhya Pradesh, Punjab, Rajasthan, Sikkim, A &N Islands
4.	Consider proposal for fresh taxation or for enhancement of existing taxes	Andhra Pradesh, Bihar
5.	Select schemes, beneficiaries and locations	Andhra Pradesh, Assam, Bihar, Karnataka, Kerala, Punjab, Rajasthan, Sikkim, Tamil Nadu and Uttar Pradesh
6.	Mobilise voluntary labour and contributions in kind and cash for the community welfare programmes	Bihar, Karnataka, Kerala, Punjab, Rajasthan, Sikkim, Uttar Pradesh, West Bengal
7.	Render assistance in the implementation of development schemes and rendering services in villages	Assam, Bihar, Karnataka, Kerala, Punjab, Rajasthan, Sikkim, Uttar Pradesh
8.	Undertake programme for adult education, family welfare within the village	Bihar, Karnataka, Kerala, Punjab, Rajasthan, Sikkim, Uttar Pradesh
9.	Promote unity and harmony among all sections of society	Bihar, Karnataka, Kerala, Punjab, Rajasthan, Sikkim. West Bengal
10.	Seek clarification from the Mukhia and members of the gram panchayat about any particular activity, scheme, income and expenditure;	Bihar, Punjab, Rajasthan
11.	Examine last audit note and replies made thereto	Bihar
12.	Consider the budget prepared by the gram panchayat and the future development programmes and the plans for the sabha area	Gujarat, Haryana, Karnataka, Madhya Pradesh
13.	Consider and scrutinise the existing schemes and all kinds of activities of panchayats	Haryana, Kerala

(*Contd.*)

Sl. No.	Functions	State(s)
14.	Maintain a complete register for all development works undertaken by gram panchayat or by any other government department	Haryana, Kerala
15.	Scrutinise the completed works and all kinds of activities of the gram panchayat	Haryana, Kerala
16.	Approval of the village plan; Approve the village budget for the year; and to review the progress of the implementation of all schemes entrusted to the village panchayat.	Tamil Nadu

Ensure Employment for the Poor

At present, a variety of self-employment and wage employment schemes are in operation. To enhance the effectiveness of these schemes in generating income-earning opportunities for the rural poor, Government will follow a four-pronged strategy with the common theme of ensuring greater involvement of Panchayati Raj institutions:

- The existing scheme of Jawahar Rozgar Yojana will be modified to ensure that all funds are placed at the disposal of Gram Panchayats for creation of rural infrastructure. They will have the sole authority for preparation of annual action planes and their implementation, including the power to execute works with the approval of Gram Sabha. The modified scheme will be called "Gram Samridhi Yojana."
- The wage employment programme of Employment Assurance Scheme will be implemented at He district/ block levels, with the selection of works being decided by the Zilla Parishads in consultation with the other elected representatives. The Employment Assurance Scheme presently operates throughout the country. We will give special priority to areas suffering from endemic labour exodus.
- The Gram Panchayat will maintain a live employment register available to the Gram Sabha and public for scrutiny. To ensure th·' the funds under the wage

employment scheme are spend with the active involvement of the elected Panchayati Raj Institutions, it is proposed that while 80 per cent of funds would be released to implementing agencies as per normal producer, the remaining 20 per cent will be released as an incentive only if the State has put in place elected and empowered Panchayati Raj Institutions.

- The plethora of self-employment programmes for the rural poor will be merged into a single programme into a single programme called "Swaran Jayanti Gram Swarozgar Yojana" which will have greater participation of the Gram Panchayats. This will be enable the implementing agencies to have greater flexibility in execution to meet the needs of the local people.

This schemes will largely benefit the poor and the unemployed youth in the rural areas, especially those belonging to the Scheduled Castes, Scheduled Tribes and Other Backward Classes.

Rural Development Schemes and Gram Sabha

According to the new rural development schemes effective from 1999, the Gram Sabha is expected to authenticate the list of families identified in the Below Poverty Line (BPL) census. The identification of individual families suitable for each key activity under Swarana Jayanti Swarozgar Yojana (SJSY) has also been entrusted to it, Self-Help Groups (SHGs) are also drawn from the BPL list approved by the Gram Sabha. The selection of individual swarozgaris also has been entrusted to the Gram Sabha. The list of swarozgaris so selected for the year should be printed by the Block Development Officer and the copies made available to the Gram Panchayat for placing it before the ensuing Gram Sabha. Persons to whom loans are sanctioned are also to be communicated to the Gram Panchayat which shall place the same in the next Gram Sabha meeting. Identification of swarozgaris for taking up designated activities will be done by a three-member group consisting of the Sarpanch by visiting each habitation (Government of India, SJSY, 1999). The rechristened Jawahar Gram Samridhi Yojana for development of rural infrastructure at the village level is also to be implemented by the Village Panchayats with the approval of the Gram Sabha. In other words, the Gram Sabha decides which all works should be taken up. The payments made under the JGSY should be informed to the Gram Sabha at its next meeting. The annual action plan prepared by the Village Panchayat should be thoroughly discussed in the meeting of the Gram Sabha. The Gram Sabha shall approve the Annual Action Plan including the individual work to be taken up for SCs and STs before May 31 every year.

Copies of muster roils duly certified shall be placed before every Gram Sabha apart from making it available to the public on demand. "In order to ensured social control of the JGSY, meetings of the Gram Sabha shall be held every quarter at a fixed date, time and place to consider the issues regarding the planning, execution, monitoring and supervision of the JGSY These meetings shall be open to all members of the village community, who shall be free to raise any issue regarding the implementation of the JGSY and all a related issues." Further, "The Gram Sabha shall appoint a vigilance committee for each village under its jurisdiction to oversee, supervise and a monitor the implementation of each work under the programme. The Committee shall consist of not more than three persons living in the village and who in the judgement of the Panchayat will be of assistance to it in this regard. The Committee should include at least one representative of the SCs/STs and one representative of women" (Government of India, JGSY Guidelines, 1999). These provisions are applicable in all states including Tamil Nadu. Given the complimentarily of the JGSY, EAS and Food for Work Programme, all of which aim at the creation of employment opportunities in the rural areas, they were revamped and merged under the new Sampoorna Grameen RozgarYojana (SGRY) scheme from September 2001.

Gram Sabha and Gram Panchayats

It is also necessary to examine the relationship between Gram Sabha and the Gram Panchayat. According to a view point there is a great possibility for establishing direct democracy at the village level wherein the Gram Sabha will function as the parent body and the Gram Panchayat will function as its executive committee. The other view is that the Gram Sabha and the Gram Panchayat should both be recognised as separate entities so that each one can function independently within their respective statutory powers. Keeping in view the ground realities, it is felt that both these institutions have to be recognised separately. However, it cannot be denied that the gram sabha cannot function as a powerful body unless it has power to control the Gram Panchayat. It is unrealistic and undemocratic to allow a Gram Panchayat to continue to work if I cannot command the confidence of the Grama Sabha. The problem is how to harmonise this relationship. If Gram Panchayat becomes a part of Gram Sabha the day-to-day working of the panchayat is likely to be affected without any corresponding advantages. Nevertheless maximum harmony and better relationship between the two institutions can be achieved by making the Gram Panchayat, though not a part of the Gram Sabha, subordinate institution to the Gram Sabha. For this purpose, it is necessary that the gram sabha should have powers to pass a vote of no confidence against the sarpanch or any member individually because the methods of electing sarpanch and the members might be different in different states and because it is necessary to ensure that personal considerations are not allowed to be brought into the picture as far as possible. There is again a problem as to how this motion of no confidence can be passed.

MPs, MLAs and PR Members with Gram Sabha

The sarpanch is expected to play a vital role in order to make the Gram Sabha an effective body and to make the deliberations of the meetings fruitful. In most of the states he is the executive office bearer of the panchayat. His guidance, sincerity and leadership and personality can play a vital role in creating enthusiasm among the Gram Sabha members. It is he who can minimise the effect of personal nature of village politics, get the cooperation of defeated persons and their followers and can create sense of responsibility amongst the Gram Sabha members who otherwise may feel that their responsibilities have come to an end just after they have elected one member. He is supposed to take the members (voters) of the Gram Sabha into confidence in carrying out the works. The role of the Sarpanch is sometimes dependent upon the nature and method of his election. This is also dependent on the fact whether the panchayat is responsible to gram sabha or not and whether Gram Sabha has powers to control the panchayat. It has been felt that the role of the sarpanch can be made more effective if the Gram Sabha has got control over the Gram Panchayat. This will compel the panchayat to work as a team.

The panchayats as a body should help the sarpanch in calling and conducting the Gram Sabha meetings. The feeling that sarpanch and/or the panches alone are responsible for convening the meetings is likely to damage the institution of Gram Sabha and the panchayat. Where the Gram Panchayat is represented by the sarpanch or a panchayat in the Panchayat Samiti as a member of the latter body, the sarpanch can effectively participate in the gram sabha meetings and can convey the feeling to the samiti in respect of the problems of the Gram Sabha areas and the steps taken or proposed to be taken by the samiti in solving the problems.

The MLAs and MPs as residents of their constituencies should make it a point to participate in the gram sabha meetings when feasible or in course of their tours in their constituencies. No evidence is available to show the role so far played by them in the gram sabha meetings. However, experiences show that MLAs and MPs can enhance the cause of political education amongst the Gram Sabha members and in minimising the personalised nature of village politics.

The Panchayat Samiti and Zilla Parishad members should also attend the meetings in a planned manner and try to function as link in carrying the feelings from top to bottom and vice-versa.

Non-officials in various fields of activities such as members of *Bharat Sevak Sangha, Sarvo Seva Sangha* and other voluntary associations, persons of special experiences in the field of agriculture, etc., retired personnel and dalapaties of the VVF should attend Gram Sabha meeting and should help in its deliberations with their knowledge in their respective fields of activities.

The officials at the village and block level should attend the Gram Sabha meetings in a planned manner. The officials at the district and sub-divisional level, whenever necessary and feasible, should also attend the meeting to stimulate the interest of the Gram Sabha members and to help make the question hour effective so as to provide opportunities to the villagers to ventilate their grievances. Social Education Organiser and the school teacher along with local NGOs can also play a vital role in making the deliberations fruitful.

MODEL GUIDELINES FOR THE CONDUCT OF GRAM SABHAS

The Government of India has declared the year 1999-2000 A.D. as the Year of the Gram Sabha. Karnataka is one of the first States to recognize the significant role of the Gram Sabha in the implementation of development programmes and in the scheme of local self-government. Section 3 of the Karnataka Panchayat Raj Act, 1993 makes it mandatory for the Gram Panchayat to convene a Gram Sabha in every village atleast twice a year. The Government is keen on strengthening the Gram Sabha so that it becomes an effective forum for participation of the rural people in the planning and implementation of different development programmes of the local bodies. The Government therefore directs that the Zilla Panchayats and the Taluk Panchayats shall consider the recommendations of the Gram Sabha and the felt needs expressed through the Gram Sabha, while formulating their action plans. With the above objectives in view, the following guidelines are stipulated for the conduct of Gram Sabha in the State:

- The Gram Sabha shall be convened atleast twice a year, once in the month of April/May and later in the month of October/November. However in order to ensured that Gram Sabhas are held in fruitful and regular manner, the Executive Officer of the Taluk Panchayat shall publish, with the concurrence of Presidents of Gram Panchayats, a detailed schedule for holding Gram Sabhas in all the villages in the Taluk over a period of one week to ten days, specified for the purpose during the months of April/May and October/November of every year. This schedule shall contain the dates and timings of Gram Sabhas in every village in the Taluk. As far as possible, in Gram Sabha shall be held in the late afternoon hours when most of the villagers are available in the village.
- The Executive Officer of Taluk Panchayat shall designate a Taluk level officer from one of the development departments of Zilla Panchayat or Taluk Panchayat as Moderator for every Gram Sabha. The names of the officers appointed as Moderators shall be shown in the Scheduled of the Gram Sabhas. It would be of help to appoint a Co-

moderator or an Assistant Moderator to assist the Moderator, wherever, it is feasible. Appointment of two or more Moderators may be imperative in villages with a large population.

- The Gram Sabhas that are convened in the month of October/November shall be used for shortlisting the works that are proposed to be taken up on priority in the next financial year out of the resources of the Gram Panchayat, the Taluk Panchayat and the Zilla Panchayat. These works shall be community works, which will benefit the entire village.
- The headmaster of the pre-primary/primary/high school situated in the village should give details of the number of children enrolled in the school, number of children who have dropped out, with particular reference to the enrollment and drop out rate of girl children, and the condition of the school including repairs, infrastructure required, if any, etc., to the Gram Sabha.
- The Medical Officer of the concerned PHC or PHU shall give details of number of children yet to be immunised in the village. He shall educate the Gram Sabha about the preventive measures to be taken by the community against common diseases like Malaria etc., and also inform them about the facilities provided by the health centre to the village.
- The Adhyaksha of the Neeru Panchayat shall give a brief report on the maintenance of water supply schemes, the quality and availability of water and the demand and collection of water tariff.
- The Gram Sabha can discuss the schemas and programmes of the Taluk Panchayat and the Zilla Panchayat in addition to the functions of the Gram Panchayat like maintenance of water supply, collection of taxes etc. For example, issues concerning the Primary School/High School in the village; issues concerning the health centre/veterinary centre; works/programmes to bed taken up by the Zilla Panchayat and the Taluk Panchayat for the development of the village etc., could also be discussed in the Gram Sabha. The Gram Panchayat shall consider such proposals/recommendations of the Grama Sabha in detail and convey its

opinion/recommendation on such issues to the Executive Officer of the Taluk Panchayat Samiti within ten days.

The Secretary, Gram Panchayat shall identify the works that could be taken up out of the Gram Panchayat grants and take action to include such works in the action plan of the Gram Panchayat and obtain the approval of the Gram Panchayat.

The Executive Officer of the Taluk Panchayat shall consider the works proposed by the Gram Sabhas of all the villages in the Taluk at the time of the finalization of the action plans of the Taluk Panchayat and obtain the approval of the Taluk Panchayat. If some works cannot be included for various reasons, this shall be informed to the Grama Panchayat for informing the Gram Sabha at a later stage. If some of the recommendations/decisions of the Grama Sabha pertain to the Zilla Panchayat, the Executive Officer shall report the same to the Chief Executive Officer of the Zilla Panchayat.

The Executive Officer of the Taluk Panchayat shall consolidated the demands, suggestions and proposals received on the schemes of the Zilla Panchayat from all the Gram Sabhas in the Taluk and send a report to the Chief Executive Officer within one week of the completion of all the Gram Sabhas in the Taluk.

- Arrangements may also be made for videography or photography of the Gram Sabha for documentation purposes. Copies of the photographs of the Gram Sabha shall be submitted to the Executive Officer of the Taluk Panchayat.
- The Gram Panchayat or the villagers may organize cultural programmes on the day of the Gram Sabha to generate enthusiasm among the villagers and ensure wider participation.
- Discussion on the functioning of the public distribution system in the village and he implementation of the old age pension, pension for the physically handicapped etc.
- Enrollment and attendance of children in the schools and issues concerning the development of the schools.
- Discussion on the functioning of Health Centres and the Veterinary Dispensaries and the preventive measures to be taken in respect of common diseases.

- The funds received by the Gram Panchayat under different programmes during the last one year and the expenditure incurred.
- The measures taken and the expenditure incurred by the Gram Panchayat/Neeru Panchayat towards the maintenance of water supply schemes.
- Details of the number of latrines built in the village and the amount of subsidy disbursed.
- Discussion on the functioning of the Anganwadi centres in the village.
- Identification and selection of individuals/families to be assisted under different schemes.
- Discussion on the schemes/programmes proposed to be taken up by the Panchayat during the succeeding year.
- Any other subject suggested by the Gram Panchayat or subject taken up with the permission of the Chairman of the Gram Sabha.
- The Secretary, Gram Panchayat shall prepare detailed notes on the items in the agenda for the Gram Sabha and obtain the approval of Gram Panchayat atleast ten days in advance. He shall prepare atleast 100 copies of the agenda notes, which among other matters shall include a report on the activities of the Gram Panchayat in the preceding year; the activities proposed during the year in question and also summary of the latest audited statement of accounts. These copies shall be made available to the public at a nominal price of Re.1 per copy. Copies shall also be available for sale at the Gram Sabha itself.
- The Gram Sabha shall be presided over by the Adhyaksha or the Upadhyaksha of the Gram Panchayat. The Gram Panchayat may also invite important persons, experts or specialists for offering their suggestions or guidance. The following persons shall be invariably invited to the Gram Sabha:
  - The Headmasters of schools situated in the village and the Chairman as well as the Members of the Village Education Committee.
  - The Medical Officer of the concerned Primary Health Centre and the Veterinary Doctor or Assistant of the concerned Veterinary Dispensary.

- Manager of the concerned Commercial Bank or Regional Rural Bank.
- Concerned Agriculture Assistant or the Assistant Agriculture Officer.
- Concerned Village Accountant and the Revenue Inspector.
- The Anganwadi workers of the village.
- Chairman of the Neeru Panchayat or the village water and Sanitation Committee.

The following subjects shall be discussed without fall in the Gram Sabha and a record prepared of the discussions:

- A report on the activities of the Gram Panchayat since the previous Gram Sabha. This should include the action taken on the decisions/recommendations of the previous Gram Sabha.
- The details of the taxes collected by the Gram Sabha and the outstanding balances during the last one year. The details of demand, collection and balance of the water rate shall be given separately. The details pertaining to the village in which Gram Sabha is being held should be furnished separately.
- The village Accountant shall notify the births and the deaths recorded in the village during the last one year and update his records in case some births and deaths have not been registered.

The Moderator shall facilitate discussion on the programmes of the Zilla Panchayat and the Taluk Panchayat in the Gram Sabha in addition to assisting in the orderly conduct of the Gram Sabha. It shall be the function of the Moderator to record a brief summary of resolutions and recommendations of Gram Sabha, on the functioning of the different Departments under the Zilla Panchayat and Taluk Panchayat and convey the same to the concerned Department and the Zilla or the Taluk Panchayat. The Moderator shall be conversant with the development programmes of the Taluk Panchayat and the Zilla Panchayat being implemented in the village concerned so that he is in a position to answer any questions raised in the Gram Sabha.

The schedule of the Grama Sabha shall be published in all Taluk Level Offices, Gram Panchayat Offices and in the Panchayat Vartha Patra. The schedule shall also be announced in the local newspapers and the All India Radio.

- The Secretary, Gram Panchayat shall announce the schedule of the Gram Sabha by the beat of tom-tom atleast one week prior to the date fixed for the Gram Sabha. The tom-tom may be repeated two or three times till a day prior to the date of the Gram Sabha.
- The Gram Panchayat shall try to ensure that a majority the members of the Gram Sabha gather at the appointed time and the date of Gram Sabha. The representation of women and weaker section of the society in large numbers shall be ensured. Adequate seating arrangements shall be made in the front rows for the women and persons belong to the weaker sections to facilitate their participation.
- If the attendance in the Gram Sabha is less than 10 per cent of the total electorate of the village, the Gram Sabha may be adjourned to a later date, which shall not in any case be later than a week.
- The Moderator shall be present at the venue of Gram Sabha at least two hours prior to the time fixed for the commencement of the Gram Sabha. The Moderator should satisfy himself that the Secretary of Gram Panchayat has taken adequate measures including advance publicity for the proper conduct of the Gram Sabha.

Conclusion

It is however, the Gram Sabha which can tackle all the traditional and modern problems in the village. The village electoral members are more powerful in connection with the implementation of respective programmes which are being provided by the governments. The dissemination of information on development and welfare programmes can also taken care by the Gram Sabha. The Gram Sabha is the key instrument in mobilising the people as well as local resources to augment the panchayats and village development. All the three-tiers of PRIs have to prepare the Annual Action Plan independently and get the approval from the Gram

Sabha in each financial year and it should be thoroughly discussed in the meetings of the Gram Sabha. In the case of ZP and intermediate panchayats, their general bodies will have full discussion before approval. Although the works implemented by the Gram Panchayats are scrutinised under social audit by Gram Sabha. In all the States, Village Vigilance Committees have been constituted and actually involved in this mechanism.

REFERENCES

1. *Harijan*, 21-12-1947.
2. R.R. Diwakar, Mahendra Agrawal, Vinoba, *The Spiritual Revolutionary*, Gandhi Peace Foundation, New Delhi, 1994, p. 73.
3. V.G. Nandedkar, *Local Government—Its Role in Development Administration*, Concept Publishing Company, New Delhi, 1979, p. 167.
4. *Seminar on Fundamental Problems of Panchayati Raj*, New Delhi: All India Panchayat Parishad, 1964, p. 69.
5. Geoffrey Ostergaard, *Non-Violent Revolution in India*, Gandhi Peace Foundation, New Delhi, 1985, p. 31.
6. N.R. Inamdar, *Functioning of Village Panchayats*, Bombay, Popular Prakashan, 1970, pp. 76-77.
7. Geoffrey Ostergaard, *op. cit.*, p. 55.
8. V.G. Nandedkar, *op. cit.*, p. 168.
9. V.G. Nandedkar, *op. cit.*, p. 167.
10. *The Hindu*, Tuesday, September 19, 1995, p. 3.
11. K.S. Singh, *A Simple Study of Comparative Local Government and Administration*, Ajanta Prakashan, Delhi, 1983, p. 35.
12. R.C. Choudhury, S.P. Jain, *Strengthening Village Democracy*, NIRD, Hyderabad, 1999.
13. Chaandan Datta, *Strengthening of Gram Sabha*, NIRD, Hyderabad, 1999, pp. 163-64.
14. Sarumathy, M. *Grama Sabha in Schedule V. Areas in Andhra Pradesh*, NIRD, Hyderabad, 1999, pp. 319-39.
15. Annamalai, V. *Gram Sabhas in Schedule V. Areas in Orissa*, NIRD, Hyderabad, 1999, pp. 353-66.

15

Empowerment of Women: Experiences of Women Elected Representatives of Grassroots Democratic Institutions: The Case of Tamil Nadu

G. PALANITHURAI

Introduction

Ever since the enactment of the 73rd and 74th Amendments to the Constitution of India, "empowerment of women at the grassroots" has become a popular concept that is used by many, (Batiwala, 1996; Batiwala, Anita, Gurumurthy and Wali, 1998; Sharma, 1992), with varied meanings and explanations. One-third of the seats at the three levels of grassroots institutions[1] have been reserved for women of all categories. This has raised expectations among different sections of the community that this group of women will become a critical mass, which, in turn, will make an indelible difference to the management of these institutions at the grassroots level. Such an expectation has grown to the extent that the existing development paradigm will undergo a drastic change in the system of benefits (Buch, 1998).

Women elected to grassroots institutions have been performing their roles and functions since 1996. The impact and the implications of the management of these institutions by women leaders have been felt in many spheres. It was expected that the newly formed critical mass of women who got power through reservation would perform a critical function. But the women-leaders who assumed responsibilities are not in a position to perform the critical function as they face a volley of problems. Despite their struggle they continue to make efforts to address the problems of the people (Krishnasamy, 2001).

An in-depth analysis will show the systematic effort on the part of the mainstream system (bureaucracy of the State Government) to project the failures of women leaders rather than their problems in handling power and institutions. It is also observed that in the Government training institutions in the name of training and capacity building, women leaders have been oriented to be submissive to the bureaucracy and obey the instructions of the officials. The women leaders' vision and their sense of self have been eroded. This has been evident since 1996 and women grassroots leaders have been silently made subordinates to the officials.

A conscientious move has been made to equip women leaders to be self-reliant by Gandhigram Rural Institute, founded as an institution for empowering women by the disciples of Mahatma Gandhi at the dawn of independence. This new initiative has also highlighted scores of problems faced by women representatives on various fronts. In order to overcome these, associations for Elected Women Representatives have been formed and they have been federated with other associations of Elected Women Representatives in South India.

The problems, issues and encounters of women leaders dealt with herein are location specific and they are confined only to Tamil Nadu. These observations, analyses and explanations cannot be generalised. All these problems are to be seen against the backdrop of the environment of the state of Tamil Nadu. This chapter, therefore, seeks to illuminate the problems faced by women representatives of the grassroots institutions of Tamil Nadu. Further, it highlights some of their experiences while trying to achieve their avowed goals. It also indicates some suggestions on the type of support needed to sustain their position of power in this space created for them.

The problems of women representatives were collected from two sources. First, while conducting training programmes for the women representatives, a specific sharing session was arranged in which all the problems faced by the women representatives were discussed and documented in detail (G. Palanithurai, 2001). Second, when the women representatives formed an association and federated themselves with the support of Gandhigram Rural Institute, they organised regional meetings in several places in order to consolidate the demands of women representatives in the local bodies. The above exercise was carried out in four zones and the exchanges and interactions with women leaders have been documented (Palanithurai, 2000, 2001).

The Reservation Debate and Process

While looking at the issues affecting women leaders, one has to bear in mind the environment in which the institutions have been created through 33.3 per cent reservation of seats for women and how they have carried out the duties and responsibilities assigned to them. Right from the 1941 Report of the Sub-Committee of the National Planning Committee[2] to the recent report of the Committee on Status of Women in India, every report (Government of India, 1975) has emphasised that the condition of women is unacceptable and that they have been denied their rights and opportunities. While commenting on women's predicament, Justice V.R. Krishna Iiyer observed: "Rethinking on the separate terms from the perspective of women who, despite the constitutional guarantees, had not achieved real justice or liberty or equality or dignity produced the holistic concept of gender justice which united all the principles into one to challenge the persistent denial of these promised objectives to the overwhelming majority of the women of India within a quarter of a century after the birth of the Republic" (Kasturi and Mazumdar, 1994).

It is true that Indian history (Altekar, 1978) provides ample proof that the rights and freedom enjoyed by women change in inverse proportion to the status of their families, especially the men in their families, within the social hierarchy. Further, it is horrifying to note from the observation of an IAS officer, based on the latest two censuses, (Agnihotri, 1996) that the only section of India's multiple people who neither destroy their baby daughters before or immediately after birth, nor allow them to die in infancy through discrimination in nutrition and health care are the Adivasis whom the rest of us have been taught to regard as the most backward and least developed/civilised members of our nation. There have been a series of reviews and observations (Moser, 1989; Sen, 1994) about the condition of women based on which new schemes and programmes have been chalked out for the welfare of women. Yet one cannot see any significant impact on the society, The marginalisation of the majority of women in the economy and the consequent neglect and demonstration of gender, class and urban bias led to a complicated situation in the general political framework of the society.

It is also true that even the opportunities that have been provided to the women have not been properly used by them for their upliftment as they are trained to be insensitive towards their own issues (Narasimhan, 1999). In a democratic country, power is always with the people and they should have the strategy to handle power. It is not the government that gives power to the people. The government derives power from the people.

To liberate oppressed women, steps have to be initiated from the point of view of the oppressed and not from the oppressor's. The government in a patriarchical society looks at issues only from a patriarchical perspective. To overcome these problems, feminists have fixed two long-term goals—freedom and empowerment (Asia Pacific Centre for Women and Development, 1979). Freedom from oppression for women involves not only equity but also the right of women to freedom of choice and the power to control their own lives within and outside their home. Control over their lives and bodies is essential to ensure a sense of dignity and autonomy for women, 'Power' refers to the sense of internal strength and confidence to face life, the right to determine choices in life, the ability to influence the social process that affects their lives as well as the direction of social change (Sahay, 1998).

Empowerment of women is prominent everywhere and has gained currency among academics and policy makers now. Empowerment has been defined differently by different scholars contextually (Batiwala, 1995). But, at present, most scholars (Sen and Grown, 1987) have come to give a broad meaning to the concept. It is a method of tackling powerlessness in encountering and combating personal and social problems. It is distinguished by its focus on developing critical awareness, increasing the feeling of collective and self-efficacy and developing skills for personal, interpersonal or social change. In other words, empowerment can be defined as control over material assets, intellectual resources and ideology. Thus empowerment is a process of awareness, capacity building, leading to greater participation, to greater decision-making power and control and to transformative action.

This process takes shape in two forms, internal and external. Women should realise their inner worth and they should be made to realise their worth. In order to perform the above tasks, the problems faced by the powerless should be first eliminated from the social environment. In the 1970s and 1980s, systematic steps were taken through the five Year Plan Proposals (Government of India, 1976; 1980), Consequent to the pressure brought on the government by the women's movement at the national and international levels commissions were constituted.[3] Yet, the struggle is still on to acquire a legitimate space in all spheres of life for women. Thus, the position of women has not changed drastically or dramatically as dreamt of. The problems of women representatives at the grassroots have to be looked at against this background.

Problems Faced by Elected Women

To empower women, first the elected women representatives have to be empowered by building the skill, capacity and support structure. In this process, it is essential to understand the problems faced by the women representatives while performing their roles and functions and to evolve solutions to these problems to the extent possible.

Women representatives elected to grassroot level institutions have been facing numerous problems, within their families, in their social, political and administrative settings, which will be spelt out hereunder. This has often led to ineffective administration of these bodies by women leaders. They do not have a common platform to express their grievances and get them redressed. Experiences from capacity building exercises conducted in various parts of the state have propelled us to prepare an action programme for empowerment of women leaders at the grassroot level. This can be done by forming an association of women representatives and federating it with similar associations of women representatives in local government in different parts of the country and making them articulate their issues on their own.

In the Indian context empowering women is a herculian task as social and cultural moorings have established strong roots in the belief system of the people. As a result, there has always been an uncommon disparity in the upbringing of women and men. All social reconstructions take place only through political activities, that too through political systems. Democracy provides enough scope for such reconstructions through polity. Hence every social segment is moving towards power. Yet, women hesitate to take part in politics as if the space is for men alone. In order to break this barrier at the micro-level, a new device has been worked out through the 73rd Constitutional Amendment Act. They have been made ineffective in administration since they have come to these institutions as fresher. Yet, laudable achievements have been scored by women leaders in panchayats.

Women leaders in panchayats are engaged in a constant struggle. Many leaders are insensitive to their own and gender issues in general. They have been oriented to lose their identity and only serve as instruments to operationalise certain processes for others. This process has made them sink in localism and become voiceless. As a result, their space is still severely limited. In order to overcome all these hurdles, an attempt has been made to associate women leaders into a federation in order to address all the issues which they face in administration and to focus on the issues of women.

Need for this Programme

The finding of the capacity building programme is that women leaders are in need of an alternative arrangement for the continuous flow of information and consultancy to stabilise their activities for development. The requirements of women leaders are not adequately fulfilled by their organisations. Hence, the demand for a full fledged professional organisation to assist women leaders of local bodies. Against this background, a series of programmes covering the entire state of Tamil Nadu was organised in four zones. The details of the programmes are given hereunder.

A facilitating centre for grassroot women leaders is being considered at the Gandhigram Rural Institute.[4] Before proceeding further, it is necessary to take a glance at the problems of women leaders.

Table 1
Network Meetings of Elected Women Representatives

Sl. No.	Category of Participants	Programme	No. of Leaders attended	Venue
1.	Panchayat Union Chairmen, Village Panchayat Presidents, Ward Members and Self-Help Groups	South Zone Network Meet on Associating Women Representatives in Local Bodies	25	Madurai
2.	Village Panchayat Presidents, Ward Members and SHG Leaders	North Zone Network Meet on Associating Women representatives in Local Bodies	32	Chengulpet
3.	Village Panchayat Presidents, and Ward Members	East Zone Network Meet on Associating Women Representatives in Local Bodies	23	Tiruvarur
4.	Panchayat Union Chairmen, Village Panchayat Presidents, Ward Members and Self-Help Groups	Central Zone Network Meet on Associating Women Representatives in Local Bodies	48	Karur
	Total		128	

Source: Computed.

The problems are drawn from the elected women representatives who have attended training programmes organised by Rajiv Gandhi Chair for Panchayati Raj studies funded by various agencies. The details of these programmes are given hereunder.

Table 2
Details of Training Programme Conducted for Elected Women Representatives

Sl. No.	Training Programme	Funding Agency	No. of Participants
1.	Empowering Panchayati Raj Institutions on the issues of Population, Health and Social Development	Population Foundation of India	6834
2.	Capacity Building for Gram Panchayat Presidents	CAPART Hyderabad	681

(*Contd.*)

Sl. No.	Training Programme	Funding Agency	No. of Participants
3.	Training of Presidents and Vice-Presidents on Panchayat Administration with Special Reference to Water and Sanitation	DANIDA Villupuram	815
4.	Training of Presidents and Vice-Presidents on Panchayat Administration with Special Reference to Water and Sanitation	DANIDA Cuddalore	416
5.	Training of Women Presidents of Gram Panchayats	Social Welfare Board	825
6.	Training of Elected Women Representatives of Urban Local Bodies	Tamil Nadu Institute of Urban Studies	2150
7.	Training of Trainers in Multi Level Planning	State Planning Commission	71
8.	Capacity Building for Weaker Sections in New Panchayati Raj System	CAPART Hyderabad	425
9.	Capacity Building for Gram Panchayat Presidents	CAPART Hyderabad	317
10.	Training Programme for Panchayat Leaders in Nilgris District on Ecological Empowerment of Panchayats	Rural Development Organisation The Nilgris	102
11.	Training for Village Panchayat Presidents and Vice-Presidents in Total Rural Sanitation	DRDA Cuddalore	682

Source: Computed.

Total Number of elected local body leaders trained	=	13,318
Total no. of panchayats covered	=	2,354
Total no. of urban local bodies covered	=	294
Districts covered	=	1

Increasing Workload

The moment the women filed their nomination for election to the grassroot level institutions, their workload doubled and so did constraints. No woman representative from the rural areas reported that her workload on the home front decreased due to her work in the public space. In a joint family system, attention to routine work cannot be reduced. At every stage, the elected women representatives have to tackle the problems of the family carefully; otherwise, she courts trouble. The family burden, coupled with the workload in the panchayat, made the elected women representatives tired of their activities in the public space. Their efficiency could neither be exhibited nor improved as they had no time. On most occasions, the elected women representatives opted for a joint workshop with the males of their families. Instead of discussing the problems faced by them among themselves, a workshop could be organised to which the elected women representatives and their husbands or any family males assisting them could be invited. All the issues affecting women representatives could be discussed in the open and that could bring about change, in their attitude.

Varied Concerns of Women Leaders

Politics has its own ramifications and dimensions–whether it is at the state or at the national level. Till they entered grassroots institutions, women had confined themselves to voting. After the reservation of seats for them in grassroots institutions, they also assumed the role of players in the political game. So far, they had not been dragged into this game and hence they are novices in this art. In order to acquaint them with politics, they need the support of men. But, while drawing upon the support of men for their work, they run the risk of men trying to make the women representatives submissive to them.

Illiteracy

Illiteracy is a basic problem among the newly elected women representatives. They are not able to write and read, but they are allowed to file their nomination. After they are elected to positions, they feel annoyed about their inability to read and write. They have the aspiration to read and write and are prepared to undergo training but their husbands prohibit this since many of them are now operating the panchayat on behalf of their spouses. Wherever the elected women representatives establish contact with NGOs, they are properly oriented and trained to manage the institutions on their own by the intervention of the NGOs. To maintain thirty-one records as a representative of panchayati raj institutions everyone requires adequate skill. The training programme is intended to impart skill in the art of management of panchayat institutions, for which literacy is a prerequisite. Nearly 9 per cent of the participants lack this skill. Hence, they have to rely on others for managing the panchayats.

Usual Shyness

Having traditionally secluded themselves from public spaces, especially the menfolk, women face difficulties in interacting with men in office and in public life, after being elected to panchayati raj institutions. They have had no previous experience of working with men but when they become leaders they have to interact with both men and women of the community. The women leaders are, therefore, inhibited in their interaction with men in public contexts. When Gram Sabha meetings are convened, the women representatives have to conduct the proceedings as chairpersons of the Gram Sabha, sitting along with men in a crowd, which is unusual in remote villages. According to Ponnikailasam, the President of the Women Panchayat Leader's Federation, in the first three or four Gram Sabha meetings, she did not comfortable sitting with men.

Domination of Males

It is clear from the experience of elected women representatives that their capacity has not been recognised by the males of their families. After their election, women representatives have been attending meetings and training programmes. They learn many things. Initially the men in the family, in the guise of helping them, accompanied the elected women representatives to offices and public places. Over a period of time, the women learnt the art of administration through interaction and training. But the males would not accept that their family women, who have been elected to panchayats, have equipped themselves to manage the institutions. It is an irony that though elected women representatives feel that they can manage the affairs of the panchayat on their own without the help of any ' male from their families, they cannot say so to the males in their families. Further, elected women representatives are facing problems in panchayats when the males of their family interfere in administration. In the absence of interference in administration by males in the families of elected women representatives, trouble from male representatives would be minimal and negligible. This is partly so because men generally feel that the women are not elected on their own merit but because of their support. This sort of attitude is very difficult to change since the women leaders too are of the belief that they have been elected to panchayat institutions only because of the influence of their husbands or other men in their families. While narrating her experience, Minnalkodi of Adhanur panchayat reported that the men in her family take decisions and impose them on her. She said that she did not have adequate courage to change this.

The women representatives pointed to yet another problem: the restriction placed on their movement. The people of the village are used to approaching their panchayat representatives with their problems at any time. Although the women representatives indicate their willingness to attend to such work at any time, they are not permitted to do so by their husbands or other family members. They need the permission of their husbands or in-laws if they want to go to the police station or the hospital at night. On such critical occasions, people want the support of leaders. If the leaders as women do not come forward to help the people, the public criticise the panchayat leaders.

Forced not to Raise Issues of Women

Although women in rural areas face a multitude of problems, men ensure that such problems are never raised openly in public fora. Women representatives feel suppressed by this. Alternatively, while women representatives feel that these problems could be raised by the affected women in the fora, the affected women feel that these problems should be raised by women representatives. The family members of elected women representatives, however, prevent the elected women representatives from articulating women's problems in public.

Environmental degradation and depletion of natural resources are affecting the life of women in rural areas, especially the poor women. Even though elected women representatives are aware of the gravity of the problem, they are unable to raise the issue in public fora as some mafia gangs are involved in such despicable activities. Only NGOs are creating awareness about this problem among the Dalit women and the poor in the rural areas.

The menace of alcoholism breeds all sorts of troubles for the family, especially women. Women face innumerable problems in the family and in society because of alcohol. Every woman and every child is affected and yet nobody has the will to oppose this practice, since everybody knows that this illicit trade takes place with the active support of politicians and with the connivance of the police. No one need create awareness about this menace among the people as they are all aware of it. But they are all afraid of the police who are behind it.

The health of womenfolk is an issue, which is not seriously viewed in rural areas by men. Even women themselves do not realise the importance of their health. In every respect, women are discriminated against in the family. No one dares to create awareness among women. Even in carrying out activities in the panchayat, men are not sensitive to issues confronting women. Worse, women are not sensitive to their own issues, be it guiding pregnant women to avail themselves of ANC or motivating girls to go to schools. In such circumstances, elected women representatives who take up these issues are not appreciated but, instead, they are criticized by the males in the Gram Sabha meetings.

Negative Attitude of Officials

Elected women representatives find it difficult to convince officials in government offices as they have a poor opinion about women representatives. The officials feel that elected women representatives are in position simply because of the reservation policy and that they do not have any opinion or vision of their own. The officials assume that women representatives will accept whatever they advise. Consequently, women representatives who go to offices with aspirations and expectations feel frustrated. Ponnikailasam, the President of the Federation of Women Panchayat leaders, while presenting the report about the plight of women leaders in her presidential address in 2001, indicated how officials were indifferent towards the demands of women representatives of local bodies.[5]

Illtreatment

It is a sorry state of affairs in government offices that elected women representatives with a high social and economic background get respect while poor elected women representatives, especially Dalits, face only illtreatment. To illustrate the tragedy of Dalit leadership, a case is narrated here. A poor Dalit woman who served as a construction worker assisting the mason got elected as Gram Panchayat President. She went to the Panchayat Union office to clear a file for her panchayat. The moment she met the concerned clerk, she was asked to bring a cup of tea from the nearby tea stall by the clerk. She readily agreed to do so and picked up a glass tumbler and got a cup of tea for the clerk without a murmur. Later she was asked to meet him at his residence. She went to his residence and she was asked to do some work in his garden. She did that work also. Later, she got the cheque from him and went home happily. When she narrated the incident in a training programme she was asked why she did not resist. She said that previously it was her routine to bring tea to the mason at the construction site. Now she was asked to do so by an official and so she obliged. Illtreatments continue unabated, despite the Dalit movement. Another gram panchayat president, Reeta, narrated her experience with officials and police in her experience sharing session at the annual convention of elected women representatives of rural local bodies in Tamil Nadu. She explained how she responded to challenges.[6]

Information Blockade

There are several hurdles and barriers to the process of women empowerment. Information blockade is the most powerful weapon used by officials to disempower women. Generally, women do not have access to newspapers. Moreover, all government information is transmitted from one department to another only among officials, The officials circulate information booklets and details only among men and not among women. Even elected men representatives are not willing to share their knowledge with women representatives. Susila, Karungulam gram panchayat president, narrated in her presentation in the group discussion in a training programme sponsored by the Social Welfare Board that she was discriminated against by officials and male gram panchayat leaders in giving copies of the Government Orders on Rural Development and Panchayati Raj.[7]

When women representatives are invited for training programmes permission is not accorded by many of their families. When elected women representatives insist, they are allowed to attend training programmes along with their husbands or other males of the family. Now, the government insists that elected women representatives should not be accompanied by their husbands or others while attending training programmes.

Domination of Caste Panchayats

Traditional caste panchayat leaders are yet another barrier to elected women representatives as they impose conditions and restrictions on women leaders. If the elected woman representative belongs to the caste of the traditional panchayat leader, they extend all support to her to remain in power but not to attend to the work on her agenda. The traditional panchayat leaders expect that the elected women representative should adhere to the advice of the traditional panchayat leaders. She is expected to carry out her work from the agenda of the traditional panchayat. If the elected woman representative belongs to other castes, particularly Dalit, she cannot do any work at all. Invariably, she has to be under the control of the traditional panchayat leader. Otherwise, she has to face problems.

Party men also expect the same. Normally, women in the panchayat do not have any political identity and hence they look at issues on the basis of the reality. On the contrary party men want elected women representatives to look at issues from the party angle, failing which the women representatives face problems from the party high command. Why do party men take such a stand? Because, it is the normal practice that when a seat is reserved for a woman, a male of the party gets permission from the party to field his wife or sister in that place. Hence, the party men feel that it is the responsibility and duty of the elected woman representative to adhere to the dictum of the party men at the local level. Issues such as domination of caste panchayat leaders over the formal panchayats headed by women and the control of political party leaders at district level over women gram panchayat leaders, repeatedly figured in the training programme while women gram panchayat presidents narrated their experience in panchayat administration.[8]

Lack of Communication Skills

Communication skills are very important for the success of any leader in the modern era. Elected women representatives never had a public space experience and hence they lack communication skills. They have to manage the council and the public with effective communication skills. Since they feel that they lack skills, they cannot achieve what they want to. Even the Federation President Ponnikailasam stated in the training programme that she was conscious of her poor communication skill.[9] But now she speaks for an hour in meetings along with ministers and higher level officials. When elected women leaders preside over the panchayat council, some men use unparliamentary words with the intention of making the elected women leaders nervous.

Poverty Prevents

There are elected women representatives from the working class who have to rely on their daily wages. Though elected women representatives have been entrusted with many responsibilities and duties there is no means of reimbursing their loss of wages. This deprives them of their livelihood and hence some are forced to use proxies in their office. V.R. Kalaiyarasi of Veppangulam panchayat argued that the Constitution has created a space even for poor scheduled caste women to occupy position in a panchayat but it has not created a conducive climate for them to work as leaders. She explained her plight in managing her family without economic compensation.[10]

Oriented to Lose Self

We generally expect women to be sensitive to women's issues. However, it is not true in the case of elected women representatives as they have been continuously oriented formally and informally not to be sensitive to women's issues. In the same way, Dalit women representatives are insensitive to Dalit issues. One argument put forward is that they are representatives of not only women or Dalits but the entire village community. Therefore, they neither address all the women's issues nor the issues of Dalit women effectively. Most of the training programmes concentrate on procedural matters and not on developmental issues. So there was further training in team building and vision building (Palanithurai, 2001).

Interference of MPs and MLAs

Elected women representatives face yet another problem in administration i.e., the interference of MPs and MLAs. They feel that everyone has his or her own domain of action. Roles are different for representatives of the different institutions. MPs and MLAs feel that the panchayats are under their control and that local body leaders have to accept whatever they say regarding rural development. This has been raised in many fora (Palanithurai, 2000).

Lack of Managerial Skills

Managerial and administrative skills are essential for any successful administrator. Elected women representatives lack accounting and managerial skills. So they are misguided by officials and males of their families. Sometimes women are trapped on this count and thereby they get involved in all the underhand dealings of officials. They say that they need managerial and accounting skills to overcome this kind of problems. To this end, the Hunger Project in India offers leadership training to women leaders in which accounting and auditing procedures have been given a major thrust.[11]

Women Leaders Made Tools

When elected women representatives meet officials with males of their family, the officials talk to the males and not to the representatives. Even the reserved seats are offered to their husbands and other males of their family and not to them. Initially, they felt this very much and later they started ignoring such insults. Only after attending training programmes, they have realised the mistake. Most of the matters transacted between their husbands and officials were not known to them. The training programmes which they attended made them understand the issues in administration. The ignorance of the women representatives is exploited at every level.

However, in local politics, muscle and money power have their due role. Hence, all activities are planned in the context of managing the muscle and the money. In order to overcome this problem, women have to rely on the family/caste/party leader. At a later stage, whoever comes to the rescue of the woman representative comes to the panchayat for personal favours and obligations. When such obligations are denied, women representatives are criticised and castigated. This was reported by the Federation leader Ponnikailasam in the network meeting organised at Thiruvarur.

Social Cleavage

The caste division in villages has been another kind of hindrance to elected women representatives. While forming Self-Help Groups (SHGs) all women are united and do not entertain any cleavage. But, after forming the same and functioning for a period of time, the women are compelled by their menfolk to look at issues from the perspective of caste. As a result, many SHGs have collapsed. In the same way, while distributing benefits to the poor, women leaders are compelled to go by caste considerations. Caste has entrenched itself everywhere and become a barrier to the smooth functioning of panchayats. Elected women representatives are often find themselves in trouble because they look at issues beyond the perspective of caste.[12]

Lack of Motivation

To perform any job, motivation is important. Elected women representatives are new to this job. All of them have not taken up this assignment willingly or voluntarily. Further, they have been facing problems without any support. There is no motivation for them. As a result, many elected women representatives are in a state of mental depression. How to solve this problem? Nobody knows the solution. The problem has reached such a stage that there is a search on for a counselling centre for mentally depressed elected women leaders.

Elected representatives are asked to carry out a variety of programmes and schemes. Before one starts one's work, one should know what role one has to perform. They filed their nominations without knowing what for! They are not aware of the 73rd Amendment to the Constitution of India and the State Conformity Act of 1994. Without knowing the basis of decentralization of powers, they have been assigned the task of realising it in practice. Normally one would expect women's organizations to start the exercise of pepping up elected women representatives. In the absence of such an initiative, elected women representatives have taken steps to form their own association through which they have decided to articulate their grievances and the problems they have been facing in panchayat administration. Gandhigram Rural Institute has decided to support such activities since women's empowerment is one of the basic objectives of Gandhigram Rural Institute. Periodical meetings of women leaders have been arranged for which the institute has generously extended its support.

Caste Discrimination

Untouchability is in practice in rural areas. For Dalit leaders, it becomes a problem. Whenever a Dalit heads the Panchayat Council and Gram Sabha, we may witness pandemonium. Dalit leaders are not respected and, in many villages, the traditional leaders conduct the proceedings. In the meeting elected women representatives merely serve as spectators. Further, the two tumbler system prevails in the rural areas where Dalit leaders are presidents. They are not able to speak on those issues as they have developed a sense of fear. It is the duty of the panchayats to administer social justice but, in reality, they are not able to do so. Only a few political parties highlight the issues and the plight of the Dalits.

Dalit Women Leaders Marginalised

Dalit women representatives, unless backed by some political party, are powerless and voiceless. Dalit leaders are not allowed to speak and that too about the problems of Dalits. Even if some Dalit oriented decisions are taken in the panchayat, they are not allowed to be executed. Genuine and basic facilities to Dalits are not allowed to be provided. In certain areas, the traditional panchayat leaders ask the Dalit women representatives to hand over the office to them. In many places, the Gram Sabha is organised and conducted by the traditional panchayat leader and the elected women representative remains one among the spectators. She has no voice and she has to sit along with other Dalit women in the audience section. Kalaiyarasi of Veppangulam panchayat explained that in Sivagangai District wherever the Dalit leaders are able to make compromises with caste Hindu traditional panchayat leaders, there is no problem in panchayat administration and where there is no cooperation between the traditional and formal panchayats Dalit panchayat leaders are in trouble.[13]

Husbands Made Tools

When the husbands of Dalit women representatives work on the farms of traditional or caste Hindu leaders, it is all the more easy to take over the panchayat. The husband insists that she has to obey the dictum of the caste leaders in order to avoid conflict and to lead a peaceful life. Officials, on their part, terrorise Dalit women leaders to execute whatever programme they want to be executed in the rural areas, irrespective of the needs of the panchayats. Dalit women representatives are easily trapped in the corrupt administrative system without any resistance. Whenever, the misdeeds are found out, the poor Dalit women are penalised and not the officials.

Non-Cooperation of Police

It is a well-known fact that police officials are always in the hands of upper class or upper caste people. Despite the repeated steps taken by Dalit women representatives, nothing favourable happens to Dalits from the side of the police. Police officials do not take cognizance of genuine grievances of Dalit representatives. Dalit representatives complain to the police about the encroachment of common properties by caste Hindus and influential party men in rural areas. As per the government order, the police have to take action and eviction has to be carried out. But, no action is taken against the encroachers despite repeated complaints. Common property resources are the lifeline of the poor. But now several hundred acres of common properties have been encroached upon by party men. When they are identified, action is initiated by the panchayat president. But there is no action from the police. But the police act in accordance with the government order in panchayats headed by caste Hindu women leaders. The basic question here is why do we have such discrimination?

Design of Caste Hindus

Since Dalit women are poor, they handover the panchayat responsibility to someone, mostly caste Hindu traditional leaders with a view to earning their livelihood. No one can refute this. But one has to look at the reality. Why is the poor Dalit woman preferred by the caste Hindu leaders, when a Dalit woman with sufficient economic background contests in the election? It is the design of the caste Hindus to elect a poor Dalit woman so that the woman could be easily coopted in their design, whereas economically sound Dalit women cannot be easily coopted in their design, as she they have required economic background to manage their livelihood.

Paucity of funds is a general problem for all panchayats in Tamil Nadu. For Dalit women, it is a serious problem because the women of the Dalit community expect that a woman representing their community would do many things in favour of Dalits. But, contrary to expectations, elected women Dalit representatives cannot do anything for Dalits due to paucity of funds. The caste Hindus do not allow elected women Dalit presidents to carry out programmes earmarked for Dalits as they also need such programmes, for which there is no sanction from the government, Even the allotted work for Dalits cannot be carried out in rural areas. Hence, Dalit presidents have got a poor image among the people of their own caste. They get neither the support of Dalits nor the support of non-Dalits.

Dalit Problems not Focused

Dalit representatives face another constraint in all public fora. They realise that there are a large number of problems which have hitherto remained unattended but could now be addressed in view of the reservation system. But it is deliberately ensured that elected women Dalit representatives do not take up Dalit issues either in the Gram Sabha or in the panchayat council meetings. This keeps Dalit representatives alienated from the Dalit community and they continue to be in the hands of others. Even if they are ready to take up such issues, their family members are not ready to support them as they are under the hold of the caste Hindu families. Thus, their expectations are belied and the Dalit youth are in an agitative mood, paving the way for social and communal conflict in villages.

Non-Cooperation of Caste Hindus

Another significant attempt is made by caste Hindu leaders in their panchayats through non-cooperation, which renders elected women Dalit leaders non-functional and unsuccessful. Thereby they declare that Dalits, especially women of that caste, are totally incompetent to manage public institutions. In many places, they have successfully done this. Wherever, elected women Dalit representatives agree to cooperate with caste Hindus, they are allowed to carry out certain works which are not favourable to the marginalised.

Elected women representatives face yet another problem in panchayats. The caste Hindus have cleverly created a design of usurping power from Dalits. Even during election time, in many gram panchayats, the caste Hindus resort to a ploy by which they get an assurance from among the candidate that the Vice-President would be elected from among the caste Hindus, and that too a male. After the election, the president is asked to agree to the proposal that a male Vice-President could be elected from among the caste Hindus, so that they can get cooperation from the caste Hindus. This renders the Dalits vulnerable as the panchayat administration is virtually under the control of the Vice-President. The elected woman Dalit president has to accede to the proposals of the Vice-President. In many places, Vice-Presidents make the presidents commit mistakes and become victims of Clause 205 of the Tamil Nadu Panchayat Act. Further, in these panchayats infrastructure facilities are created in the settlements of caste Hindus and not in Dalit settlements. If this is raised in the Gram Sabha by the Dalit youth the Vice-President gives a vague reply. The Dalit president is at the receiving end at the hands of the Dalit community.

Neglect of Vital Issues in Training

Training and orientation are given to elected women representatives by the Government but these programmes do not touch upon the vital issues of the marginalised people. In the training programme, orientation is given to the leaders to take up the schemes and programmes of the government. There is no scope for discussion on gender issues, issues of Dalits and participation of the people in the planning process. Proper orientation is not given to women leaders in training programmes conducted by the government and some of the non-governmental agencies. So, Gandhigram Rural Institute has designed a training module to train elected women panchayati presidents. This initiative was supported and approved by the Rajiv Gandhi Foundation. (The training module which runs to 120 pages is available with the Rajiv Gandhi Chair, Gandhigram Rural Institute.)

No Support Base

Another pertinent question discussed by women is the support base of women leaders. Discussions have been held on all relevant aspects based on which women leaders have taken the initiative to carry out certain schemes and programmes. They have faced a variety of problems in the field. To overcome these problems they are in need of some supportive organizations. But there is no such support base for women leaders. In the absence of such a support mechanism, one cannot expect exemplary achievements from the women leaders at the grassroot level.

Encroachment Encounters

As per the New Panchayat Act, the president of the Gram Panchayat can take action against encroachments. To evict an encroacher, panchayat presidents have to get the village map from the village administrative officers. In many of the villages, the administrative officers do not give the village map to the presidents of the Gram Panchayats. With great difficulty the Gram Panchayat Presidents take the initiative to retrieve the common property from the encroachers. This act has incited encroachers to fight against women leaders. This is yet another challenge to elected women representatives. Menaka of Urapakkam panchayat paid with her life for taking steps to remove encroachments. This issue was discussed in many meetings of the women leaders' association. Women leaders have exerted pressure on the government to support the move of panchayats to remove encroachments.

Crowd Management

Another problem that elected women representatives face is the problem of crowd management. Gram Panchayat presidents have to convene Gram Sabha meetings four times every year. Our rural masses normally tend to shout in a crowd. Even the Speaker of the Lok Sabha is not able to manage enlightened representatives and the Legislative Assemblies do not fare any better. But in a Gram Panchayat, even if it is four hundred people in an open place, it is always a free for all. When women representatives are presiding, anti-social elements deliberately use unparliamentary words in order to drive away the womenfolk. Nobody regulates the meeting except the family members of the elected women representatives. When family members come to the rescue of elected women representatives other members of the Gram Sabha oppose it. But the same Gram Sabha members do not help elected women representatives while they are facing problems in the Gram Sabha due to anti-social elements. People under the influence of alcohol participate in and disturb the proceedings. But no one is ready to control them. What is the way out of this?

Local body leaders are invited for public functions and they are asked to address the public. Elected women representatives are not in a position to speak like others in public meetings as they do not have the required communication skills. It is the felt need of every elected women representative. This deficiency is responsible for poor management of crowds also.

Representatives' Perception of Women's Issues

The above posited issues are the problems faced by women leaders in panchayat administration. They have perceived the problems faced by women in rural areas. The issues are classified and presented hereunder. Primarily, the aspirations and feelings of women are not respected and are not taken into consideration for decision-making. It is common at the family level and at the community level. There is not much difference between the rich and the poor. Gender discrimination prevails in the family, community, office, parties, cultural organisations, and religious organisations. Women are discriminated against in providing facility, service and benefits. From the family level to the Central Government level one can find discrimination on the basis of gender. Girl children are poorly fed and malnourished. They are not given fair treatment on par with male children. Women are harassed in the family and sexually exploited in the workplace.

Girls are generally not permitted to go in for higher studies or even beyond primary school. Women discharge dual responsibilities with great difficulty, yet, their burden is not appreciated properly. When women move beyond the routine, their workload increases with nobody to share it. For the poor women, there are no proper amenities in the workplace. Health facilities are not provided to women in the same way as they are extended men. Women are also not sensitive to their health problems. Female infanticide and foeticide are the problems that women face in many villages. Due to non-availability of water, fuel wood, medical facilities, proper public distribution system, women are the worst victims. Women are denied property rights even though the Equal Property Rights Act has been passed in the Tamil Nadu Legislative Assembly. Women workers are paid poor wages compared to men. Women are made dependent. Assertive women are subjected to character assassination. Panchayats have no perspective plan for women's empowerment.

What They Need?

These are some of the vital issues women have perceived as problems of the elected representatives Solutions can be found to all these problems. The women representatives themselves have identified some solutions. They are listed hereunder: (*a*) Proper orientation has to be given to elected women representatives by way of periodical training. (*b*) Women representatives are to be sensitised on issues concerning women. (*c*) They have to be organised at a larger level and enabled to address their issues on their own by creating a suitable support base. Institution based legal support has to be provided to women who take up the struggle to administer social justice. (*d*) Periodic interface between successful women and women leaders who lead struggles has to be organized. (*e*) Managerial skills, leadership qualities, accounting skills and communication skills have to be developed through periodic capacity building exercises. (*f*) Comprehensive awareness programmes have to be conducted in rural areas on the problems of women. Information has to be provided to women representatives on all vital matters pertaining to improvement in the quality of their life. Women's participation has to be ensured in Gram Sabha meetings. (*g*) A Women's component plan has to be initiated at every level. (*h*) Stringent laws are to be enacted to deal with individuals committing atrocities against women. (*i*) Women segmented on the lines of political party, caste, religion and class have to be united and they should be helped to stand as a single entity. (*j*) As a prelude to this, elected women representatives have to be organised at state level and further federated with other state level organisations so that they will gain added strength. (*k*) They can espouse the cause of women and legitimately claim political space in order to address women's issues effectively.

Where do They Stand?

Though elected women representatives face innumerable problems while discharging their duties, they continue their struggle to succeed in their mission. But their perception of their self and their desire vary from individual to individual and from group to group. There are six kinds of leaders, namely aggressive leaders, sober capacitated leaders, ambitious capacitated leaders, leaders with aspiration, leaders in a mood of withdrawal and leaders without an idea. A few cadre parties and a few committed NGOs have been continuously orienting a set of leaders and extending all their support to women leaders having links with the parties and the NGOs. They always exhibit an aggressive character which enables them to discharge their duties more effectively than other leaders. Twelve per cent of the representatives belong to this group.

There is yet another category of leaders, who have been oriented and trained but are not committed to any ideology or organization. But they are committed to their work. They have participated in the programmes organized by NGOs but they do not have continuous linkage with the NGOs. They are capacitated leaders concentrating much on their responsibilities and they have performed very well as they have enhanced their capacity. They have aspiration to continue in public service but no specific position. Whether they win the next election or not they will remain in the public sphere. This group constitutes 22 per cent.

There is another category which is slightly different from the previous one. The capacitated leaders have concentrated much on enhancing their capacity continuously and performing their duties. While performing their duties, they see the response of the people, based on which they have a desire to continue in office. But this category has an ambition to continue in the same position, for which they have developed the art of managing the people in local bodies. All their deficiencies are compensated by their public relations. Their linkages with people are strong as they have always been. Nearly 24 per cent of the leaders belong to this category.

The fourth category of leaders have a different aspiration. Though they have a number of deficiencies, by keeping themselves very active in discharging their duties, they want to demonstrate to their party leaders that they are the apt candidates for membership in the Legislative Assembly. They are always busy meeting people and familiarizing themselves with them. They consider the Panchayati Raj Institution as a launching pad for their political career. Though their number is very small they are certainly the models for emulation. Eighteen per cent of the leaders have this type of aspiration.

Another category of leaders are unable to meet the challenges of their role and bear the pressures of society and their family. They have expressed their desire to withdraw from public life. These leaders were brought to public life forcefully by their husbands. In most of the cases, the relationship between the husband and wife has undergone a change in the whole process of administering development through Panchayati Raj Institutions. Many husbands realise the fact that their wives have acquired the required capacity and, hence, they have to withdraw from the support space. But there is another segment of men who are determined not to allow their wives to attend to their duties on their own. Most women leaders have stated that they have been facing problems in the local body institutions because of the interference of their husbands. This factor cannot be explained to their husbands by women leaders of panchayats on their own. This group constitutes 20 per cent of the leaders.

There is yet another category which has no idea. They are in the hands of the males of the family, despite the pronouncements of the Government. The women leaders do not move out of their houses for public work. They do not meet people. Their husbands virtually run the show for them. They are not bothered about it. It is a money spinning device which is ably tackled by their husbands by their muscle and money power. Officials also cooperate with such leaders. They have no idea about the panchayats and they have no aspiration to contest in the next election. If their husbands ask them to contest they will contest; otherwise, they will not bother about it. They are only 4 per cent; yet their cases have been repeatedly quoted in public. It is true that a withdrawal symptom is visible among many women leaders in local bodies. They face a volley of problems from officials, caste groups, family members and even their own political party leaders.

Yet, the majority of the leaders have exhibited their determination to occupy public space. Having entered and tasted power, women leaders have come to the stage of enlisting themselves as members of various organizations to fight for their rights and legitimate spaces. In their struggle, they have identified the organizations and institutions which support empowerment of women and, through them, they are determined to continue their struggle. Further, they have started forming their own organizations and federating their organizations with other organizations. Another interesting development is that a large number of women are being trained in the Self-Help Groups (SHGs) to move over to this power domain. Women leaders have come to the public sphere and they will continue to keep their hold over institutions and try to expand their space.

Observation and Conclusion

Women have come to positions in the local bodies, as a provision has been made in the Constitution. The attitude of society towards women has started changing. But, in the process of empowering women, hurdles continue to remain. Steps are being taken by women of their own accord to overcome hurdles. It is a long drawn process. A structure which has been created over centuries to work against the interests of women cannot be dismantled within a short span of four or five years. It can be changed only by creating a women's movement for which this provision of one-third reservation of seats for women will help. To fight against the designs of the structure, an organized movement of the masses is an imperative. In order to make women achieve results in their positions an array of interventions are necessary.

Women need orientation, sensitization, capacity building, information and counselling continuously through organizations. The ongoing experiments and experiences suggest that periodical training, orientation and sensitization make women leaders perform their assigned role in a better way. When women leaders respond to socio-political challenges, they are to be supported by organizations and institutions which work for their empowerment. Wherever such interventions are available, the achievements of women leaders are substantial and impressive. The Government will respond to the needs of these women leaders only when they are supported by organisations well-known for their credentials and are to be reckoned with as a force.

NOTES

1. Gram Panchayat, Block Panchayat and District Panchayats.
2. This report was published in 1941 but it was missing and later it as decided to republish the document by the Centre for Women Development Studies in New Delhi.
3. The details of these activities are recorded in the article entitled "Women: From Equality Empowerment" by Vina Mazumdar in *Independent India: The First Fifty Years* (Ed.) Hiranmay Kariekar, Oxford University Press, New Delhi, 1988, pp. 262-263.
4. A State Resource Centre would be created in Gandhigram Rural Institute. This centre would provide needed information to the panchayat leaders through regional resource centers which would be created in different regions through NGOs.
5. For more details see Rajiv Gandhi Chair, The *Annual Convention of the Elected Women Representatives of Rural Local Bodies in Tamil Nadu,* Rajiv Gandhi Chair for Panchayati Raj Studies, Gandigram, 2001.
6. *Ibid.*
7. Rajiv Gandhi Chair, *Report of the Training Programme Conducted for Women Presidents of Gram Panchayats in Five Districts of Tamil Nadu,* Gandhigram: Rajiv Gandhi Chair for Panchayati Raj Studies, Gandigram, 1998.

8. Rajiv Gandhi Chair, Report of *the Training Programme Conducted for Gram Panchayati Women Presidents of Madurai, Ramanathapuram and Pudukkottai Districts,* Rajiv Gandhi Chair for Panchayati Raj Studies, Gandhigram, 2000.
9. Rajiv Gandhi Chair, *Report of the Training Programme Conducted for Women Presidents of Gram Panchayats in Five Districts of Tamil Nadu,* Rajiv Gandhi Chair for Panchayati Raj Studies, Gandhigram, 1998.
10. Rajiv Gandhi Chair, *Report of the Training Programme Conducted for Gram Panchayat Presidents,* Rajiv Gandhi Chair for Panchayati Raj Studies, Gandhigram, 1998.
11. Rajiv Gandhi Chair, *A Report on Elected Women Representatives Network Meeting,* Singamma Sreenivasan Foundation, Gandhigram, 2002.
12. G. Palanithurai, *Role of Case Groups in New Panchayati Raj System: A Case Analysis of Tamil Nadu,* presented in the UGC National Seminar organized in the University of Madras from 4th to 5th January, 2001.
13. Rajiv Gandhi Chair, *Report of the Second Annual Convention of the Elected Women Representatives of Rural Local Bodies in Tamil Nadu,* Rajiv Gandhi Chair for Panchayati Raj Studies, Gandhigram, 2002.

REFERENCES

1. Satish Agnihotri, 'Juvenile Sex Ratios in India: A Disaggregated Analysis', *Economic and Political Weekly,* (Special Number), 28 December, 1996.
2. A.S. Altekar, *The Position of Women: Hindu Civilization,* Motilal Banarasidass, Agra, 1978.
3. Asia-Pacific Centre for Women and Development, *Feminist Ideology and Structures: Report of an International Seminar,* UNESCAP, Bangkok, 1979.
4. Srilatha Batiwala, Empowerment of Women's Autonomy, Proceedings of a Consultation on women's Health and Rights: Rethinking Population, HIVDS Technical Report Series, 1996, 1: 4.
5. Srilatha Batiwala, B.K, Anitha, Gurumurthy Anita and S. Wali, *Chandana, Status of Rural Women in Karnataka,* National Institute of Advanced Studies, Bangalore, 1998.
6. Srilatha Batiwala, "The Meaning of Women's Empowerment", *Women's World,* 1995, pp. 23-34.
7. Nirmala Buch, "Decentralised Governance, Women's Participation and Poverty Eradication", in Bidyut Mohanty and S. Haider (Eds.), *Women and Political Empowerment,* Institute of Social Sciences, New Delhi, 1998, p. 82.
8. *Towards Equality: Report of the Committee on the Status of Women in India,* Government of India, New Delhi, 1975.
9. *The Fifth Five Year Plan,* Government of India, Planning Commission, New Delhi, 1976.

10. *The Sixth Five Year Plan,* Government of India, Planning Commission, New Delhi, 1980.
11. Leela Kasthuri and Vina Mazumdar, *Women and Indian Nationalism,* Vikas Publishing House, New Delhi, 1994.
12. P. Krishnaswamy, "Women Panchayati Leaders more Sinned against than Sinning", *The New Indian Express,* 22 August, 2001, p. 3.
13. Vina Mazumdar, "Women: From Equality to Empowerment" in Hiranmay Kariekar (Ed.), *Independent India: The First Fifty Years,* Oxford University Press, New Delhi, 1998.
14. Moser Caroline (1989), "Gender Planning in Third World: Meeting Practical and Strategic Gender Needs," *World Development,* Vol. 17, No. 11, November, 1989.
15. Sakuntala Narasinhan, *Empowering Women: An Alternative Strategy from Rural India,* Sage Publications, New Delhi, 1999, pp. 44-45.
16. G. Palanithurai, *Report on Capacity Building for Gram Panchayati Presidents,* Rajiv Gandhi Chair for Panchayati Raj Studies, Gandhigram, 2000.
17. G. Palanithurai, *Report of the Workshop on Networking of Associations of Elected Women Representatives in Local Bodies,* Rajiv Gandhi Chair for Panchayati Raj Studies, Gandhigram, 2001.
18. G. Palanithurai, *Report on the Capacity Building for Weaker Sections in New Panchayati Raj System,* Rajiv Gandhi Chair for Panchayati Raj Studies, Gandhigram, 2001.
19. G. Palanithurai, *Capacity Building for Local Body Leaders,* Concept Publishing Company, New Delhi, 2001.
20. Sushama Sahay, *Women Empowerment: Approaches and Strategies,* Discovery Publishing House, New Delhi, 1998, pp. 8-9.
21. Kumud Sharma, "Grassroots Organisations and Women's Empowerment: Some Issues in the Contemporary Debate", *Samya Shakti,* Vol. 6, 1992.
22. Gita Sen, Gita, "Poverty, Economic Growth and Gender Equity: The Asian and Pacific Experience" in Heyzer Nocleen and Gita Sen (Eds.) *Gender Economic Growth and Poverty,* Kali for Women, New Delhi. 1994.
23. Gita Sen and Grown Caren, *Development Crises and Alternative Visions: Third World Perspectives,* Monthly Review Press, New York, 1998.

16

Status of District Planning Committees in India: Experiences of a Decade

S. HARSHA

The 73rd and 74th Amendments effected to the Constitution have brought in new status and role to the rural and urban local bodies. One of the salient features of 74th Amendment is the provision for constituting District Planning Committees (DPCs) by the State Governments. The DPCs are expected to consolidate the plans prepared by the Panchayats and Municipalities in the district and on their basis formulate a draft development plan for the district as a whole. Some of the States and Union Territories (UTs) have passed conformity legislation to constitute DPCs. After a decade of passing these enabling Acts, it is time to take cognizance of the status of DPCs in India. This article seeks to analyze the status of DPCs with reference to some major States and Union Territories in India based on the reports of working groups and other secondary sources. It also aims at suggesting remedial measures for the efficacious functioning of DPCs.

Article 243-ZD of the 74th Constitution Amendment Act states:

1. There shall be constituted in every State at the district level a DPC to consolidate the plans prepared by the Panchayats and Municipalities in the district as a whole.
2. The legislature of a State may, by law, make provision with respect to—
   (*a*) the composition of District Planning Committees (DPC);

(*b*) the manner in which the seats in such communities shall be filled; provided that not less than four-fifths of the total number of members of such committee shall be elected by and from amongst, the elected members of the panchayat at the district level and of the municipalities in the district in proportion to the ratio between the population of the rural areas and of the urban areas in the district;

(*c*) the functions relating to district planning which may be assigned to such committees;

(*d*) the manner in which the chairpersons of such committees shall be chosen.

3. Every District Planning Committee shall, in preparing the draft development plan:

(*a*) have regard to—

(*i*) matters of common interest between the panchayats and municipalities including spatial planning, sharing of water and other physical and natural resources, the integrated development of infrastructure and environmental conservation;

(*ii*) the extent and type of available resources whether financial or otherwise;

(*b*) consult such institutions and organizations as the governor may, by order, specify.

4. The chairperson of every District Planning Committee shall forward the development plan, as recommended by such committee, to the Government of the State.

From the above account it is clear that the main function of the DPC is to consolidate the plans of panchayats and municipalities and to prepare a development plan for the district as a whole. Details regarding the choice of the Chairperson and Vice-Chairperson, manner in which the seats are to be filled are left to the State Governments. However, the Act has mandated that not less than four-fifths i.e. 80 per cent of the total number of persons in the DPC shall be elected by and from amongst the elected members of panchayats at the district in proportion to the ratio between the population of the rural areas and of the urban areas in the district.

The 73rd and 74th Amendment Acts have ushered in participatory kind of governance and planning involving people and their representatives. The DPC is a pivot which facilitates this participatory governance and planning. Having given the blueprint of DPC, it would be appropriate to analyze its status in some of the Indian States/UTs.

Table 1
State-wise/Union Territory-wise Status of DPCs

	State/UT	*Status*
1.	Andhra Pradesh	Constituted
2.	Arunachal Pradesh	No
3.	Assam	No
4.	Bihar	No
5.	Chattisgarh	Yes
6.	Goa	Yes
7.	Gujarat	No
8.	Haryana	Constituted
9.	Himachal Pradesh	Constituted
10.	Jharkhand	No
11.	Karnataka	Constituted
12.	Kerala	Constituted
13.	Madhya Pradesh	Constituted
14.	Maharashtra	Constituted
15.	Manipur	Constituted
16.	Nagaland	No
17.	Orissa	Constituted
18.	Punjab	No
19.	Rajasthan	Constituted
20.	Sikkim	No
21.	Tamil Nadu	Constituted
22.	Tripura	No
23.	Uttaranchal	Constituted
24.	Uttar Pradesh	Constituted
25.	West Bengal	Constituted
26.	A & N Islands	Constituted
27.	Chandigarh	No
28.	Dadra & Nagar Haveli	Constituted
29.	Daman & Diu	Constituted
30.	Pondicherry	No

Source: Website rural.nic.in Information updated on 11.12.2003.

From the Table 1, it is clear that 19 States/UTs have set up DPCs. The constitution of DPCs is still under consideration in 6 States/UTs. In Jharkhand and Pondicherry DPCs have not been set up because of the non-holding of elections to urban local bodies. The DPCs have not been set up in the States of Meghalaya, Mizoram, Sikkim and Lakshadweep because of the absence of urban local bodies. The J&K and Delhi have been exempted from constituting DPCs. In the States of Nagaland and Gujarat, district planning boards are functioning as DPCs. It is unfortunate to note that about eight States/UTs have not yet shown any commitment to constitute DPCs.[1]

Chairman of DPC

The very idea of decentralization envisages that the powers should be vested in the elected representatives heading either Panchayats or Municipalities. However, the Table 1 indicates that some of the States have followed this principle only in the breach. Some States have nominated cabinet minister as Chairman of DPCs. The demerits of this system as illustrated by MP, Andhra Pradesh, Orissa, Maharashtra and Uttar Pradesh is that since the Minister is a very busy person the proceedings of DPCs either gets postponed or held under Vice-Chairperson performing the function of Chairman. Moreover, vesting of powers in the State Minister symbolizes undermining the powers and functions of PRIs. Elected representatives of the local bodies might feel that Minister is being thrust on them. The Minister can bring in State politics to local level and as a consequence spoiling local level good will. In this context, it is pertinent to note that many Working Group reports have recommended exclusion of MLAs and MPs from the deliberations of panchayats (Government of Karnataka, 1996).

Persistence of District Rural Development Agencies (DRDA) and other Rural Development Agencies (RDA)

Even after 73rd and 74th Constitution Amendment Acts giving constitutional recognition to PRIs, District Rural Development Agency and other bodies continue to implement large number of Central and State Government schemes. DRDA's have not been abolished in States like Tamil Nadu, Andhra Pradesh, Orissa, Uttar Pradesh, Gujarat, Bihar and Maharashtra. In Andhra Pradesh apart from DRDA, Drought Prone Area Development Programmes (DPAP) is constituted.

A study by Babu (2001) of Post-73rd Amendment Panchayat System in Andhra Pradesh states that a large number of rural development activities especially in the area of poverty alleviation and employment schemes are executed through DRDA, DPAP and incidentally they function independently under the administrative control of project directors who are ultimately accountable to the District Collector. In Kerala (World Bank, 2000), District Development Councils (DDCs) have usurped the planning functions of rural local bodies. Thus, the existence of DRDAs and other agencies have imperiled the powers and functions of DPC, since they continue to implement the large number of schemes and wield enormous powers.

Existence of Area Development Funds Outside the Purview of DPCs

The measure which is considered as most retrogressive by the advocates of decentralization is the decision to place under the disposal of the members of parliament Rs. 1580 crores per year for local area development. The Member of Parliament Local Area Development Scheme (MPLADS) was introduced to enable MPs to execute in their constituencies small works of a capital nature based on locally felt needs. Under this scheme, each Member of Parliament has the freedom to suggest to the District Collector, works to the tune of Rs. Two crore per year within his or her constituency.

Obviously, the MPs local area development scheme is 'an assault on the letter and spirit of the Seventy-third Constitution Amendment. There is an overlapping between PRIs and the scheme. How can there be any planning by DPCs when MPs have their own priorities and huge funds under their disposal. Many State Governments have also been disbursing MLAs area development fund. Such separate funds defeat the very rationale for DPCs.

Emergence of Parallel Bodies

Some of the State Governments have initiated several parallel bodies to delimit the powers of the panchayats. The Janmabhoomi Programme of Andhra Pradesh, Joint Forest Management Committees of Gujarat, Watershed Programme of Rajasthan, water user groups and site implementation committees of UP, District Government in Madhya Pradesh, Area Development Boards in Karnataka are some of the cases in point. These are blatant attempts by the State Governments to strengthen the hands of ministers, other powerful elements nominated to these parallel bodies and above all, the District Collector. This fact was also underscored by Karnataka's High Power Committee for redressal of regional imbalances. The Committee has pointed out, "the boards are functioning according to their own style, not so much in line with the charters and guidelines." The report has alluded to the fact that Panchayat Raj Institutions are expected to play a significant role after the enactment of 73rd and 74th Amendment Acts and they could take over the functions which have been assigned to Area Development Boards.

Apart from these, DPCs are beset with meagre powers and resources placed at their disposal. In Andhra Pradesh only a few functions have been delegated to PRIs. The functions actually transferred to Zilla Parishad (ZP) and Mandal Parishad (MP) are rural roads, rural drinking water supply and education up to secondary level. The line departments and ZPs have been kept outside the purview of ZP.

No Provision for Experts and NGOs in DPCs

The different spatial entities at the local level (the village, the blocks, the district and the various urban local bodies included in it) empowered for local governance and planning, constitute a system of "nested hierarchy" (Sundar Ram, K.V., 1997) for the performance of planning and development functions. This would mean that each one of them would prepare their own "area plans", which will get coordinated at the next higher level. Further each of the area plans will be independent so far as their spatial focus is concerned, but interdependent with the other area plans, so far as their linkages and complementarities are concerned. This is what "nesting" implies. In this system of planning, the district level, which at the apex of the local level, needs a strong coordinating mechanism to "nest" and coordinate the various plans and programmes. The DPC would appear to have been conceived for this purpose. Though the choice of schemes will be a social and political judgement by the individual local bodies, the "nesting" and "coordination" and the fine tuning of the plan, taking "consistency" and "linkages" into account would be, by and large, a technical exercise. This calls for co-opting technical experts and prominent local NGOs into DPCs. However, the experience of the States shows that experts and NGOs are hardly co-opted in the DPCs. Usually District collector serves as a technical expert in DPCs. In Karnataka, Chief Executive Officer and Chief Planning Officer act as technical guides. In Kerala, the planning by elected representatives at each level is supplemented by expert committee at district (DLEC), block (BLEC), municipal and corporation levels. The expert committees, at various levels, are an advisory arm of the DPC helping it to appraise the plans and projects. But this provision is absent in most of the States. Even the Sen Committee (Government of Kerala, 1997) has suggested the cooption of experts to DPCs.

Integration of District Plans at the State Level

All the District Plans have to be harmonized and integrated with the State Plan taking into account compatibility with the state and national development objectives, policies and priorities. In this connection (State Planning Commission, Chennai, 1997) it is obligatory on the part of state planning commission to consider the District Plans prepared by the District Planning Committees while finalizing the Draft Plan of the State. In this context, Tamil Nadu Working Group has recommended that the State Planning Commission should hold discussions with the chairpersons of district planning committees of each district in order to decide on the inclusion of the various schemes and projects into the State Plan. In fact, this aspect of state planning commission holding consultations with all the DPCs in the state while finalizing the State Plans is absent in most of the states. For instance in Karnataka, allocations for state sector schemes are made by the departmental heads at the State level and for district sector schemes government fixes the target for which the ZPs have to prepare the plans.

Furthermore, the Karnataka Government (GO. No. RDP 229 ZPS/2000) issued guidelines for constituting a fund for DPC and suggesting that State Government should provide grants as deemed necessary to the DPC for effectively discharging its functions. Notwithstanding this, DPC do not receive any funds of their own nor does the government provide them any funds. Thus owing to these deficiencies DPCs have become rubber stamps in Karnataka.[2]

Integration of Rural and Urban Plans

One of the crucial functions of DPCs is to facilitate interface between municipal bodies and panchayati raj institutions. In addition to plan coordination, the DPC will be required to resolve certain conflicts on issues relating to peripheral areas. For example, certain important questions concerning rural urban interface are likely to arise, like the fringe area of a town, where urbanization is taking place, may lie within the Panchayati Raj Institutions. Similarly, zilla parishads, municipalities and block panchayat might have to share the drinking water. Such issues could better tackled in DPCs. Working groups of several State Governments have recommended the constitution of block planning committees on the model of DPC in order to provide for the organic linkages between panchayat unions, town panchayats and municipalities at the block level.

Having outlined the functions and drawbacks of DPCs in some States, it is imperative to suggest remedial measures in order to enable its effective functioning. Some of the remedial measures are as follows:

1. With regard to selection of chairperson, it is necessary to select always Chairperson of District Panchayat or Mayor of Municipality, to uphold the spirit of decentralisatior The prevailing view is that depending on the urbanisation status of the particular district, the chairperson may be elected either from the rural or urban local bodies. Thus, if a district is predominantly rural, then the chairperson will be from among the elected rural district panchayat members. If the district is predominantly urban, then the chairperson may be elected from among the urban elected members or they could hold the chairmanship by rotation.
2. Parallel bodies like DRDAs and others should be merged with the district panchayats. Special programmes like

Janmabhoomi and others should be implemented by PRIs. Given the technical nature of the functions, it is necessary to co-opt experts and NGOs into DPCs.

3. MPs and MLAs area development funds should be placed at the disposal of DPCs and it should be spent with the concurrence of DPCs.
4. There is a need to insist the State Governments/UTs to hold regular elections to local bodies, to devolve powers and functions to PRIs and to abolish parallel bodies.
5. Centre should take stringent action against erring State Governments which do not constitute DPCs by withholding grants and programmes. Central Finance Commission and State Finance Commissions, appointed once in five years, should examine the status and functioning of DPCs in all the states and the latter should examine the status and functioning of DPCs in the respective State's while giving its recommendations relating to devolution of funds to Panchayat Raj Institutions.
6. According to Expert Committee reports contentious issue of regional disparities bedeviling many States could be better addressed by abolishing regional development boards and transferring their funds to Panchayat Raj Institutions. In this context, it can be said that the DPCs of the respective backward districts could play a pivotal role in planning for the respective backward districts.

NOTES

1. As of October 2006, Ministry of Rural Development has not updated the information pertaining to DPCs put up on its website as on 31st December, 2003.
2. This is told to the author in an interview by Director, Panchayat Raj, Rural Development and Panchayat Raj Department, Bangalore.

REFERENCES

M. Devendra Babu, 2001, "Process and Performance of Panchayats in Andhra Pradesh" in Abdul Aziz (Ed.) *Decentralised Governance and*

Planning: A Comparative Study in Three South Indian States, Macmillan, New Delhi, 2001.

Report of the Expert Committee on Karnataka Panchayat Raj Act, Nayak Committee, Government of Karnataka, Bangalore, 1996.

High Power Committee for Redressal of Regional Imbalances, Final Report, Government of Karnataka, Bangalore, 2002.

Committee on Decentralisation of Powers (S.B. Sen Committee) Final Report, Government of Kerala, Trivandrum, 1997.

Report of the Task Force on Devolution of Powers and Functions upon Panchayati Raj Institutions, Government of India, Ministry of Rural Development, New Delhi, 2001 (a).

Report on the Working Group on Decentralized Planning and Panchayat Raj Institutions (for the Tenth Five Year Plan), Government of India, Ministry of Rural Development, New Delhi, 2001(b).

Report of the Steering Group on Rural Poverty Alleviation, Watershed Development, Decentralised Planning and Panchayat Raj Institutions (for Tenth Five Year Plan), Government of India, Planning Commission of India, New Delhi, 2001.

Report of the Task Force on Panchayat Raj Institutions (PRIs), Government of India, Planning.

Commission of India, New Delhi, 2001.

Report of the Working Group on Decentralised Planning and Panchayati Raj, Government of Tamil Nadu, State Planning Commission, Chennai, 1997.

K.V. Sundar Ram, "*Decentralised Multilevel Planning: Principles and Practices—Asian and African Experiences*", Concept Publishing Company, New Delhi, 1997.

World Bank, *Overview of Rural Decentralisation in India*, Washington D.C., 2000.

17

The Experiences of Empowering Women Panchayat Members in India: Problems, Challenges and Opportunities

NUPUR TIWARY

Since the passing of the 73rd Constitutional Amendment Act, the major change that took place in context of women functionaries of PRIs was political representation of women through reservation. About one million women entered in the first election of Panchayats after 73rd Constitutional Amendment Act. About 40 per cent of the elected women represented the marginalized sections. However, about 70 per cent women representative were illiterate and most of them had no previous political experience. But the apprehension that they will be manipulated by men has been largely disapproved. The entry of women has deep impact on gender equity. We can say that women have to go a long way to make an impact on the rural power structure, but they have certainly made their presence in the power struggles once dominated by men.

Now some of the pertinent questions are—What has been the impact of PRIs on women individually? Why is it that so many of them say they do not wish to contest elections again, in spite of the tact that it has given them power and status? Is it that they have only male role models that they do not wish to follow? Is it that this experience has taught them they cannot change the system without joining it, in all its corruption? This needs deeper probing.

The experiences of women in the PRIs has been so varied, across the three levels of the PRIs and the different states that except for some "tautological" statements little can be said.

We need to distinguish between women who hail from families with political background and those who, can be termed "first generation political aspirants"— women who drifted into PRIs due to the 73rd Amendment. Even though the amendment made the "space" for both these to enter the PRIs, the alacrity with which they take to the new role will vary.

The point to be noted is that hitherto, space for women to participate in institutions like the PRI, which are in the "public sphere", were negligible. Consequently, the early entrants have had only "male role models" of political leadership. Thus, we have had women in a double blind—to be seen as effective, they have to take to masculine ways and when they do that they cease representing women's interests.

From everywhere, an often-heard comment is that many of these women would not like to contest in the next round of elections. Why is that so? Is it a pointer to their "unsuitability" to assume leadership? Or an inability to cope with multiple and conflicting role demands? Or is it time to ask ourselves what is it about PRIs (and politics) that makes it unpalatable to half of humanity, even when it can determine the quality of life.

Added to this is the fact that the women who have come under reservation have come in with their social and economic disadvantages—mostly non-literate, with little productive assets, largely dependent on wage labour and into a rural society that has fixed places for various castes and gender. These cannot be changed by a wave of the constitutional amendment wand.

Experience has taught people to go slow to approach their goal indirectly. They have to decide if attending Panchayat meetings is sometimes worth missing their daily wage. This is even more so in the case of women, who have to worry about crying babies and hungry husband. Thus, as of now, it is unrealistic to expect much in terms of their response. It has first to be demonstrated that the system is indeed here to stay.

The new system co-exists with traditional institutions. The elders wield power in a way the constitution may not have foreseen. If the PRIs are to succeed in their main goals, then they must work in harmony with these traditional institutions, not confront them head-on. This is easier said than done.

The traditional institutions have not given space for women. Many of the factors that hindered women in the earlier system continue to exist and operate in rural areas. In fact, gender as a phenomenon hardly ever appears in a pure form. It is almost always alloyed with caste, class and religious factors. In matters where there is a clash between gender and caste or class, it is impossible to expect women to align themselves with other women, going against their caste or class loyalties. Some women have developed political ambitions too, especially when it is seen as a quick means for upward mobility. And political survival will be difficult if they betray class and caste interests. This is why the reservation of the post of President to the SC/ST category is so resented. The problem is in society, not in the Panchayat that only reflects social reality.

The women functionaries of PRIs are not only showing their active presence in the grassroot politics but have also played a significant role to fulfill the requirements of women. Nevertheless, women functionaries of PRIs face different kinds of problems in carrying out their duties and discharging their responsibilities in the panchayats. During the last twelve years of Panchayati Raj, there has been a strong argument to mobilise, train, inform and equip women in leadership skills and strengthen their understanding of the processes that enhance their abilities to claim their due share of power and resources. Given the foregoing, The Rajiv Gandhi Foundation launched a project "Strengthening the role of Women in Grassroots Democracy." The overall aim of the Project was to address the political and social learning needs of women in Panchayati Raj Institutions. Women elected members of the Panchayats, many of whom are first timers and neo-literates, need special affirmative measures and need-specific capability building interventions. It is recognised widely that the absence of appropriate training software and training technology are serious impediments in this regard.

As a first step a Training Needs Assessment workshop was organised to assess needs of women members of PRIs for performing their statutory role in the panchayats so that a need based training system can be developed for them as required under the project. Towards that end the following objectives were set for the workshop:

- Assessing the problems and difficulties faced by women panchayat members and how training interventions could address them;

- Examining the state level capacity building efforts focused on women PRI members and how they can be improved;
- Developing the basis for a systematic training intervention on conceptual understanding of self-governance, and what appropriate participatory training methodologies would work in different contexts of training of women PRI members.

Knowing the major problems confronting the women functionaries of PRIs was the first task, so it was essential to understand the basic problems faced by women PRI functionaries. However, only discussing problems may provide only an unbalanced picture of the status of women in PRIs. Hence, we worked on "problems, challenges and opportunities" of women functionaries of the PRIs in different states in India.

The participants, principally the members of the panchayats, pointed out that the main problem they face is per se in the exercise of the powers and function as a whole which have been provided by the Constitution to them. This was because of lack of delegation, lack of resources and 'archaic' mindset of men in their home, in society and in the bureaucracy.

The most important issue raised by women Panchayat representatives relates to the difficulties they are facing in the form of "interference of Government official and other influencial persons in their-jurisdiction." The types of influence that the participants identified as problems are in Table 1.

Table 1
Types of Interference Faced by Women Functionaries in Panchayats

- Interference of MLAs in panchayat administration.
- Pressures of contractors for getting work.
- Secretary is not accountable to gram panchayat.
- Proper support from Government Official (is not forthcoming).
- No respect for women from Administration
- Problem of 'Pradhan Pati'
- Political interference (from other sources).
- Social forestry not entrusted to panchayats.
- There is no official/formal relationship between Self-Help Groups (SHGs) and Gram Panchayats.

If we look at the issue to political interference, the crux of the problem again boils down to non-delegation of powers and lack of ability of the women functionaries to resist interferences (from politicians, contractors, husbands and 'other sources', which was explained as bureaucrats and lumpen elements). The core-strategy to ward off external interference to the working of the PRIs, would be to empower the women in panchayats and create a "body" of such women which can act as a source of support to them and as a pressure point against insidious interference by outsiders.

Problem of Resources

Second set of problems that women functionaries relate is to planning. Developing a village level plan according to the demands of the community and implementation of the approved plan in the village are major roles of panchayat members. Starting from the preparation to implementation of the plan these representatives face a series of problems as given in Table 2 below:

Table 2
Problem of Resources

- Problem in implementation on plans prepared by the panchayat body in the block/district.
- It takes longer time to pass gram panchayat proposal for implementation at the district level.
- There is insufficient funds available for development of panchayat.
- MP-MLA funds not linked to panchayats. There is no consultation with panchayats for use of MP/MLA area development funds.
- Funds are not transferred fully (there are cuts and leakages).
- Funds come indirectly to GPs — bribes need to be paid (to the sanctioning/ disbursing authority).

The key issues relating to planning are paltry devolution of resources and public thievery. Because resources do not come to the gram panchayats, funds pass through bureaucratic channel which delays execution of works and more importantly, takes its slice of the cake. The participants ascribed it various appellations: bribe, speed money, lubricant and dasturi. The seriousness of the "cuts" assumes even greater importance because, the resources base of PRIs being small, a cut makes it even smaller.

Challenges

The women and challenges are almost synonymous terms. Because the Indian society is not very open for women, women face challenges both at the political and social levels. The participants from different states/regions however face different kinds and intensity of the same set of problems. As indicated earlier, the process for generating the list of challenges facing women members of PRIs was co-terminus with the process of identifying the problems and opportunities. The different groups worked out the challenges they thought were critical in their states and came to the plenary to present the same. These were discussed and debated. Clearly, barring one exception, participants argued that most of the challenges faced by women functionaries in the PRIs in the different states had a lot of commonality.

Table 3
Challenges Faced by Women Members of PRIs

S. No.	*Challenges*	*No. of Votes*	*Rank*
1.	Securing 50% representation (of women in PRIs)	7	3
2.	Establishing rapport with government officials	1	8
3.	Stop the interference of MLAs / MPs and other state leaders	5	5
4.	Arranging to provide knowledge about duties and roles to women and men members of PRIs	4	6
5.	Increase the transparency in Panchayats	2	7
6.	Form 'panchayat maitri' groups	4	6
7.	Demonstrate that we are "as good or better than men"	6	4
8.	Commission to government officials to approve the work	10	2
9.	Raising funds	16	1

An analysis of the challenges clearly spelt out that there are structural, social and administrative issues. Changes in social mores and mindset of people at large are critical for women in PRIs to be effective. With archaic social mores and mindset, family support for women working in PRIs is hesitant at best and outright hostile at worst. This is a major issue that must be tackled.

On the structural issues, the challenge of increasing the representation of women in PRIs via the reservation route seemed well entrenched. It was argued that quantity often leads to quality: if the mass of women in PRIs increases to match the proportion of women in the total population, the number of women in PRIs will increase. With the increase in "mass" of women in PRIs, the quality of the performance of women in PRIs will also improve which in turn will lead to better governance at the local level. It *was* not lost on the participants that the challenge of increasing reservation of seats for women members from the existing 33 per cent to 50 per cent is formidable. In presenting the issue of 50 per cent reservation of seats for women in PRIs, the participants seemed well informed of the struggle experienced by successive governments to pass laws allowing reservation of seats for women in the Parliament.

On the administrative issues, building "bridges", with the bureaucracy came up as a big challenge, several times over. With "restrained" devolution of resources and limited delegation of powers, the bureaucracy still holds the key to the success of women in PRIs. Starting from changing the bureaucrats' perception about women, their attitudes and behaviour towards panchayat functionaries, to their willingness to let go their hold on the PRIs for the good of the greatest number, all make up a complex interlocking challenge for the women in PRIs.

Opportunities

Together with problems and challenges, the participants also identified the opportunities that are available to women functionaries in PRIs. It was frankly recognised that the 73rd Constitutional Amendment has opened up vistas of opportunities for women to prove their significant role in the development process. The fact that women are in PRIs itself is an enabling factor for women. And that women are in PRIs in a particular percentage was even more enabling. However, the scope for opportunities did not limit itself to reservations alone. Against this backdrop, the opportunities identified by the groups are detailed in Table 4. Adopting the voting methods described for prioritizing the problems, the opportunities were also prioritized. The rank that the opportunities got are indicated in column 4 of Table 4, as in case of problems some of the opportunities were also clubbed together in terms of their ranks.

Table 4
Opportunities

S.No	Opportunities	No. of Votes	Rank
1.	33% reservation in Panchayats	21	1
2.	To participate in national level discussions/events	3	4
3.	To raise women's issues in Panchayat like—lack of access to water, health, electricity	7	2
4.	Opportunities to take up issue specific to women and children	3	4
5.	To take decisions in development of Panchayats	3	4
6.	Opportunities provided by Gram Sabhas—an occasion for large number of women to participate and raise their concerns	21	1
7.	Establish a relationship between public and women representatives	7	2
8.	Opportunity in proper identification of BPL families	3	4
9.	Creation of women SHGs through Women Panchayat Members	3	4
10.	Opportunity for Women Presidents to express their views and ideas	6	3

The most important opportunities that women in PRIs have relate to 33 per cent reservation and the opportunities provided by Gram Sabhas to participate and raise their concerns. The opportunity of establishing a relationship with the public (ranked as second) was also considered a big boon to the participants. Thus, the opportunities predominantly relate to raising issues and participating in decision-making process. That women can participate in making decisions has provided them with opportunities for providing basic services to the masses. Nevertheless, during the discussion on the "opportunities" it came out that women in PRIs still lack the capacity and capability to force an issue, and that they are hamstrung by their ignorance (of laws, rules, processes) and widely dispersed location in accomplishing what they want to achieve: empowerment of all women.

Self-Empowerment

As a natural follow-up, once the participants identified the problems, challenges and opportunities facing women members/functionaries of PRIs, the issue of empowerment of women members of panchayats was taken up for examination. During the course of the workshop, women representatives repeatedly mentioned one specific area for improving the effectiveness of women panchayat leaders and that was self-empowerment. The participants themselves identified the skills and abilities as in Box 1 that need to be developed in the women leaders, to call them "empowered".

Box 1
Skills and Abilities for Empowerment

(*i*) Self-confidence.
(*ii*) Ability to understand the public.
(*iii*) Ability to view public equally without discrimination.
(*iv*) Ability to march forward.
(*v*) Ability to take decision.
(*vi*) Ability to insure public participation.
(*vii*) Ability to provide total literacy.
(*viii*) Financial independence.

Having identified the skills and abilities that are critical for empowerment of women members of PRIs, the participants were taken through participatory process of assessing the level of empowerment of women members/functionaries in the different states, namely, preparing and analysing the empowerment circle. The process followed was somewhat like the following:

A circle was drawn with eight radii. Each radius represented one skill / ability along which the relative skill/ability was written. The point at the centre of the circle for a particular radius indicated the position that the skill/ability represented by the radius as zero. As against this, the point where the relative radius met the circumference of the circle indicated the presence of 100 per cent of the relative skill/ability represented by the radius. This was explained to all the participants.

Each of the participants were then given eight "bindis" with the advise to place one bindi along one radius indicating the level of availability of skills/abilities in the women members/functionaries of PRIs in the states they represented (on a "zero to hundred" scale explained above). The participants had the option of not indicating the skill/ability if they were not sure or ambivalent about the position she should indicate. The result is the empowerment circle.

An analysis of the empowerment circle is at Table 5 below:

Table 5
Skills and Abilities for Empowerment of Women Functionaries in PRIs (Diagram is Attached as Appendix-3)

S. No.	*Percentage → Skills and Abilities for Empowerment ↓*	*Total no. of Responses*	*0-25*	*26-50*	*51-75*	*76-100*
1.	Self-confident	23	—			86.95
2.	Ability to understand the public	21	14.28	33.33	52.38	—
3.	Ability to view public equally without discrimination	20	5	40	55	—
4.	Ability to march forward	24	—	16.66	41.66	41.66
5.	Ability to take decisions	20	—	—	30	70
6.	Ability to ensure public participation	22	—	18.18	40.90	40.90
7.	Ability to provide total literacy (educate)	22	4.54	0.09	27.27	59.09
8.	Financial Independence	22	—	13.63	31.81	54.54

The empowerment circle indicates fairly clearly that women functionaries of PRIs have fairly high levels of skills and abilities to feel that they are empowered. However, about 40-60 per cent of them still fall short of the "optimum levels" of ability to march forward, ability to ensure public participation and educate their constituencies impartially. Thus, the picture that the empowerment circle and its analysis, present is a mixed one. While most of the elements of empowerment were present in the women functionaries, it was somewhat surprising that many of them had the characteristics of empowerment at levels, just above the 50 per cent mark and only a few saw themselves as fully empowered. Thus while women functionaries/members in PRIs are in the decision-making process, there is something that is left to be desired on many of the elements. The message was clear much more work on empowerment of women in PRIs is urgently called for.

Social Mobilization with Gender Focus

Social mobilization is the process by which communities are empowered through the formation of groups to meet their basic needs and those of their communities. (A community can be loosely defined as any grouping of people such as a village, a small town or neighbourhood or part of a neighbourhood in a larger town or city). It is important that people form groups they are comfortable with or with common interest and muster up support for each other through joint efforts to raise their state of well-being. When we talk about gender focus social mobilization, it includes alliances of women and for the women. But for social mobilisation it is critical to have a mass of social capital. Thus, social capital was the issue that was then examined. All women member motioned the importance of alliance building for women PRI members. In Box 2 are the some of the elements of social capital, for a community that the participants identified.

Box 2

Some Elements of Social Capital

(*i*) Willingness to do communal good.

(*ii*) Unity (amongst the members of the community).

(*iii*) Concern for community well being.

(*iv*) Mutual trust.

(*v*) System of participatory community decision-making.

(vi) Existence of social institutions.

A circle was drawn with six radii. Each radius represented an element of social capital written along it. The point at the centre of the circle for a radius indicated total absence represented by the particular radius. As against this, the point where the relative radius met the circumference of the circle indicated that generally 100 per cent availability of the relative element of social capital.

Each of the participants was then given six bindis. They were advised to place one bindi along one radius indicating the level of availability of the particular element of social capital in the state they represented (on a "zero to hundred" scale explained above). The participants had the option of not indicating the status of availability of any or of all the elements of social capital if they were not sure or ambivalent about the position she should indicate.

The picture that thus emerges is at Figures-2 to 15. An analysis of Figures 2 to 15 thus indicates a very varied picture, consistent with the general beliefs about the different levels of development in the States. Attention is invited to Table 6 below:

Table 6
Levels of Different Elements of Social Capital in Different States (diagrams is attached as Appendix-4)

S. No.	Levels → Elements of Social Capital ↓	0- 25%	26-50%	51-75%	76-100%
1.	Willingness to do communal good	Uttaranchal (25%) Madhya Pradesh, Ujjain (20%) Uttar Pradesh (20%) Maharashtra (25%) Orissa (10%) Bihar (10%)	Assam (40%) Haryana (50%)	Goa, South (75%) Himachal (70%)	Andhra Pradesh (100%) Kerala (90%) Tamil Nadu (80%) Goa, North (90%) Madhya Pradesh, Betul (80%)
2.	Unity		Andhra Pradesh (50%) Madhya Pradesh, Ujjain (30%) Uttar Pradesh (30%) Maharashtra (40%) Kerala (50%) Goa, South (50%) Orissa (30%) Bihar (30%)	Uttaranchal (75%) Assam (70%) Goa, North (75%) Himachal (55%)	Tamil Nadu (85%) Haryana (80%) Madhya Pradesh, Betul (100%)
3.	Concern for community well being	Uttaranchal (25%) Maharashtra (10%) Bihar (5%)	Madhya Pradesh, Ujjain (30%) Kerala (40%) Assam (30%)	Orissa (60%) Himachal (60%) Haryana (50%)	Andhra Pradesh (80%) Uttar Pradesh (80%) Tamil Nadu (95%) Goa,South (90%) Goa, North (100%) Madhya Pradesh, Betul (100%)

(Contd.)

S. No.	Levels → Elements of Social Capital ↓	0- 25%	26-50%	51-75%	76-100%
4.	Mutual trust	Uttaranchal (25%)	Andhra Pradesh (40%) Maharashtra (40%) Goa,South (50%) Orissa (50%) Assam (50%) Himachal (20%) Bihar (50%)	Kerala (75%) Tamil Nadu (70%) Goa, North (75%)	Madhya Pradesh, Unjjain (100%) Uttar Pradesh (80%) Haryana (90%) Madhya Pradesh, Betul (100%)
5.	System of participatory community decision-making		Andhra Pradesh (40%) Uttaranchal (50%) Madhya Pradesh, Ujjain (50%) Uttar Pradesh (40%) Maharashtra (35%) Orissa (30%) Himachal (10%) Bihar (50%)	Tamil Nadu (70%)	Kerala (80%) Goa, South (100%) Assam (80%) Goa, North (100%) Haryana (80%) Madhya Pradesh, Betul (100%)
6.	Existence of social institutions	Andhra pradesh (20%) Maharashtra (%) Goa, South (20%) Haryana (20%)	Uttaranchal (50%) Uttar Pradesh (30%) Goa, North (50%) Himanchal (10%)	Madhya Pradesh, Ujjain (70%) Kerala (60%) Tamil Nadu (60%)	Orissa (90%) Assam (90%) Madhya Pradesh, Betul (100%) Bihar (80%)

If we examine columns of Table 6, signifying the levels of the elements that make the social capital of PRIs, it seems that different states are at different levels of achievement on the different elements. On the whole it comes out that most of the states have rather low level of social capital (in the range of 26-50%). It is striking that all southern states (A.P., Kerala, T.N. and Goa) and Haryana, have higher levels of all the elements of social capital. The under developed states (Bihar, M.P., U.P., H.P. Uttaranchal, Orissa and Assam) are still struggling to develop their strengths in social capital. Curiously enough, contrary to popular understanding, Maharashtra does not come out as a front-runner in this regard. The undeveloped states (Assam and Orissa) having large tribal populations, otherwise fairly low on different elements, have scored high on the existence of social institutions. This is probably because tribal communities traditionally have their own very strong social institutions.

A notable exception has been Madhya Pradesh. The participant from Madhya Pradesh had indicated in their Cob-web Analysis that Betul, M.P. have every element of social capital at or nearly 100 per cent level, which is unlikely. The matter is being further examined and we are in correspondence with the participants to clarify the matter.

Attitudes and Behaviour

When we talk about alliances or collective effort, we require changes in every individual as attitudes and behaviour. The participants themselves have talked a great deal about attitudes and behaviour of men and of the bureaucracy and Government Departments. To have a quick glimpse of what attitudes and behaviour the participants have, as a mirror image of the attitudes and behaviours of women in PRIs, a participatory game was played. The participants were taken through the exercise of "solving a picture puzzle" to realise their attitudes and behaviours, when they work in groups. For the purpose, the participants were divided into two groups in the workshop hall forming two circles.

Each group was given pieces of pictures and they were required to put the pieces together and create the picture. (There were three simple rules to follow: *one,* members of the groups cannot speak to each other in their group but can help each other and communicate through gestures; *two,* the two groups had "advisers" who could speak and guide them but not touch the pieces; *three,* the task had to be finished in 30 minutes.

What happened at the workshop hall was very interesting. The groups struggled with the pieces within the groups, but they did not consult the other group. Some dominant members of Group-II (within the group) took charge of a large number of pieces and attempted to form the picture by themselves while others were left out of the activity.

After a while, a member from Group-I went over to Group-II, to find out what they were doing and without any discussion came back to her own group and requested (through gestures) a dominant member of her group to collect as many pieces as she can and attempt at completing the picture, which the dominant member attempted but did not succeed. In none of the groups, the participants examined the reverse of the "picture pieces" to realise that there were different colour schemes on the reverse and hence, the pieces belonged to different picture puzzles. Finally, none of the groups succeeded in completing the two pictures within the allocated time of 30 minutes.

After 30 minutes, the lead facilitator analysed the attitudes and behaviour displayed by both the group, as under:

(*a*) We do not "listen" (we hear but not listen).

(*b*) "We do not talk to each other (communicate) well." While the group members could not talk amongst themselves, there was no bar to communicate with the other group. Inter-group communication was not barred but none realised so and none attempted it.

(*c*) We are more comfortable to work in "our own group"—reflecting some kind of groupism and anti-inclusiveness. In the process, important members of the community are left out and marginalised by the process.

(*d*) "We are quick to imitate." While there is merit in not inventing the wheel, it is important to bear in mind that imitation is not possible all the time. There is need to adapt.

(*e*) "We are dominant." We want to do things our way, unconcerned about what others may be feeling.

(*f*) "Some of us just want to flow with the tide." Let other do the job we will get the credit anyway.

The participants were asked to quietly reflect within themselves and see if the analysis of their attitudes and behaviour corresponded with their own perception of what attitudes and behaviours they have and exhibit in their real life. The participants agreed with the analysis and confirmed that in their functioning at the panchayat levels, they do reflect similar attitudes and behaviour. The need to change attitudes and behaviour for women in PRIs to succeed was brought out in bold relief.

Solutions to the Problem of Women Members in PRIs

The participants worked on the solutions to the problems, which they were facing and explored ways and means to meet the challenges. The objective was to identify solution to overcome the hindrances in meeting the challenges. The participants were divided in four groups representing different regions/states, having due regard to their language competencies. The process followed was similar to what was followed in developing the problems, challenges and opportunities. Each group presented their solutions in the plenary and then a common list of solutions was worked out using the Delhpi method. The solutions were as in Table 7.

Table 7
Solutions to Problems of Women in PRIs

1. Raise Funds.
2. Commission to Government Officials for approving work of PRIs be stopped.
3. Demonstrate that "we" are better than men.
4. Establish a network of women Gram Panchayat members.
5. Stop the interference of MPs, MLAs and other state leaders.
6. Increase the knowledge of women members so that they have less difficulty in functioning properly.
7. Assume responsibility to create environment for women's empowerment.
8. Eliminate male domination.

Some of the activities on how to operationlise the solutions suggested are reflected below:

Activities to Operationalise the Solutions

1. Raising Funds
   - 40 per cent of state plans funds to be transferred to GPs.
   - Direct (flow of) funds to GPs.

- Funds related to the following to be transferred to the GPs—fisheries, agriculture, dairy, social welfare, social forestry, rural development, and SC/ST development.
- Birth, death, marriage registration to be handed-over to GPs in all states.
- Clarification, demarcation and handing-over of Panchayat lands for development—revenue mobilization.
- Ponds to be handed-over to GPs.

2. Payment of commission to government officials for approving the work of PRIs be stopped
   - To form watch-groups based on legal rights.
   - (Carry out) Social Audit.
   - Power to write CR (Confidential Report) of Govt. officials be vested in PRIs.
   - Knowledge of anti-corruption bill.
   - Unity amongst the women PRIs.
   - Collectively develop an alternative culture of integrity.
   - 33 per cent reservation (for women) in State Assemblies and Parliament.

3. Demonstrate that we are as good or better than men
   - Women representatives concentrate more on child and women welfare.
   - Women feel more comfortable with women representatives.
   - Consider women's opinion in framing/changing systems and rules.
   - Obtain training on legal matters.
   - Appoint legal adviser for women representatives.
   - Women representatives be (made) more confident.
   - Empower women.
   - Work with a challenging mindset.

4. Establishing a network of women Gram Panchayat members
   - Establish contact with women Panchayat members.
   - Discuss with the women members about the network.

- Networks should be at the village, block and district level (and be federated).

5. Stop the interference of MLAs, MPs and other state leaders

- Additions/amendments to be done in the Constitutional Law.
- Funds to be given to panchayats directly. No interference of district officials.
- Inter co-ordination between MLAs, MPs—PRIs to be established.
- As per 73rd Amendment total powers to be entrusted to panchayats.
- Women members of PRIs to be trained in Panchayat Acts.
- Panchayat Acts should be available in local languages.
- 50 per cent of State Government funds to be released to panchayats directly.
- Panchayat Presidents to be elected through direct election.
- Remove provisions for no confidence motion.

6. Increase knowledge of women members so that they have less difficulty in functioning properly

- Regular training programme for women functionaries by Government.
- Regular information flow to Panchayat members through informal network and group.
- Develop reading habit for journals on Panchayats.
- Use of low cost media for information dissemination.

7. Responsibility to create suitable environment for women's empowerment

- Increase income through creating livelihood opportunities for women.
- Entrust GPs (not NGOs) with responsibility for promoting SHGs.
- Majority representation of women in statutory and village development committees
- Prohibition of liquor.

8. Eliminate Male Domination
   - Ensuring that only elected representation, not proxies, represent GPs formally.
   - Monthly meetings, specifically between women representatives and administration.
   - Men should be sensitized about women's right.
   - Special effort to raise self-confidence of women representatives.
   - Impart trainings—on how to run panchayats, conduct meetings, and provide information about rules of business and procedures to be followed.
   - Increase awareness amongst women representatives.
   - Legal literacy for all women.

There is a need for free flow of information to the women members/functionaries of the panchayats, building a system by which the members/functionaries of PRIs can exchange data and information, building the capability of the members/functionaries of PRIs to build and sustain alliances to take forward issues of governance at local level (including tackling interference, building bridges with the bureaucracy and cutting out payment of bribes) and establishing a network of members of panchayats to lobby for changes and for advocacy. Significantly the participants were earnest in acquiring knowledge of how to govern panchayats and the urge in them to acquire knowledge, skills and attitudes necessary for good governance was clearly discernible.

To facilitate the capacity building of women members/ functionaries of PRIs training has to be imparted on philosophy, law, panchyati raj governance, structure, gender and the Indian Constitution which would be relevant to PRIs.

Skills have to be deveioped in elements of planning for social and economic development and programme management at the village level. The women functionaries have to be trained in finding ways and means to offer effective challenge and resistance to invidious social mores; customs, beliefs and stereotyping that disempower women functionaries. These could be organizational, institutional or structural. Further they also require guidance on building and sustaining mechanisms and systems to counter rampant public thievery of panchayat funds.

It is important to Create platforms that would act as pressure points to force powers that—be to bring about changes in attitudes and behaviour of political and bureaucratic executive towards women functionaries of PRIs is a critical requirement for proper functioning of the PRI.

There is also a need to emphasize the issue of local power structure to make the elected women members understand the importance of social capital. There should be a session on leadership behaviour for empowerment of women PRI members. Every Gram Panchayat has a steering committee in their panchayat. To highlight this fact, there is a need to emphasize on working committees in the module. Language should be simplified in the module, so that trainer can easily grasp it. There is a need to define the terms, like social mobilization, social capital and transformative strategy etc. A separate session should be added on group process.

Stressing the need for making these provisions truly effective, there is a critical necessity of empowering women and doing away with surrogate representatives for this purpose. "Training of women representatives must not begin with the promise that women are themselves responsible for the lack of social and cultural capital. The situation is a systematic failure. Therefore, even the trainer must start from what the participants know and then take them to the arena of the unknown. ... Building up community support networks for women members should be an important component of training intervention" (RGF Task Force Report, 2001).

Emphasis on procedures and programmes, rather than political process and critical issues that women encounter, is not going to usher in a qualitative change in the participation of women. Majority of women representatives are now showing their determination to occupy public space and are fighting for their rights and legitimate space. In their struggle against entrenched systems disempowering them, they have to overcome many hurdles, such as conditions of poverty, social responsibility for the domestic unit, growing criminalization of political process and interlocking of other social relations with gender relations. This is just a small beginning, though, and much remains to be done before we can actually claim to have empowered the women elected members of panchayati raj.

REFERENCES

Abdul Nazir Saheb State Institute for Rural Development: Training of Gram Panchayat Members Mysore: ANSSIRD, 2002.

Agnihotri, V.K., S. Krishna and A. Mukherjee, "Human Resource Development for Panchayats, in Amitava Mukherjee," ed. *Decentralisation, Panchayats in the Nineties,* Vikas Publications, New Delhi, 1994.

Andhra Pradesh Academy of Rural Development: Manual for Management of Gram Panchayats, Hyderabad: Andhra Pradesh Academy of Rural Development, 2002.

Bohra, O.P., "Decentralisation and Devolution of Powers and Functions to Panchayats, *Journal of Rural Development,* Vol. 19(2), 2000.

Cente for Rural Studies and National Society for Promotion of Development Administration: Capacity Building of the PRIs in Uttaranchal State, Mussoorie, Uttaranchal: Centre for Rural Studies and National Society for Promotion of Development Administration, 2002.

Indira Gandhi National Open University: Set of IGNOU Modules, New Delhi: IGNOU, 1997.

Kaushik, S., "Women and Panchayati Raj," Haranand Publications, New Delhi, 1993.

Kerala Institute for Local Administration: Training Module for Panchayati Raj Functionaries, Thrissur: KILA, 2001.

Kerala Institute of Local Administration: Modulc for Training Programme on "Women Empowerment" for Elected Representatives of Gram Panchayat in Kerala, Thrissur: KILA, 2002.

Kerala Institute of Local Administration: Report of the Operational Level Training for Gram Panchayat Functionaries, Thrissur, Kerala: Kerala Institute of Local Administration, 2001.

Madhya Pradesh Institute of Social Science Research: Operational Training for Gram Panchayat Officials, Ujjain: Madhya Pradesh Institute of Social Science Research, 2001.

Mukherjee, Amitava Participatory Rural Appraisal: Methods and Applications in Rural Planning, New Delhi: Vikas Publishing House 1995 and 2nd revised edition by New Delhi: Concept Publishing.

Mukherjee, Neela, Participatory Learning and Action: With 100 Field Methods, New Delhi: Concept Publishing Company, 2003.

National Institute of Rural Development: Training Modules for Panchayati Raj Functionaries, Hyderabad: NIRD, 1994.

Omeo Kumar Das Institute of Social Change and Development: Modules for Training Programmes for PRIs of Tripura, Guwahati: Omeo Kumar Das Institute of Social Change and Development, 2002.

Participation and Governance Institute: Report on One day Orientation

Programme for Newly Elected Representatives, Nainital: Participation and Governance Institute, 2003.

Sharma, Kumud From Representation to Presence, The Paradox of Power and Powerlessness.

Sharma, Kumud, "Transformative Politics: Dimensions of Women's Participation in Panchayati Raj, " *Indian Journal of Gender Studies*, Vol. 5(1), Sage Publications, Delhi, 1998.

Stephen, F., "Empowering Women in Panchayats through Training, in Building Women's Capacities: Interventions in Gender Transformation" (ed.) Ranjini K. Murthy, Sage Publications India Pvt. Ltd., New Delhi, 2001.

Task Force on Panchayati Raj, Rajiv Gandhi Foundation: Empowering Panchayats—Handbook for Master Trainers, Using Participatory Approach, (New Delhi: Concept Publishing Co.), 2003.

The Hunger Project: Women's Leadership Workshop, New Delhi: The Hunger Project, 2003.

Appendix-I

The Constitution (Seventy-Third) Amendment Act, 1992 on the Panchayats

Further to Amend the Constitution of India

Be it enacted by Parliament in the Forty-third Year of the Republic of India as follows:

1. *Short Title and Commencement*—(*a*) This Act may be called the Constitution (Seventy-third Amendment) Act, 1992.

(*b*) It shall come into force on such date as the Central Government may, by notification in the Official Gazette, appoint.

2. *Insertion of New Part IX*—After Part VIII of the Constitution, the following Part shall be inserted, namely—

PART IX
THE PANCHAYATS

243. *Definitions*—In this Part, unless the context otherwise requires:

(*a*) "District" means a district in a State,

(*b*) "Gram Sabha" means a body consisting of persons registered in the electoral rolls relating to a village comprised within the area of Panchayat at the village level;

(*c*) "Intermediate level" means a level between the village and district levels specified by the Governor of a State by public notification to be the intermediate level for the purposes of this part;

(*d*) "Panchayat" means an institution (by whatever name called) of self-government constituted under Article 243B, for the rural areas;

(*e*) "Panchayat area" means the territorial area of a Panchayat;

(*f*) "Population means the population as ascertained at the last preceding census of which the relevant figures have been published;

Assented by President of India on April 20,1993 and brought into effect on April 24, 1993.

(*g*) "Village" means a village specified by the Governor by public notification to be a village for the purposes of this Part and includes a group of villages so specified.

243A. *Gram Sabha*—A Gram Sabha may exercise such powers and perform such functions at the village level as the Legislature of a State may by law, provide.

243B. (1) *Constitution of Panchayats*—There shall be constituted in every state, Panchayats at the village, intermediate and district levels in accordance with the provisions of this part.

(2) Notwithstanding anything in clause (1), Panchayats at the intermediate level may not be constituted in a State having a population not exceeding twenty lakhs.

243C. (1) *Composition of Panchayats*—Subject to the provisions of this Part, the Legislature of a State may, by law, make provisions with respect to the composition of Panchayats:

Provided that the ratio between the population of the territorial area of a Panchayat at any level and the number of seats in such Panchayat to be filled by election shall, so far as practicable, be the same throughout the State.

(2) All the seats in a Panchayat shall be filled by persons chosen by direct election from territorial constituencies in the Panchayat area and, for this purpose, each Panchayat area shall be divided into territorial constituencies in such manner that the ratio between the population of each constituency and the number of seats allotted to it shall, so far as practicable, be the same throughout the Panchayat area.

(3) The Legislature of a State may, by law, provide for the representation:

(*a*) of the Chairpersons of the Panchayats at the village level, in the Panchayats at the intermediate level or, in the case of a State not having Panchayats at the intermediate level, in the Panchayats at the district level;

(*b*) of the Chairpersons of the Panchayats at the intermediate level, in the Panchayats at the district level;

(*c*) of the members of the House of the People and the members of the Legislative Assembly of the State representing constituencies which comprise wholly or partly a Panchayat area at a level other than the village level, in such Panchayat;

(*d*) of the members of the Council of States and the members of the Legislative Council of the State, where they are registered as electors within:

(*i*) a Panchayat area at the intermediate level, in Panchayat at the district level.

(ii) a Panchayat area at the district level, in Panchayat at the district level.

(4) The Chairperson of a Panchayat and other members of a Panchayat whether or not chosen by direct election from territorial constituencies in the Panchayat area shall have the right to vote in the meetings of the Panchayats.

(5) The Chairperson of:

(*a*) a Panchayat at the village level shall be elected in such manner as the Legislature of a State may, by law, provide; and

(*b*) a Panchayat at the intermediate level or district level shall be elected by and from amongst, the elected members thereof.

243D. *Reservation of Seats*—(1) Seats shall be reserved for: (*a*) The Scheduled Castes and (*b*) the Scheduled Tribes, in every Panchayat and the number of seats so reserved shall bear, as nearly as may be, the same proportion to the total number of seats to be filled by direct election in that Panchayat as the population of the Scheduled Castes in that Panchayat area or of the Scheduled Tribes in that Panchayat area or of the Scheduled Tribes in that Panchayat area bears to the total populations of that area and such seats may be allotted by rotation to different constituencies in a Panchayat.

(2) Not less than one-third of the total number of seats reserved under clause (1) shall be reserved for women belonging to the Scheduled Castes or as the case may be, the Scheduled Tribes.

(3) Not less than one-third (including the number of seats reserved for women belonging to the Scheduled Castes and the Scheduled Tribes) of the total number of seats to be filled by direct election in every Panchayat shall be reserved for women and such seats may be allotted by rotation to different constituencies in a Panchayat.

(4) The offices of the Chairpersons in the Panchayats at the village or any other level shall be reserved for the Scheduled Castes, the Scheduled Tribes and women in such manner as the Legislature of a State may, by law, provide;

Provided that the number of offices of Chairpersons reserved for the Scheduled Castes and the Scheduled Tribes in the Panchayats at each level in any State shall bear, as nearly as may be, the same proportion to the total number of such offices in the Panchayats at each level as the population of the Scheduled Castes in the State or of the Scheduled Tribes in the State bears to the total population of the State:

Provided further that not less than one-third of the total number of offices of Chairpersons in the Panchayats at each level shall be reserved for women.

Provided also that the number of offices reserved under this clause shall be allotted by rotation to different Panchayats at each level.

(5) The reservation of seats under clauses (1) and (2) and the reservation of offices of Chairpersons (other than the reservation for women) under clause (4) shall cease to have effect on the expiration of the period specified in Article 334.

(6) Nothing in this Part shall prevent the Legislature of a State from making any provision for reservation of seats in any Panchayat or offices of Chairpersons in the Panchayats at any level in favour of backward class of citizens.

243E. (1) *Duration of Panchayats etc.*—Every Panchayat, unless sooner dissolved under any law for the time being in force, shall continue for five years from the date appointed for this first meeting and no longer.

(2) No amendment of any law for the time being in force shall have the effect of causing dissolution of a Panchayat at any level. Which is functioning immediately before such amendment, till the expiration of its duration specified in clause (1).

(3) An election to constitute a Panchayat shall be completed

(*a*) before the expiry of its duration specified in clause (1);

(*b*) before the expiration of a period of six months from the date of its dissolution:

Provided that where the remainder of the period for which the dissolved Panchayat would have continued is less than six months, it shall not be necessary to hold any election under this clause for constituting the Panchayat for such period.

(4) A Panchayat constituted upon the dissolution of a Panchayat before the expiration of its duration shall continue only for the remainder of the period for which the dissolved Panchayat would have continued under clause (1) had it not been so dissolved.

243F. (1) *Disqualification for Membership*—A person shall be disqualified for being chosen as and for being, a member of a Panchayat:

(*a*) If he is so disqualified by or under any law for the time being enforce for the purposes of elections to the Legislature of the State concerned:

Provided that no person shall be disqualified on the ground that he is less than twenty-five years of age, if he has attained the age of twenty-one years;

(*b*) If he is so disqualified by or under any law made by the Legislature of the State.

(2) If any question arises as to whether a member of a Panchayat has become subject to any of the disqualifications mentioned in clause (1), the question shall be referred for the decision of such authority and in such manner as the Legislature of a State may, by law, provide.

243G. *Powers, Authority and Responsibilities of Panchayats*—Subject to the provisions of this Constitution, the Legislature of a State may, by law, endow the Panchayats with such powers and authority as may be necessary to enable them to function as institutions of self-government and such law may contain provisions for the devolution of powers and responsibilities upon Panchayats at the appropriate level, subject to such conditions as may be specified therein, with respect to:

(*a*) the preparation of plans for economic development and social justice;

(*b*) the implementation of schemes for economic development and social justice as may be entrusted to them including those in relation to the matters listed in the Eleventh Schedule.

243H. *Powers to Import Taxes by and Funds of the Panchayats*—The Legislature of a State may, by law:

(*a*) . authorise a Panchayat to levy, collect and appropriate such taxes, duties, tolls and fees in accordance with such procedure and subject to such limits;

(*b*) assign to a Panchayat such taxes, duties, tolls and feels levied and collected by the State Government for such purposes and subject to such conditions and limits;

(*c*) provide for making such grants-in-aid to the Panchayats from the Consolidated Fund of the State; and

(*d*) provide for constitution of such Funds for crediting all moneys received, respectively, by or on behalf of the Panchayats and also for the withdrawal of such moneys therefrom as may be specified in the law.

243-I. *Constitution of Finance Commission to Review Financial Position*—(1) The Governor of a State shall, as soon as may be within one year from the commencement of the Constitution (Seventy-third Amendment) Act, 1992, and thereafter at the expiration of every fifth year constitute a Finance Commission to review the financial position of the Panchayats and to make recommendations to the Governor as to:

(*a*) the principles which should govern:

(*i*) the distribution between the State and the Panchayats of the net proceeds of the taxes, duties, tolls and fees leviable by the State, which may be divided between them under this Part and the allocation between the Panchayats at all levels of their respective shares of such proceeds.

(*ii*) the determination of the taxes, duties, tolls and fees which may be assigned to, or appropriated by, the Panchayats;

(*iii*) the grant-in-aid to the Panchayats from the Consolidated Fund of the State;

(*b*) the measures needed to improve the financial position of the Panchayats;

(*c*) any other matter referred to the Finance Commission by the Governor in the interests of sound finance of the Panchayats.

(2) The Legislature of a State may, by law, provide for the composition of the Commission, the qualifications which shall be requisite for appointment as members thereof and the manner in which they shall be selected.

(3) The Commission shall determine their procedure and shall have such powers in the performance of their functions as the Legislature of the State may, by law, confer on them.

(4) The Governor shall cause every recommendation made by the Commission under this article together with an explanatory memorandum as to the action taken thereon to be laid before the Legislature of the State.

243J. *Audit of Accounts of Panchayats*—The Legislature of a State may, by law, make provisions with respect to the maintenance of accounts by the Panchayats and the auditing of such accounts.

243K. *Elections to the Panchayats*—(1) The superintendence, direction and control of the preparation of electoral rolls for, and the conduct of all elections to the Panchayats shall be vested in a

State Election Commission consisting of a State Election Commissioner to be appointed by the Governor.

(2) Subject to the provisions of any law made by the Legislature of a State, the conditions of service and tenure of office of the State Election Commissioner shall be such as the Governor may by rule determine;

Provided that the State Election Commissioner shall not be removed from his office except in like manner and on the like grounds as a Judge of a High Court and the conditions of service of the State Election Commissioner shall not be varied to his disadvantage after his appointment.

(3) The Governor of a State shall, when so requested by the State Election Commission, make a valuable to the State Election Commission such staff as may be necessary for the discharge of the functions conferred on the State Election Commission by clause (1).

(4) Subject to the provisions of this Constitution, the Legislature of a state may, by law, make provision with respect to all matters relating to or in connection with elections to the Panchayats.

243L. *Application to Union Territories*—The provisions of this Part shall apply to the Union Territories and shall, in their application to a Union Territory, have effect as if the references to the Governor of a State were references to the Administrator of the Union Territory appointed under Article 239 and references to the Legislature or the Legislative Assembly of a State were references, in relation to a Union Territory having a Legislative Assembly, to that Legislative Assembly.

Provided that the President may, by public notification, direct that the provisions of this Part shall to any Union Territory or part thereof subject to such exceptions and modifications as he may specify in the notification.

243M. *Part not to Apply to Certain Areas*—(1) Nothing in this Part shall apply to the Scheduled Areas referred to in clause (1), and the tribal areas referred to in clause (2), of Article 244.

(2) Nothing in this Part shall apply to:

(*a*) the Sates of Nagaland, Meghalaya and Mizoram;

(*b*) the hill areas in the State of Manipur for which District Council exist under any law for the time being in force.

(3) Nothing in this Part:

(*a*) relating to Panchayats at the district level shall apply to the hill areas of the District of Darjeeling in the State of West Bengal for which Darjeeling Gorkha Hill Council exists under any law for the time being in force;

(*b*) shall be construed to affect the functions and powers of the Darjeeling Gorkha Hill Council constituted under such law.

(4) Not with standing anything in this Constitution:

(*a*) The Legislature of a State referred to in sub-clause (1) of clause (2) may, by law, extend this Part to that State, except the areas, if any, referred to in clause (1), if the Legislative Assembly of that State passes a resolution to that effect by a majority of the total membership of that those and by a majority of the total membership of that House and by a majority of not less than two-thirds of the members of that House present and voting;

(*b*) Parliament may, by law, extend the provisions of this Part to the Scheduled Areas and the tribal areas referred to in clause (1) subject to such exceptions and modifications as may be specified in such law, and no such law shall be deemed to be an amendment of this Constitution for the purposes of Article 368.

243N. *Continuance of Existing Laws and Panchayats*—Notwithstanding anything in this Part, any provision of any law relating to Panchayats in force in a State immediately before the commencement of the Constitution (Seventy-third Amendment) Act, 1992, which is inconsistent with the provisions of this Part, shall continue to be in force until amended or repealed by a competent Legislature or other competent authority or until the expiration of one year from such commencement, whichever is earlier: Provided that all the Panchayats existing immediately before such commencement shall continue till the expiration of their duration, unless sooner dissolved by a resolution passed to that effect by the Legislative Assembly of that State or, in the case of a State having a Legislative Council, by each House of the Legislature of that state.

243O. *Bar to Interference by Courts in Electoral Matters*—Notwithstanding anything in this Constitution:

(*a*) the validity of any law relating to the delimitation of constituencies or the allotment of seats to such constituencies, made or purporting to be made under Article 243K, shall not be called in question in any court;

(*b*) no election to any Panchayat shall be called in question except by an election by an election petition presented to such authority and in such manner as is provided for by or under any law made by the Legislature of a State.

3. *Amendment of Article 280*—In clause (3) of Article 280 of the Constitution after sub-clause (*a*) the following sub-clause shall be inserted, namely:

(*b*) the measures needed to augment the Consolidated Fund of a State to supplement the resources of the Panchayats in the State on the basis of the recommendations made by the Finance Commission of the State;

4. *Addition of Eleventh Schedule*—After the Tenth Schedule to the Constitution, the following schedule shall be added, namely:

ELEVENTH SCHEDULE
(Article 243G)

1. Agriculture, including agricultural extension.
2. Land improvement, implementation of land reforms, land consolidation and soil conservation.
3. Minor irrigation, water management and watershed development.
4. Animal husbandry, dairying and poultry.
5. Fisheries.
6. Social forestry and farm forestry.
7. Minor forest produce.
8. Small scale industries, including food processing industries.
9. Khadi, village and cottage industries.
10. Rural housing.
11. Drinking water.
12. Fuel and fodder.
13. Roads, culverts, bridges, ferries, waterways and other means of communication.
14. Rural electrification, including distribution of electricity.

15. Non-conventional energy sources.
16. Poverty alleviation programme.
17. Education including, primary and secondary schools.
18. Technical training and vocational education.
19. Adult and non-formal education.
20. Libraries.
21. Cultural activities.
22. Market and fairs.
23. Health and sanitation, including hospitals, primary health centres and dispensaries.
24. Family welfare.
25. Women and child development.
26. Social Welfare, including welfare of the handicapped and mentally retarded.
27. Welfare of the weaker sections, and in particular of the scheduled castes and scheduled tribes.
28. Public distribution system.
29. Maintenance of community assets.

Appendix-II

The Provisions of the Panchayats (Extension to the Scheduled Areas) Act, 1996

To provide for the extension of the provisions of Part IX of the Constitution relating to the Panchayats to the Scheduled Areas.

Be it enacted by Parliament in the Forty-seventh Year of the Republic of India as follows:

1. This Act may be called *The Provisions of the Panchayats (Extension to the Scheduled Areas) Act, 1996*.
2. In this Act, unless the context otherwise requires, 'Scheduled Areas' means the Scheduled Areas as referred to in clause (1) of Article 244 of the Constitution.
3. The provisions of Part IX of the Constitution relating to Panchayats are hereby extended to the Scheduled Areas subject to such exceptions and modifications as are provided in Section 4.
4. Notwithstanding anything contained under Part IX of the Constitution, the Legislature of a State shall not make any law under that Part which is inconsistent with any of the following features, namely:—

   (*a*) a State legislation on the Panchayats that may be made shall be in consonance with the customary law, social and religious practices and traditional management practices of community resources;

   (*b*) a village shall ordinarily, consist of a habitation or a group of habitations or a hamlet or a group of hamlets comprising a community and managing its affairs in accordance with the traditions and customs;

(*c*) every village shall have a Gram Sabha consisting of persons whose names are included in the electoral rolls for the Panchayat at the village level;

(*d*) every Gram Sabha shall be competent to safeguard and preserve the traditions and customs of the people, their cultural identity, community resources and the customary mode of dispute resolution:

(*e*) every Gram Sabha shall:

(*i*) approve the plans, programmes and projects for social and economic development before such plans, programmes and projects are taken up for implementation by the Panchayat at the village level;

(*ii*) be responsible for the identification or selection of persons as beneficiaries under the poverty alleviation and other programmes;

(*f*) every Panchayat at the village level shall be required to obtain from the Gram Sabha a certification of utilisation of funds by that Panchayat for the plans, programmes and projects referred to in clause (*e*);

(*g*) the reservation of seats in the Scheduled Areas at every Panchayat shall be in proportion to the population of the communities in that Panchayat for whom reservation is sought to be given under Part IX of the Constitution:

Provided that the reservation for the Scheduled Tribes shall not be less than one-half of the total number of seats;

Provided further that all seats of Chairpersons of Panchayats at all levels shall be reserved for the Scheduled Tribes;

(*h*) the State Government may nominate persons belonging to such Scheduled Tribes as have no representation in the Panchayat at the intermediate level or the Panchayat at the district level:

Provided that such nomination shall not exceed one-tenth of the total members to be elected in that Panchayat;

(*i*) the Gram Sabha or the Panchayats at the appropriate level shall be consulted before making the acquisition of land in the Scheduled Areas for development projects and before settling or rehabilitating persons affected by such projects in the Scheduled Areas; the actual planning and implementation of the projects in the Scheduled Areas shall be coordinated at the State level;

(*j*) planning and management of minor water bodies in the Scheduled Areas shall be entrusted to Panchayats at the appropriate level;

(*k*) the recommendations of the Gram Sabha or the Panchayats at the appropriate level shall be made mandatory prior to grant of prospecting license or mining lease for minor minerals in the Scheduled Areas;

(*l*) the prior recommendation of the Gram Sabha or the Panchayats at the appropriate level shall be made mandatory for grant of concession for the exploitation of minor minerals by auction;

(*m*) while endowing Panchayats in the Scheduled Areas with such powers and authority as may be necessary to enable them to function as institutions of self-government, a State Legislature shall ensure that the Panchayats at the appropriate level and the Gram Sabha are endowed specifically with—

- (*i*) the power to enforce prohibition or to regulate or restrict the sale and consumption of any intoxicant;
- (*ii*) the ownership of minor forest produce;
- (*iii*) the power to prevent alienation of land in the Scheduled Areas and to take appropriate action to restore any unlawfully alienated land of a Scheduled Tribe;
- (*iv*) the power to manage village markets by whatever name called;
- (*v*) the power to exercise control over money-lending to the Scheduled Tribes;
- (*vi*) the power to exercise control over institutions and functionaries in all social sectors;
- (*vii*) the power to control local plans and resources for such plans including tribal sub-plans;

(*n*) the Stale Legislations lliat may endow Panchayats with powers and authority as may be necessary to enable them to function as institutions of self-government shall contain safeguards to ensure that Panchayats at the higher level do not assume the powers and authority of any Panchayat at the lower level or of the Gram Sabha;

(*o*) the State Legislature shall endeavour to follow the pattern of the Sixth Schedule to the Constitution while designing the administrative arrangements in the Panchayats at district levels in the Scheduled Areas.

5. Notwithstanding anything in Part IX of the Constitution with exceptions and modifications made by this Act, any provision of any law relating to Panchayats in force in the Scheduled Areas immediately before the date on which this Act receives the assent of the President, which is inconsistent with the provisions of Part IX with such exceptions and modifications, shall continue to be in force until amended or repealed by a competent Legislature or other competent authority or until the expiration of one year from the date on which this Act receives the assent of the President:

Provided that all the Panchayats existing immediately after such date shall continue till the expiration of their duration unless sooner dissolved by a resolution passed to that effect by the Legislative Assembly of that State or, in the case of a State having Legislative Council, by each House of the Legislature of that State.

Appendix-III

A Charter for Panchayats*

PROLOGUE

Searching for an institutional frame for a caring, humane and responsive administration at the local level;

Recognising the strength and the weakness of the present district administration dominated by elite services;

Noticing that administration was not adequately accountable to those whom it was designed to serve, in spite of the administrative and political wings being generally efficient and enlightened;

Recalling numerous instances and complaints of callous, indifferent, negligent even cruel responses of the district administration to the individual and/or small group/community causes;

Finding that the lack of responsiveness of the administration was due to non-accountability;

Affirming that administration can be made responsive only if it is made representative;

Rajiv Gandhi conceived of a third-tier of representative governance at the district level and below thereby bringing in a basic change in the architecture of Indian polity;

Developing the aforesaid idea, Parliament enacted the Seventy-third and Seventy-fourth Amendments to the Constitution of India with the explicit purpose of transferring power to the people.

---

* Released by the Task Force on Panchayati Raj, Rajiv Gandhi Foundation, New Delhi, on 20 August, 1994.

Source: Issues for discussion in Sub-regional Workshops 1994-95 and other Documents, Task Force on Panchayati Raj, Rajiv Gandhi Foundation, New Delhi, October 2, 1994.

ARTICLES

1. It is noticed with grave concern that the basic ideology behind the Seventy-third Amendment of making Panchayats institutions of self-government has been largely ignored in the recent State legislation. It is urged that all sections in such legislation which militate against these over reaching objective should be deleted or appropriately further amended to make Panchayats genuine institutions of participatory self-governments.
2. Panchayats cannot develop as genuine units of self-governance without corresponding drastic reduction and restructuring of the powers and administrative set up of the Central and State Governments at least in respect of items included in Eleventh Schedule of the Constitution. Stifling overhang of enormous Central and State administrative structures is a serious impediment to development of autonomous Panchayat administrative structure. To ensure this reduction of functions and structural readjustment of Central and State Governments, a National Commission should be constituted.
3. There should be a single Ministry of Panchayats and Nagarpalikas.
4. The democratization of our pluralistic society cannot be ensured merely through legislative and administrative actions of the State. These enabling provisions would require massive mobilisational support. NGO's, academic and professional bodies, trade unions, political and other groups and individuals should involve themselves in exerting pressure "to restore power to where it belongs."
5. In the preparation and implementation of plans for economic development and social justice, NGO's and Co-operatives should be functionally associated with Panchayats.
6. There are numerous Central and State Acts, regulations, manuals, government orders which go against appropriate devolution of powers and functions to Panchayats. All these items require to be identified for appropriate remedial legislative and executive action by the Central and State Governments. Either the Law Commission or any other expert body should be immediately entrusted with this job

so that it may make recommendations within six months. The Central and State Governments should then initiate action on both sets of recommendations, for amending the laws and regulations and restructuring the administrative set up by redeployment/reduction of excess manpower.

7. Elected Panchayats should not be subordinate to government officials. Elected representatives should be enable to exercise superintendence and control over government officials to be placed under Panchayats along with devolution of functions.
8. The power of dissolution as well as of accountability of lower level Panchayat units must rest with the next higher levels of Panchayats and not with government officials so that peer group accountability is established.
9. Requirements of financial accountability should be designed and supervised by the Comptroller and Auditor General.
10. The artificial divide between development and general administration should be done away with. Since the Eleventh Schedule only provides the floor, there is no legal bar to empower Panchayats with necessary judicial and police powers to settle petty cases both of civil and criminal nature and to defuse any potential conflict-situation both among individuals and groups.
11. The basic principles of allocation of powers and functions should be that what can be done at the lower level must necessarily be done at that level and not at a higher level. Functions and powers should be given by the legislature. There should not be any scope for executive fiat in this respect.
12. Inter-Zilla Parishad or Panchayat Council should be constituted in every State with the Chief Minister as the Chairman, all the Zilla Parishad elected Chiefs, Leader of Opposition and Ministers of concerned Departments as members to discuss and thrash out matters relating to Panchayat in general and Zilla Parishad in particular, and the State Governments in respect of legislative, financial, administrative and other relevant issues.
13. Panchayat should not merely be implementing agencies of preconceived schemes passed on to them with funds as

centrally or State sponsored schemes. To become self-governing institutions there should be true decentralized planning so that district level Panchayats but not handed over to them from above. Panchayats at three levels should have reasonable percentages of the funds of the State Plan and other financial resources which should be totally united so that they can use these funds on the basis of their own priorities and choices. These together with other sectoral outlays should constitute a district plan budget reflecting the sum total of allocations under the district sector plan. This should be clearly and transparently shown in the State budget to be voted upon by the State Legislature. The District Planning Committee should be headed by the elected Chairman of the Zilla Parishad.

14. Panchayats should be constituted for every part of the country including the areas covered under the Fifth and Sixth Schedules of the Constitution. In these areas the basic principles of the Seventhly-third Amendment should be harmonised with the local ethos, traditions and institutions so as to have democracy with continuity. The central law contemplated in Article 243 M of the Constitution should be enacted early.
15. A constitutional amendment should be brought for ensuring elections to co-operatives as the successful functioning of the co-operative system is crucial to attainment of the objectives of Panchayat Raj.

EPILOGUE

"We trust the people. We have faith in the people. It is the people who must determine their own destinies and the destiny of the nation. To the people of India, let us ensure maximum democracy and maximum devolution. Let the people be empowered."

Rajiv Gandhi

Appendix-IV

State-wise Panchayati Raj Acts Passed in Conformity with the 73rd Amendment of the Constitution of India

Sl. No.	*Name of the State*	*Year*	*Name of the Act*
1.	Andhra Pradesh	1993	The Andhra Pradesh Panchayati Raj Act, 1993
2.	Bihar	1993	The Bihar Panchayati Raj Act, 1993
3.	Gujarat	1993	The Gujarat Panchayat Act, 1993
4.	Himachal Pradesh	1994	The Himachal Pradesh Panchayati Raj Act, 1994
5.	Karnataka	1993	The Karnataka Panchayati Raj Act, 1993
6.	Kerala	1994	The Kerala Panchayati Raj Act, 1994
7.	Madhya Pradesh	1994	The Madhya Pradesh Panchayat Act, 1994
8.	Maharashtra	1994	The Bombay Village Panchayats and the Maharashtra Zilla Parishad and Panchayat Samities (Amendment) Act, 1994
9.	North East:		
	(*i*) Assam	1994	The Assam Panchayat Act, 1994
	(*ii*) Tripura	1993	The Tripura Panchayat Act, 1993
	(*iii*) Manipur	1994	The Manipur Panchayati Raj Act, 1994
	(*iv*) Arunachal Pradesh	1994	The Arunachal Pradesh Panchayati Raj Ordinance, 1994
10.	Orissa	1993	The Orissa Gram Panchayats, Taluk Panchayats, Zilla Parishads (Amendment) Act, 1993
11.	Punjab	1994	The Punjab Panchayati Raj Act, 1994
12.	Rajasthan	1994	The Rajasthan Panchayati Raj Act, 1994
13.	Tamil Nadu	1994	The Tamil Nadu Panchayati Raj Act, 1994
14.	Uttar Pradesh	1994	The Uttar Pradesh Panchayat (Amendment) Act, 1994
15.	West Bengal	1994	The West Bengal Panchayati (Amendment) Act,1994

Source: Prof. B.K. Chandrashekar (Editor), Panchayati Raj in India Status Report 1999, Task Force on Panchayati Raj, Rajiv Gandhi Foundation, New Delhi, March, 2000.

Number of Elected Members in the Three-tier Panchayati Raj System: State-wise as on 1st April, 2006

States/Union Territories	Gram Panchayats		Panchayat Samiti		Zilla Parishad		Remarks
	Number	Elected Representatives	Number	Elected Representatives	Number	Elected Representatives	
Andhra Pradesh	21913	208291	1095	14617	22	1095	as on 1.4.2005
Arunachal Pradesh(#)	1744	9046	150	2216	15	181	Excluding Tirap Dist.
Assam	2489	15620	203	1402	20	273	as on 1.4.2005
Bihar	8471	116029	531	11611	38	1162	as on 1.4.2005
Chhattisgarh	9139	124211	146	2639	16	274	as on 1.4.2005
Goa	189	1450	*	*	2	50	
Gujarat	13819	109209	224	4161	25	817	
Haryana	617	66256	119	2833	19	384	
Himachal Pradesh	3037	18549	75	1658	12	251	as on 1.4.2005
Jharkhand	3746	$	211	$	22	$	Elections not held
Karnataka	5652	91402	176	3683	27	1005	
Kerala	991	8458	152	1009	14	202	as on 1.4.2005
Madhya Pradesh	22029	208356	313	4297	45	486	as on 1.4.2005
Maharashtra	28553	178132	349	2877	33	1423	as on 1.4.2005
Manipur	166	1111	*	*	4	39	as on 1.4.2005

(Contd.)

Orissa	6234	93781	314	6227	30	854	
Punjab	12445	48860	140	1667	17	190	as on 1.4.2005
Rajasthan	9189	114282	237	5257	32	1008	as on 1.4.2005
Sikkim	166	905	*	*	4	100	
Tamil Nadu	12618	109308	385	6524	29	656	
Tripura	513	5352	23	299	4	82	
Uttar Pradesh	52000	377518	820	33290	70	1338	as on 1.4.2005
Uttaranchal	7227	53961	95	3247	13	373	
West Bengal	3354	49545	341	8483	18	720	
A&N Islands	67	498	7	42	1	20	as on 1.4,2005
Chandigarh	17	162	1	15	1	10	as on 1.4.2005
D&N Haveli	11	114	*	*	1	11	
Daman & Diu	14	73	*	*	1	20	
Lakshadweep	10	49	*	*	1	14	as on 1.4.2005
Pondicherry	98	$	10	$	$	$	Elections not held
Total	232088	2010528	6117	118054	536	13038	

Meghalaya, Mizoram & Nagaland are Traditional Councils.

NCT of Delhi—Panchayati Raj System is yet to be revived.

* = Two-tier Panchayat.

Appendix-VI

Recommendations of Bhuria Committee

Report of the Committee of Members of Parliament and Experts to make Recommendations on law concerning extension of provisions of the Constitution (Seventy-third Amendment) Act, 1992 to Scheduled Areas, Ministry of Rural Development, Government of India, January 1995.

SUMMARY OF RECOMMENDATIONS

1. The Committee has been called upon to suggest:

   (*a*) Steps for harmonization of Fifth, Sixth, Eleventh and Twelfth Schedules of the Constitution as they impinge upon the Panchayati Raj Institutions.

   (*b*) Salient features of the law that may be taken up for enactment by Parliament for extending the provisions of Para IX of the Constitution to the Scheduled Areas referred to in clause (1) of Article 244 of the Constitution subject to such exemptions and modifications as may be necessary under Article 243 M(4) (*b*); and

   (*c*) Variations and modifications in other articles relevant to the Fifth Schedule Areas in order to strengthen institutions of local government in Fifth Schedule Areas.

2. The Committee fell that while certain provisions of 'The Constitution Seventy-third Amendment Act, 1992 on the Panchayats' were wholesome and should be incorporated in the law to be passed by Parliament under Article 243 M(4) (*b*), certain unique characteristics of tribal societies and tribal areas need to be kept in view. Important among them are that many tribal societies have had their own

customary laws, their mode of living, organization, cultural mores, etc., and their present-day predicament of exploitation, deprivation, marginalization etc., would have to be kept in focus. Since many tribal communities have been living autonomously, cut off from the rest of the society, they have exercised control over and had access to natural resources moulding their institutions. Their gram sabhas and village councils have been vibrant institutions in the fields of administration, religion, politics, economics, justice, etc. The Committee felt that while shaping the new panchayati raj structure in tribal areas, it is desirable to blend the traditional with the modern by treating the traditional institutions as the foundation on which the modern supra-structure should be built.

3. As per Article 243M (4) (*b*) Parliament may, by law, extend the provisions of Para IX to Scheduled Areas and Tribal Areas covered by clause (1) and clause (2) respectively of Article 244 subject to such exemptions and modifications as may be specified in such a law. Parliament may consider our recommendations for such legislation. The law passed by Parliament will be applicable to Scheduled Areas and Tribal Areas to the supersession of corresponding provisions of any State law.

Objects and Reasons

4. Most of the tribal societies in India have been practising democracy, having been characterized by an egalitarian spirit. Cognizance has to be taken of their indigenous institutions and ethos while considering democratic decentralization in tribal areas.

   (*a*) Time-honoured customary usages and arrangements in tribal areas should be respected and allowed to continue. Traditional tribal conventions and laws should continue to hold validity. Harmonization with the modern systems should be consistent therewith.

   (*b*) Panchayati Raj bodies in tribal areas should be made more effective and more participative in the context of the foregoing. More than in the past they have to function as institutions of self-governance and development. They have to work for socio-economic goals like the removal of poverty, illiteracy and ill-health among the people.

(*c*) For the attainment of the aforesaid goals, a flow of adequate funds has to be ensured. Such funds should be utilized for the purpose for which they are set apart and should not be diverted. Suitable financial mechanisms should be created for proper utilization of funds.

(*d*) Since the 1992 Act does not take into account the unique features of tribal areas, we make recommendations as embodied in this report.

5. In drafting the law under Article 243M (4) (*b*), advantage should be taken of both the Fifth and Sixth Schedules. The Fifth Schedule should be deemed as a broad and powerful overarching frame, serving as the fountainhead of essential and beneficial legislation. The design and contents of the Sixth Schedule could serve as a relevant reference frame for a district within the broader canvas of the Fifth Schedule. However, ethnic regional and other related variations should be given due consideration. The Sixth Schedule should be regarded with such reformation and changes as are necessary, as a broad charter of autonomy at the district level and be adopted.
6. The Tribes Advisory Council, envisaged by the Fifth Schedule as a consultative body at the state level, needs to be reformed to make it an effective and functional organization. The Chief Minister of the State should be its chairman and its meetings should be held once every three months.
7. At the centre, the Central Advisory Council should be revived, serving the purpose of (*a*) a sounding board for tribal policies and programmes and (*b*) advice in disputes between a State Government and the tribes advisory council or between a district council and the tribes advisory council. Its advice should normally be binding. The Prime Minister should chair its meetings and its

members may be welfare minister, home minister, rural development minister, deputy chairman, planning commission, etc.

8. Many of the present-day administrative boundaries were determined during colonial times. Notwithstanding changes, by and large, the earlier boundaries have stayed. Reorganization of boundaries based on geographic, ethnic and demographic considerations may be considered and finalized within a couple of years.
9. The tribal societies are characterized by a communitarian and co-operative spirit, visible in many undertakings like shifting cultivation, house construction. The potential of this ingrained attribute has not been taken advantage of so far. Cooperative organizations among tribals should be constituted in a manner suitable to their oral traditions and milieu.
10. It has been observed that in tribal areas, the lower functionaries of departments like Police, Excise, Forest, Revenue, have generally been acting against tribal interest and not unoften have even become repressive and exploitative. While their role in tribal areas is minimal, they tend to overbear on the tribal and village communities. Hence, they should be assigned minimal role and should work under the control of concerned panchayats.
11. The 1992 Act envisages a panchayat at village level in addition to panchayats at intermediate and district levels, as per Article 243B. The concept of a panchayat at village level may fit in well for non-tribal areas, since villages there are generally large. But in tribal areas with mostly hilly topography, the villages are usually scattered and population-wise, small. These small villages or hamlets are known as *tolas* in some areas. But a small village or group of hamlets or habitations may have its own *gram sabha* (hereafter gram sabha). The gram sabhas should be allowed to exercise their customary traditional role unhindered. Further, a gram sabha may have a traditional village council, which may be a traditional body and may delegate to it functions like execution of development works.

12. A number of hamlets aggregated may constitute a village panchayat, called variously a gram panchayat, anchal or parha *or pargana* panchayat (hereafter pargana panchayat). This tier corresponds to the lowest tier envisaged in the 1992 Act. Its members may be elected.
13. Constituencies may be delimited for the election of members to the intermediate—and district-tier panchayats. The district level panchayat may be called Autonomous District Council (ADC).
14. In certain districts, scheduled tribe population may be less than 50 per cent of a district's total population, but it may be concentrated in a part or parts of the district, say in some blocks or a sub-division or sub-divisions. We have recommended that sub-district councils may be constituted for such areas and designated as Autonomous Sub-District Councils (ASDCs). ASDCs should be at par with ADCs. However, this may be regarded as an interim arrangement, pending reorganization of administrative boundaries which we have recommended elsewhere.
15. So far as the organizational structure of an ADC is concerned, we recommend the adoption of a broad frame-design of autonomous district councils contained in the Sixth Schedule of the Constitution in force in the states of Assam, Meghalaya, Mizoram and Tripura. The Sixth Schedule has been conceived to be an instrument of self-management and socio-economic development. It may not be too wrong to say that, to an extent, it has fulfilled the ethnic aspirations of the tribal communities. We have enumerated in this Report (Para 16) some shortcomings of the Sixth Schedule and these would need to be reformed. In addition, we feel that setting apart seats (may be not exceeding 5 in number) would open scope for nomination in the district councils of minority tribal communities which cannot find place through the election process. The nominations may be made in consultation with the governor.
16. The 1992 Constitution Amendment Act provides for representation of members of the house of people and members of the legislative assembly of the state, representing constituencies which comprise wholly or

partly a panchayat area, at a level other than the village level. We recommend that Lok Sabha Scheduled Tribe MPs should be associated with intermediate (block) level of panchayat and with the district council. But the representation should not be restricted to Scheduled Tribe MLAs and even non-ST MLAs should be associated with the two-tiers.

17. Since the Scheduled Areas and Tribal Areas are expected to have the majority of tribal population, the different-tier panchayats therein should have a majority of Scheduled Tribe members. Further, both the chairman and vice-chairman should belong to STs.
18. The Sixth Schedule confers powers of legislation and administration of justice on the district councils apart from executive, developmental and financial responsibilities. We should adopt for districts in Scheduled Areas, the Sixth Schedule format, but expand it to include subjects that are indicated in the Eleventh Schedule of the Constitution.
19. The legislative powers of the autonomous district councils in the Fifth Schedule Areas have been proposed more or less on the same lines as in the Sixth Schedule with some amendments. Insofar as administration of justice is concerned, the committee has been emphatic that a traditional jury-based legal system evolved by tribal societies should be recognized and should be enabled to continue to function. There should be no police interference in cases not involving non-heinous offences. Such cases should be under the domain of the Gram Sabha. Insofar as development functions are concerned, this too is a vital area. Our proposal therefore, is that the functions enumerated in the Sixth Schedule as well as in the Eleventh Schedule should be discharged by the ADCs. We have given a list of such functions in Annexure 'D'.
20. In Article 243H, the sources of funds for panchayats have been detailed. These should be applicable to panchayats in Scheduled Areas. While the panchayats in these areas may receive funds as per Articles 243H and 2431, funds as per the first proviso to Article 275(I), should continue to be available normally.
21. For the purposes mentioned in the first proviso to Article 275(I), funds received from sources other than the

panchayats' own, should be placed in 'charged' category in the respective governments' budgets as opposed to 'voted' category. This will enable funds to remain fully available for purposes related to tribal interest, without fear of misutilization or diversion.

22. In order to prevent wrong financial practices occurring in the tribal sub-plan fields, the tribal sub-plan funds (whether relating to state plan or special central assistance or any other) pertaining to different sectors of development should be quantified and placed at the disposal of the autonomous district councils for distribution among the panchayats in the districts. Moreover, the Central and State Governments should devise to the extent possible, procedures for direct allotment of funds to the autonomous district councils.
23. Education and health sectors should be the first charge on the funds received by a panchayat in Scheduled Areas and, notwithstanding any other provision, the panchayat will have power to appropriate funds from any other head for meeting this obligation.
24. All government servants and functionaries of institutions concerned with the functions of a panchayat in a Scheduled Area and located within its jurisdiction will be under its control.
25. As per the provision in the Sixth Schedule, the Governor may appoint a Commission to examine and report on all matters relating to the administration of autonomous district councils. Representation should be given to Scheduled Tribes in the membership of the Commission.
26. The tribes advisory councils and autonomous district councils in the Scheduled Areas should review the existing laws for their relevance and applicability and take action necessary for the exclusion of those that are not relevant and inclusion of those that are useful. Such action should be completed within a stipulated period of about two years.
27. We understand that states have already passed legislation in pursuance of the Seventy-third and Seventy-fourth Constitution Amendment Acts and that the provisions of those laws apply to Scheduled Areas also. The law passed

by the Parliament will supersede such and any other related law.

28. The process of Scheduling of tribal areas in the country commenced earlier, has remained incomplete. It is necessary that the remaining tribal sub-plan and MADA areas as well as similar other pockets should be included in the Scheduled Areas.

29. We have dealt in this report with proposals and provisions that we think should apply to the Fifth Schedule Areas in the country as declared by the President under Para (6) of that Schedule. Article 243M of the 1992 Act covers 'tribal areas referred to in Clause (2) of Article 244'. We feel that the benefit of self-government at different tiers should be made available to these areas. We leave this matter to the judgement of the states concerned. But since we have examined the Sixth Schedule, we suggest that the framework of that Schedule should be looked afresh in the north-eastern region in the light of our suggestions contained in Annexure 'D' which may be helpful for reformulation.

30. We recommend for the gram sabhas, gram panchayats, intermediate panchayats and autonomous district councils, powers, functions and procedures enumerated respectively in Annexures 'A', 'B', 'C' & 'D'.

Appendix-VII

Overview of Efforts at Decentralized Planning*

Background

Efforts at outlining decentralized planning of development commenced with the First Five Year Plan (1951-56), which recognized the need to break up the planning exercise into National, State, District and Local Community levels, but did not spell out how this was to be operationalised. Two new elements for the planning process were introduced in the Second Five Year Plan, namely, the establishment of the District Development Council and the drawing up of village plans and peoples' participation in planning through democratic decentralization. However, the attempt at decentralization of planning did not succeed as a proper enabling framework was not devised, both for planning and for integration of development activities at the micro level.

In 1957, as recommended by the Balwant Rai Committee, village, block and district level Panchayat institutions were established in many States. However, they were not assigned any meaningful role or resources and were not given any place in the planning framework. The Administrative Reforms Commission, in its Report of 1967, highlighted that district planning needed to be focused in those areas where local variations in the pattern and process of development were likely to yield quick results in terms of growth. It was emphasized that district authorities should be given a clear indication of the resources that would be made available so as to enable them to prepare purposeful plans at their

---

* Excerpts from the Report of the Expert Group on Planning at the Grassroots Level— An Action Programme for the Eleventh Five-Year Plan, 2006, Ministry of Panchayati Raj, Government of India, New Delhi, 2006.

level. In 1969, the Planning Commission communicated guidelines to the States for formulating district plans detailing the concept and methodology of drawing up such plans within the framework of annual, medium term and perspective plans.

The guidelines on district planning led to several States formulating district plans during the Fifth Five Year Plan. However, except in Maharashtra, Gujarat and Karnataka these were not integrated into the annual plans of the States.

From the Fourth Five Year Plan (1972-73) to the beginning of the Ninth Plan, a central scheme was operated to assist States for strengthening their planning set-up at the State level. In 1982-83, this scheme was extended to the district level. At about the same time, the Reserve Bank of India directed the lead bank in each district to prepare a district credit plan. However, there was scarcely any link between district development plans and district credit plans.

A Working Group on Block level Planning headed by Prof. M.L. Dantwala (1978) identified the remoteness of planning agencies at the district level from the actual scene of action as the cause for mismatch of financial allocations with location specific needs. The Group recommended the Block as the appropriate sub-state planning level for proper appreciation of the felt needs of the people. It also asserted that the block level provides the vital link between clusters of villages and the district level and thence to the region, State and National levels. The Planning Commission issued guidelines on formulation of Block level plans in tune with these recommendations.

Initiatives in strengthening Panchayati Raj closely paralleled those for district planning. Though Panchayati Raj Institutions got off to a good start in the early sixties, these hopes were short lived. With the possible exception of Maharashtra, Gujarat, Karnataka and West Bengal, elsewhere these institutions were either superseded or allowed very little freedom to operate, which inevitably led to their decline. In the period of plan holiday-between the third and Fourth Plan, in many States, Panchayats were superseded. The Ashok Mehta Committee on Panchayati Raj recommended in its report (1978) that Panchayats ought to be strengthened into agencies capable of undertaking local planning.

Studies connected with the Planning Commission's report on district planning (by the Working Group on District Planning headed by C.H. Hanumantha Rao May 1984), brought out the fact that planning from below was undermined by different streams of funding the district plan. As States had to prepare their annual plans within the framework prescribed by the Government of India, they, in turn, prescribed rigid guidelines, which left little scope for flexibility to District Development Councils in preparation of their annual plans. Substantial funds were also retained at the State level and schemes were formulated by sectoral departments without much consultation with the District Development Council. The Working Group recommended the following steps to achieve the objective of meaningful district planning:

- For good district planning, functions, powers and finances need to be decentralized. States should outline the sharing of functions with districts.
- Each district plan must reflect the basic objectives of the national plan and the divisible plan outlay ought to be distributed to districts on the basis of population, area and level of development.
- District Planning Bodies consisting of a Chairman, Member-Secretary and about fifty members, in which the Collector is the Chief Co-ordinator should be set up. The District Planning body should be assisted by a Chief Planning Officer assisted by Block level planning officers and technical experts from various disciplines.

The G.V.K. Rao Committee (1985) to review the administrative arrangements for rural development, recommended that the District Panchayat should be the principal agency to manage all development programmes at the district level. The Sarkaria Commission on Centre-State relations highlighted the need for participation of people's representatives in the planning and administrative machinery at the local level. A notable recommendation was the creation of a body akin to the Finance Commission at the State level for devolution or transfer of resources to the districts on an operational and objective basis.

The details of the history of attempts to promote decentralized planning from the First Plan onwards to the mid-eighties is summarized in the table below:

Decentralisation—Chronology of Attempts and Committee Reports

Year	*Item*	*Ideas and Concepts*
First Plan, 51-56	Community Development Blocks	To break up planning exercise into National, State, District and Local Community levels.
Second Plan, 56-61	District Development Councils	Drawing up of village plans and popular participation in planning through the process of democratic decentralization.
1957	Balwant Rai Mehta Committee	Village, Block, District Panchayat institutions established.
1967	Administrative Reforms Commission	Resources to be given/ local variations accommodated, purposeful plan for Area.
1969	Planning Commission	Formulated guidelines; detailed the concept of the district plan and methodology of drawing up such a plan in the framework of annual plans, medium term plans and perspective plans.
1978	Prof. M.L. Dantwala	Block level planning to form a link between village and district level planning.
1983-84	Centrally Sponsored Scheme/ Reserve Bank of India	Strengthen District Plan/ District Credit Plan.
1984	Hanumantha Rao Committee	Decentralisation of function, powers and finances; Setting up of district planning bodies and district planning cells.
1985	G.V.K. Rao Committee	Administrative arrangements for rural development; district panchayat to manage all development programmes.

Panchayat involvement in rural development was enlarged during the Sixth and Seventh Plan period. Greater involvement of Panchayats was institutionalized with the launching of the Jawahar Rozgar Yojana (JRY) in 1989-90, under which there was a substantial flow of funds to Village Panchayats. In addition, Village Panchayats were required to prepare an inventory of assets and give details of the projects taken up under JRY. The works to be taken up were decided in the meetings of the Gram Sabha.

Thus, over a period of four decades since the beginning of planned development, there were several suggestions and attempts at decentralized planning. The conditions required were also outlined and repeated. However, the increase in the number of ministries, departments and parastatals at the Centre and in the States and the vertical planning, preparation of programmes and methods of funding stood in the way of decentralized planning becoming a reality.

The 73rd and 74th Amendments to the Constitution gave constitutional status to local self-governments and provided a new, more politically underpinned, universalized platform for decentralized planning from below. However, though it is now nearly 14 years since the amendments were made and there has been progress in implementing some of the mandated provisions such as conduct of elections, the concept of development planning from below has still not taken root, even in the few States in which there is relatively larger devolution of powers and provision of untied funds to local governments.

Recent Initiatives

We have already referred to the initiative taken by the Ministry of Panchayati Raj to convene seven Round Table Meetings with the State Ministers in charge of Panchayati Raj and the points for action decided upon therein. The recommendations of the Second Round Table regarding decentralized planning were briefly as follows:

- District Planning Committees ought to be constituted in every State, by the end of the Current Financial Year (2004-05), in according with the procedure laid down in Article 243ZD (2).
- All States ought to make provision, by law, outlining the functions and procedures of DPCs.
- District planning ought to take into account the area's resource endowment, people's felt needs and their relative absorptive capacity.
- Each level of Panchayat and Municipalities ought to prepare perspective Five Year Plan and Annual Plans as provided in the Constitution, which would be consolidated by the DPC.
- The State must specify institutions, organizations and individuals to assist Panchayats, Municipalities and DPCs in preparing plans in accordance with Article 243ZD (3) (*b*).

- States must indicate extent and type of available resources to each Panchayat level and Municipalities as per Article 243ZD, in order to facilitate planning.
- States must, to the extent possible, provide resources as untied funds to Panchayats and Municipalities. Where grants are scheme specific, guidelines for implementation ought to be broad and simple.
- Central Government could consider establishing a mechanism to pool all Central Government and Finance Commission's resources, for channellising them to Panchayats.
- States must strengthen the finances of the PRIs so that planning at the District and Sub-District level is based on an indication of the resources available and those that would be made available for the activities devolved on them.
- States ought to consider incorporating a Panchayat sector in each departmental budget within their budget.
- The Planning Commission, in consultation with the Central Ministries concerned, could work out appropriate arrangements for incorporating a Panchayat sector in each departmental budget.
- A distinction must be maintained between administrative grants and development grants in allotting financial resources to PRIs.
- State Governments could consider incorporating in their State laws provisions for Standing Committees in Panchayats for planning and implementation of allotted subjects, with an earmarked budget. Standing Committees could handle implementation from conception to approval, calling of tenders, finalization of vendors; conducting supervision of on-going works and certifying issue of utilization certificates.
- In local planning, priority ought to be given for basic minimum needs; provision of services; facilitating Rural Business Hubs.
- The Planning Commission may ensure that the Eleventh Plan begins with and is founded on District Plans prepared in accordance with Part-IX and IXA of the Constitution.

Taking note of the fact that annual plan proposals were to be called from States in November 2005, this Expert Group recommended to the Planning Commission that certain important aspects relating to district planning may be included in the circular issued to the State Governments. Based on the recommendations of the Group, the Planning Commission wrote to the State Governments that the following points would be taken into consideration before approval of the Annual Plan proposals for 2006-07:

(*a*) The District Planning Committees (DPC) should be constituted in accordance with the provisions of the Constitution by the time the Annual Plan Proposals are presented.

(*b*) The composition of the District Planning Committees is to be decided by the law made in this connection by the Legislature of the State. Taking into account the imperative need to increase the professional competence of the DPCs, whose main responsibility and function is to consider the Gram Panchayat and block Panchayat development plans, as also the municipalities of districts, and to consolidate and prepare a draft development plan for the district as a whole, the DPC should be required to consult institutions and professionals, as may be specified for this purpose by the Governor under Article 243 ZD (3)(*b*).

(*c*) At least in respect of items dealing with minimum needs as listed below, the Annual Plan proposals have to indicate the detailed activities of the different levels of Panchayats:

(*i*) Literacy (adult literacy) and elementary education.
(*ii*) Primary health and sanitation.
(*iii*) Rural water supply.
(*iv*) Rural roads.
(*v*) Housing for the poor (rural and urban).
(*vi*) Nutrition, children and women and crèches.
(*vii*) Livelihood and employment guarantee.
(*viii*) Rural electrification.

(*d*) As regards each of the items, the proposals have to indicate the funds, if any, received from (*i*) recom-mendations of the Twelfth Finance Commission, (*ii*) Back-ward Regions

Grant Fund (BRGF), (*iii*) Centrally Sponsored Schemes, (*iv*) Different Development institutions at the Center and in the States like Scheduled Castes Commission, Women's Commission, etc., (*v*) Fin-ancial Institutions, (*vi*) Externally assisted schemes, and (*vii*) their own resources, if any.

(*e*) The Annual Plan Proposals should also indicate the detailed deployment of funds received from the above different sources for a specific subject in each of the districts of the State.

(*f*) The Annual Plan Proposals should indicate the criteria followed by the State Government for allocating the resources for the above items, district-wise. The State Government may also indicate how the district allocation will be distributed between the District, Block and Gram Panchayat levels taking into account the conditions in the State.

(*g*) The detailed exercise in respect of items of minimum needs are suggested as a first step and they do not exclude the need for a similar exercise in respect of the entire set of items to be implemented through/by PRIs as part of the Plan.

(*h*) In order to enable Panchayats at different levels to formulate and implement locally relevant schemes in respect of functions that have been devolved to them, the Annual Plan Proposals should work towards a target District Plan outlay of 30 per cent of State Plan outlay and untied funds of 25 per cent of the District Plan outlay.

(*i*) Recognizing the importance of accounting and audit, dissemination and capacity building, four per cent of the untied block grants should be earmarked for strengthening these activities. Earmarking may be done for these activities in the Annual Plan Proposals.

The inclusion of the above points in the Annual Plan circular of the Planning Commission for 2006-07, marked an important step towards district planning. In continuation of those measures, this Report aims at addressing the challenge and draws attention to the elements in the current scenario that need revision so as to make local planning a reality by the end of the Eleventh Plan.

FORMULATION OF DISTRICT AND SUB-DISTRICT PLANS AT ALL LEVELS OF PANCHAYATS

The object of district planning is to arrive at an integrated, participatory coordinated idea of development of a local area. An essential step in this direction is to ensure that each Panchayat at any level or Municipality is treated as a planning unit and the 'district plan' is built up through consolidation and integration of these plans as well as by considering the development of the district as a whole. It is a two-way interactive exercise, the district being viewed as a convenient local area.

As now practised, the concept of district planning is considerably diluted by the fact that most department schemes envisage in their guidelines, separate and self-contained 'planning' processes. One way of curbing this tendency is to ensure that the word "plan" is used restrictively, to mean only that "plan" that is prepared at the level of each local government. Sectoral planning efforts ought to be termed as "programmes". Thus a "Plan" would be a composite whole which consists of several programmes in a mutual interdependent way. In Hindi, this would translate into one 'yojana' with several sectoral "karyakrams". It will emphasize mutual reinforcement of sectoral programmes. It will also ensure that resources are not wasted. Another important aspect is that it would entail a back-and-forth consultation as participants strive to temper and prioritize needs to fit the availability of resources. Lack of structure in this consultative process can delay planning indefinitely yet too much hierarchy and rigidity can inhibit discussion and end up keeping essential participants out of the exercise. Avenues of consultation have to be open, but without too many steps before plan approval.

The Expert Group visualizes the process of decentralized planning as falling into a broad sequence of steps. The sequence of preparing the Eleventh Five Year Plan from grassroots upwards could be to undertake a decentralized envisioning and stocktaking exercise, followed by a planning exercise at each local body level and then the consolidation and integration exercise. The envisioning process, would look at how the main priorities are determined as also the participatory processes that enable all stakeholders to be involved. Issues such as the representative profile of Panchayat elected members are critical here—for instance, the fact that women are represented to more than 40 per cent of the seats and SC & ST representation is in excess of the seats reserved for them would all have a huge impact on the visioning process. Indeed, Panchayati Raj represents the most potent means for women to lead governance, both in envisioning and implementation. Next would come the actual processes involved in the planning process at each level of Panchayat. Thirdly, comes the process involved in consolidation and integration of plans by the District Planning Committee. This Chapter deals with the first two steps-decentralized envisioning and planning. Consolidation and integration of plans is dealt with in the next Chapter, along with the functions of the District Planning Committee.

Building a District Vision

The early part of the year 2006-07 should be devoted to preparing for each district a vision, through a participative process starting from the grassroots, as to what would be the perspective for development over the next 10 to 15 years. In basic terms, the articulation of a vision is best done in each planning unit, right down to the Gram Panchayat level, stating with respect to each area what the needs and potential are, what the attainable levels are and what the goals to be reached could be. A basic requirement is that the preparation of the vision is not conditioned by schemes and programmes. The vision would be primarily articulated in terms of goals and outcomes and would address basically, three aspects of development, namely, *human development* indicators, *infrastructure development* and *development in the productive sector*. The idea is that the envisioning process, being participative, would build a spirit of teamwork and hopefully break down the department-wise 'planning' process that is now dominant.

Building a vision *for basic human development* indicators would essentially cover health, education, women and child welfare, social justice and availability of basic minimum services. Each Panchayat could propose, in its envisioning exercise, that they will achieve the levels specified for each such aspect within a particular period of time. Building a stage by stage approach is not pre-cluded—for instance, in districts that are below the national average in literacy, the first step would be to reach the average level and the next would be to attain the desirable level. Similar envisioning could be undertaken in respect of attainments regarding education, health, water supply and sanitation etc. Special attention has to be given to women and disadvantaged groups so as to enable them to take a lead in planning. The current means for inclusion of women in development planning and implementation as well as in allocation of funds is to offer a special women's component plan to ensure that part of sectoral funding is available and used for women. However, what is needed is that, equality has to be built into the envisioning process as a whole, by ensuring that women have an important role in the design of the entire Panchayat plan, rather than only in the womens' component. For example, in surveys involved in the planning process, it needs to be ensured that women's views are especially sought, including through focus group discussions. Women community leadership will need to be identified and included in committees that may be formed under various sectors, to ensure that women are included in planning for sectors other that social development, such as infrastructure, use of common lands, natural resources and employment. In ensuring meaningful participation of traditionally muted and excluded groups like dalits and women in the envisioning exercise, there is need for special capacity building for them. Networks of elected women members ought to be encouraged so that they can exert collective pressure as well as throw up leadership for a meaningful development of village and district plans with womens' views embedded in them. Capacity building programmes ought to ensure womens' empowerment as a cross cutting theme so that womens' empowerment is understood by others and development priorities identified by women are respected. These processes can become part of the participatory exercises in building the district vision.

With respect to the vision for infrastructure, the targets aimed under Bharat Nirman could be adopted in the manner as applicable for each district. The vision for the productive sector would consider what is the potential of the district and what can be reached within the plan period, considering the natural and human resources available in the district. There ought to be a close look at all aspects of natural resources use such as food and agricultural production, land and its improvement, irrigation and attainment of water security etc. The vision should also cover the possible local response to the changes taking place as a result of national, state and private development efforts.

There are several districts in the country where the basic targets concerning human development indicators have been already achieved. In such districts, the concentration could be on the next level of envisioning, basically in infrastructure and economic development, modernization of traditional industry and technical development of peoples' skills.

Evolution of the District Vision through Discussion in Panchayats and Other Local Bodies

It is essential that the district vision is owned by all. This will require a high degree of Participation in the preparation of the vision. The Ward and Gram Sabhas will have to be involved fully in the preparation of the district vision. One of the processes that is suggested in the exercise for planning, namely, undertaking participative citizen surveys is itself a good way of starting the process, through giving every citizen surveyed an opportunity to voice his or her needs and vision.

The district vision document should be given wide publicity. There are several means by which DPCs could ensure wide dissemination of the vision, one of them being to progressively cover all Intermediate Panchayats and Gram Panchayats on a block-wise basis through a series of workshops for all Panchayat leaders for creating awareness. Copies and brief abstract of the same should also be made available to the people as a priced publication.

Undertaking a Parallel Stock Taking Exercise

Paralleling the envisioning process, a stock-taking exercise would need to be undertaken, comprising both an assessment of the human condition in the District, as also the availability of natural, social and financial resources and infrastructure. For doing this, data pertaining to these aspects of development already existing in different forms would need to be compiled, assessed and described in a simple fashion. Using a common manner of describing and displaying the results of stock taking would be useful. This Group has elsewhere made suggestions concerning the work of preparing and maintaining databases for planning. The data base prepared would be an invaluable resource for the stocktaking exercise. In this connection, the concept of using development radars,* already used by the Planning Commission for preparing the National Human Development Report, 2001, merits wider adoption. Development Radars are a pictorial depiction of the performance of a unit of planning in respect of various sectors such as health, education, poverty alleviation, drinking water, housing etc. These can be redrawn over a time sequence and the difference in attainment measured. Apart from aiding stocktaking and envisioning, DRs could even be used as a report card that can measure progress on the development parameters that comprise it. With the strides being made in electronic data compilation, if a listing of Panchayats with the constituent revenue villages is made available by States, development radars can be prepared for Gram Panchayats too. We strongly recommend that the preparation of Developmental Radars be taken up, on priority, as part of the stock taking exercise.

Developing HDR Reports for States and Districts

Several States have prepared HDR reports, which have become the basis for the development planning exercise in them. It is suggested that HDR reports be prepared district-wise, so that there is a common framework within which the envisioning exercise takes place in each district.

Other Aspects of the Stock Taking Exercise Would be as Follows:

- Determination of cumulative physical and financial achievement regarding the availability of government provided services, from data available with implementing officers.
- Verification of physical assets, both community and individual assets, undertaken at each Panchayat level.
- Determination of works spilling over from the earlier plan and the funds required for the completion of the same.
- In many areas of service delivery, the private sector has supplemented insufficient government provision and the stocktaking exercise has to take into account the extent of such supplementation.

---

* From the work undertaken by Dr. N.C. Saxena and Jayanthi Ravi.

- The credit plans of the district can be used as a starting point for taking stock of the resources that are available through credit for planning. This will need to be supplemented by taking stock of the growth of the self-help movement and micro-finance.

Taking Stock of the Own Revenue Raising Capability of Panchayats

Raising of local revenues by Panchayats remains neglected in stocktaking, planning and implementation. No serious effort has been made nationwide to implement the recommendations of the Eleventh and Twelfth Finance Commissions in this regard. In several States, while taxes are assigned to local bodies by law, collection is unsupervised and neglected in practice. Experience suggests that given encouragement and with adequate capacity building, panchayats are capable and enthusiastic about collection of taxes. There has to be a substantial emphasis in local planning processes to estimate local revenues, entailing categorization of taxable properties, setting of tax rates for different categories, measurement of properties and self-declaration of taxes. Developing a framework for assessment of own tax and non-tax revenues of Panchayats would be part of the stocktaking exercise. While local variation in legislative provisions relating to taxation may exist, it is useful to look at the policies and practices of States that have undertaken successful reform of taxation at the Panchayat level.

Intimating Available Order of Resources for Planning at Local Levels

It is necessary that an exercise is done to make known the resources that will be available for planning at all levels. Even if a complete indication of funds available is not possible, an indication of the order of resources that will be available from different sources such as CSSs, externally assisted schemes, if any, and state plan funds is possible. Details of funds flowing from bilateral projects and MP and MLA Local Area Development programmes should also be given so that an overall picture of resources is available and could be made public. United funds for local plans could be added wherever they are available. As regards the broad time frame within which these processes need to be undertaken, it is suggested that during 2006-07 itself it should be possible to indicate with reasonable precision the resources that will be available for planning at each level of Panchayat. Since the process will take a year to be completed, intimation need to go out from the Planning Commission and the State Governments early in 2006-07.

Some States, such as Kerala have Issued Detailed Guidelines on Local Planning, Including Taking Stock, which could be Adapted and used by other States

After the envisioning and stock-taking exercise, the DPC will need to determine a strategy for the development of the district as a whole and accordingly provide guidelines to the Panchayati Raj Institutions and Municipalities for formulating their Plans. The objective is to ensure that all DPCs prepare and update at least once in five years synchronous with the Five year plans of the Centre, a five year plan for the development of the district, defining the goals of development in each sector and outlining the strategy to be followed for each sector based on local conditions. Such plans may also be prepared with taluk as a unit for the rural areas and a town/city as the unit for the urban areas.

The planning process at each level of Panchayat. Keeping in mind that the entire focus is on bottom up planning, the sequence followed is to first outline the process recommended at the Gram Panchayat level followed by higher levels.

Participative Planning at the Gram Panchayat Level

Given below are suggestions on how the planning process could be taken up at the Gram Panchayat level so as to ensure full peoples' participation.

The Gram and Ward Sabhas

For proper planning at Gram Panchayat level, Gram Sabhas have to function effectively. Their meetings would have to be representative of all people living in a Gram Panchayat. Several States have devised consultative mechanisms below the Gram Sabha, such as Ward Sabhas and Mahila Sabhas to ensure that every socio-economic section is properly represented in the Gram Sabha. Even so, the general picture is that meetings are few and far between and that attendance is low, especially of weaker and disadvantaged sections. The following steps are suggested to be carried out on a campaign mode to ensure good participation in Gram Sabhas and Ward Sabhas:

- Dates for meetings to be determined in advance by the Panchayats.
- Notices to be printed and distributed and adequate awareness created through display of fixed notices in public places particularly about the responsibilities of the Gram and Ward Sabhas in Plan formulation.
- Special interest groups such as SHGs etc., to be contacted for attending the Ward and Gram Sabhas.
- Information to be given through NGOs, libraries, schools, anganwadis and cooperatives functioning in the area about Ward and Gram Sabhas.
- Campaigns through National Service Scheme and Nehru Yuvak Kendra (NYK) volunteers, NCC cadets and College students could be undertaken.
- House visits through squad work, particularly mobilized through the Ward member could be arranged.
- The Gram Panchayat nominating two facilitators one male and one female identified unanimously for each Ward Sabha. These facilitators could also be earmarked for special training at the Block/Municipal levels.
- Having a proper structure for the Gram and Ward Sabha with scope to break up into smaller groups for discussion.
- It would be useful to meticulously keep records of the meetings, such as attendance register with details photographs, etc., where feasible.

Participative Citizen Surveys

Information is a basic tool for planning, but information relevant to each area and its population is rarely available. A citizen survey leading to a data-base for each Gram Panchayat to know more about themselves, developed in a participative manner, is a desirable prerequisite for participatory planning. The process of data collection on citizens could be so dealt with that Gram Panchayats see in it, their own empowerment. This also builds a climate of participation even before the actual planning process starts. A good design of data collection by the Gram Panchayat will result in:

- The Gram Panchayat will own the data it collects.
- A basic framework will be developed and local initiatives and add-ons encouraged.
- Data collection would involve the local elected representatives. Gram Panchayat members or their literate assistants could carry out the surveys.
- Data collection is a process, not an event. Data will be continuously refined.
- Gram Panchayats will begin to act on their findings even before the data is correlated.

A Natural Resources Database

Systems for collecting natural resources data are already available, often GIS supported. Data from an existing GIS system can be transferred into a series of static slides that can be given to the Gram Panchayat on a CD.

Taking Stock of Gram Panchayat Level Resources

While the importance of this exercise has been mentioned earlier, at the Gram Panchayat level this exercise would, specifically look at the following points:

- Increasing local resource mobilization through taxes, user charges and contributions.
- Innovative means of financing through cess, BOT, Community contribution and borrowings.
- Other efforts at promoting development through local action without significant outflow of funds from the local government. This could include tapping of funds from local philanthropists, NRIs, the Corporate sector and NGOs.

The Use of IT in the Maintenance of Databases

It tought to be positioned as a tool that enhances the quality of decision-making at the Gram Panchayat level. Several simple processes, such as giving a standard identity number to the family, could help in linking up one database with another, thus adding greater value to it.

Making Commitments to the People on Good Governance

A housekeeping plan ought to also be part of the Planning Exercise. Each Panchayat may give details of how it is adequately equipped to handle the workload associated with decentralized planning and implementation. This will also take stock of devolution of adequate functionaries to them for better administration. Some of the priorities under the housekeeping plan would be as follows:

- Updating of records,
- Completion of Asset Register,
- Prescribing performance standards for institutions and officers,
- Steps to reduce waste and leakages,
- How procurement would be undertaken for the implementation of the plan,
- Other measures to improve the performance of obligatory functions mandated by law.

Matching of Resources to the Plan

Ideally speaking, each Gram Panchayat should be free to allocate resources in accordance with the assessed needs. However, at this stage of our development, the local planning exercise has to take into account the diversity of sources of funds. The attempts should be to put them to best possible use.

Therefore, once the order of resources for the plan are known, it is best to place them into a matrix that is divided into three categories, namely, purely untied funds, partly untied funds (where there is some flexibility in use) and tied funds. Such a matrix would give each Panchayat an idea of how it can slot its priorities into the conditionalities associated with funding. This would ensure that funds, which are inescapably tied should be first used and then untied funds are applied. Once needs are assessed at the Panchayat level, a process of linking each need to the source of funding can be adopted, through the steps detailed below:

Step 1: Classifying Each Need into a Matrix

Discussions with people would throw up several needs, such as housing, sending children to schools, nutrition, roads, health care etc. Each of these will need to be classified under broad headings irrespective of the source of funds.

Step 2: Assigning Specific Purpose Grants

Having classified the needs, the next step would be to identify the specific purpose grants that address such needs and match these resources to each need.

Step 3: Assigning Part-Untied Funds

Part-untied funds are available for certain purposes and allow for a certain measure of convergence with other schemes. Examples are SGRY and funds from award of Central and State Finance Commission. These funds can be used for gap filling within limits.

Step 4: Assigning Fully Untied Funds

The final step is the placement of fully untied funds. These are typically own sources of revenue, general or untied State Plan Grants, SFC grants. In this connection, it would also be very useful to consider the assignment of non-monetary contributions, such as voluntary labour, as fully or partly untied resources.

The Adaptability to Change of a Plan

Several factors may call for a change in the Plan. One is the possible impact of general development and technological change on a given area and the need to adjust, respond and make use of the opportunity. There could also be a natural calamity which may necessitate leaving incomplete plans aside and concentrating on immediate relief and rehabilitation. Currently there is no formally designed mechanism that integrates a calamity relief operation, even in a slow acting calamity such as a drought, with the existing Panchayat plan. This leads to duplication of work and irregularities. Systems will have to be put in place for a calamity relief plan to act in concert with a local plan. There will also be a need for frequent monitoring of calamity relief programmes, including through an appropriate social audit mechanism too.

Sequencing and Processes of Planning at the Gram Panchayat Level

The planning exercise ought to lead to a five-year plan for the period corresponding with the national plan period, and annual plans that define and priorities areas and schemes from such a plan. The longer term plans would capture the overall picture of the Panchayat and allow people to understand what planning and governmental funding could hold out for them. Once a five year plan is prepared, the annual plan can be drawn out from it.

Considering the size and availability of personnel of Gram Panchayats, it is obvious that they would need assistance and help in the preparation of projects and schemes, but the decision should be that of the Gram Sabha. Development Meets/Workshops at gram sabha level would be necessary leading to the emergence of a draft plan, with schemes and projects listed in priority.

General Format of a Gram Panchayat Level Plan

A basic point to be stressed is that everybody should be able to understand the plan, more so the people of the village and the Gram Panchayat members. The Gram Panchayat level plan could follow a broad and simple pattern.* Drawn from best practices, given below is a possible framework:

- The Vision.
- Citizens' Profile.
- Natural Resources and Infrastructure Profile.
- The Financial Resources Profile.
- The Anti Poverty Programme.
- The Gender Justice Programme.
- The Special Component and Tribal Programmes.
- Programmes for Social Security.

* The only state that now has a system of detailed Gram Panchayat level plans is Kerala, where the plan follows a broad pattern of first stating out the human development condition, the resources available and then chapters relating the action points pertaining to each department.

- Implementation.
- Monitoring and Evaluation.

The Planning Process at the Intermediate Panchayat

The process and format of the Intermediate Panchayat plan will be largely the same as that suggested for the Gram Panchayats. However, the actual components would be dependent on the Activity Mapping for the Block Panchayat and the vision envisaged by the Intermediate Panchayat. An important role of this level of panchayat is to act as a facilitator in the various steps of planning at the Gram Panchayat level. The tasks of the Intermediate Panchayat as regards planning would be:

- Prepare five year and annual plans in accordance with activity mapping and covering inter village-panchayat issues, through a participators process following the steps listed in the case of Gram Panchayats (as appropriate).
- Maintain multi-disciplinary technical teams (which could include NGOs) for assisting Gram Panchayats in planning and implementation. This would especially synergize inter-tier coordination for watershed development and Rural Business Hub initiatives. There is urgent need to equip each Intermediate Panchayat with a planning support unit.
- Maintain and manage multi-panchayat cadres, such as teachers, engineers, watershed managers, social forestry supervisors, anganwadi supervisors, and intermediate level health supervisory workers.
- Feedback from Gram Panchayats regarding works outside their purview, such as inter-village road formation and multi-panchayat irrigation structures could be included in Intermediate Panchayat Plans.

The Planning Process at the District Level

We deal at length with the composition and functions of the constitutionally mandated District Planning Committees. Their task would include assistance in planning to different levels of panchayats as well as the integration of their draft plans.

As regards district Panchayats, the role would be one of preparing plans in accordance with activity mapping and overall coordination in planning, providing capacity building and technical support, to lower levels of panchayats. Quite often, districts are themselves highly uneven in development. The District Panchayat has the responsibility to provide for equitable development of backward regions within the district. This could be done through guidelines as well as differential allocation of resources to low levels of panchayats under special component plans and programmes in the earmarked fund. The District Level, in preparing its plans will particularly need to take into account gender issues, tribal sub-plans and Special Component Plans for the development of SCs.

It is essential that the District Panchayat plan also looks into several issues that may lie outside activity mapping, but are critical to the overall development of the district as a whole. While all of them cannot obviously be tackled at the district level, the plan could cover measures that would help to promote them. We indicate below some of these issues that need to be addressed in the District Panchayat plan. These are particularly relevant to the district plans in the 200 backward districts where poverty is chronic.

Agricultural Land Related Issues

Several land related regulatory issues often lie at the root of continuing and chronic poverty. These include backlogs in land survey, confirmation of grant of title to those who do not have title, identification of land alienated illegally, restoration of alienated land so identified through Gram Sabhas under powers vested in them under Provision of Panchayat (Extension to the Scheduled Area) Act 1996 (PESA) and in an analogous manner in non-Scheduled Areas and recognition of Community control over traditional Jhum/Podu areas and promotion of programmes of tree culture and husbandry, as a step towards self-sufficient and sustainable use of resources.

Forest Land Related Issues

These would include completing the process of conversion of forest villages into revenue villages and settlement of other old habitations, regularisation of pre-1980 occupations and resolution of other disputed claims over forest land in terms of Government of India directions, livelihood rehabilitation of those whose occupation cannot be regularized, identification of all occupied lands and preparation of maps authenticated by the Gram Sabha concerned, the Forest Department and the Revenue Department.

Credit and Usury Related Issues

These would include the following initiatives:

- assessing the debt liabilities of members of the Scheduled Castes and Scheduled Tribes and other weaker sections.
- revival and restructuring of the Large Area Multi-purpose Cooperative Societies (LAMPS) and Primary Agricultural Cooperative Societies (PACS) with the specific targets of providing all credit needs of the Scheduled Castes and Scheduled Tribes and weaker sections.
- providing special arrangements for provision of long-term loans for purchase of long-term loans for purchase of land by asset less poor and resource less families, who are dependent upon agriculture for their livelihoods.
- Providing effective support price operation for all items of agriculture and minor forest produce.
- Strengthening of the public distribution system, through a system of buffer stock within a village from out of local produce, supplementing the same from outside, to the extent of deficiency.

Livelihood Issues

These would, in particular, deal with steps for effective implementation of the National Employment Guarantee Act, through assistance to the panchayats in the preparation of appropriate shelf of works for each area.

Primary Health Care and Nutrition Issues

These would include the following:

- Discontinuing commercial vending of liquor and other intoxicants in terms of the excise policy for tribal areas and institutionalize control of the Gram Sabha over the preparation and use of traditional drinks.

- Ensure functioning of health facilities as per national norms.
- Ensure that all sanctioned posts are mandatorily filled in by trained professionals/para professionals, if necessary through local recruitment.
- Ensure universal full immunization of all children, guaranteed safe deliveries through accredited health provides/skilled birth attendants and management/ treatment of communicable diseases together with supply of essential drugs, up to health Sub-Center level.
- Establish an identifiable and effective nutrition chain for all pregnant women and nursing mothers in rural areas all mal-nourished children and for all children studying in schools.

Reinforcing Administration and Planning through delegation of powers, setting up an effective grievance redressal system, and creation of necessary infrastructure, service conditions, and facilities for all personnel working in these areas would also need to be specifically addressed in the District Plan. The plan for provisioning of larger infrastructure would also be part of the Plan. The thrust areas of Bharat Nirman, such as connectivity of roads, and electrification of all villages and habitations together with electrification of all unelectrified below poverty line households could also be addressed in the District Plan through supplementation of plans of lower levels as well as through attention to inter-panchayat issues.

There is need to ensure close collaboration between levels of Panchayats, without converting the relationship into either a hierarchical or an effort-duplicating one. The principle of financial subsidiarity will need to be followed, by which even if a higher level of Panchayat, such as a District or Intermediate Panchayat sanctions a work of a value less than a prescribed floor limit, it transfers the money allocated for that work to the Gram Panchayat concerned for implementation. This will lead to a clear understanding and separation of who implements what, regardless of who sanctions it. In addition, just as district and intermediate levels of Panchayats would be mandated to delegate implementation of schemes below a certain outlay ceiling to the level below, it ought also be open to lower levels of Panchayats to recommend to the immediate higher level such schemes that ought to be undertaken at the higher level. In addition, there is a need to enable clustering of Gram Panchayats for the purpose of building a sufficient scale for efficient planning. This is particularly relevant for States that have a large number of very small and spread out Village Panchayats. Thus an enabling mechanism could be provided that allows Panchayats, either at the three levels or amongst the same level, to form collaborative arrangements with each other. This could be through a system of contracts and MOUs concerning the assignment of functions in planning to each level.

Some of the ground rules for planning at the intermediate level would include mandating prior consultation with Gram Panchayats. It is suggested that Intermediate and District Panchayats ought to hold meetings of all elected local government members of the levels of Panchayat within its jurisdiction and carry out a detailed consultation exercise. In the case of District Panchayats a meeting of all Village Panchayat Presidents along with all elected members of the District and Block Panchayats may be held, in order to ensure a structured consultation. West Bengal has developed a system, which may be considered for adoption with suitable modifications. Though an amendment to the Panchayati Raj Act in 2003, each Intermediate Panchayat is to have a Block Sansad, consisting of all members of the Gram Panchayats pertaining to the Block and all members of that Panchayat Samiti. One half-yearly and one annual meeting of the Block Sansad are held every year. A 10 per cent quorum is fixed. The Block Sansad has powers to guide and advise the Panchayat Samiti for all matters relating to development including preparation of annual plans and budget and implementation of development programmes for economic development and ensuring social justice. The deliberations, recommendations and observations passed in the meeting of the Block Sansad shall be considered in the meeting of the Panchayat Samiti within one month from the meeting of the Block Sansad. A similar system for District Panchayats is through the Zilla Sansad, which is comprised of Pradhans of all Gram Panchayats in the district, *Sabhapatis* (Presidents), *Sahakari Sabhapatis* (Vice-Presidents) and *Karmadhyakshas* (Standing Committee Chairpersons) of all Panchayat Samitis and all members of the Zilla Parishad.

At the District and Intermediate Panchayat level, it is also essential that there is detailed consultation with other key stakeholders such as farmers, traders, industrialists, the labour, the poor and the academics and professionals, through well publicized consultations.

Time Table for Plan Finalisation

It is suggested that a time-table be followed by States starting from 2006-07 to prepare for and draw up the Eleventh Five Year Plan. The following schedule is suggested for completing various phases in the Planning process. The dates are suggestive and States may make changes within the over-all time frame in accordance with local needs. The object should be that by the beginning of the Eleventh Plan, a district vision document, draft Five Year Plan for 2007-12 as also an annual plan for 2007-08 would be ready for implementation.

S. No.	*Activity*	*Activity to be Completed (Period or by the Date)*
1.	State Level Workshop for all Chairpersons, vice-chairpersons and member convenors of all DPCs.	May 2006
2.	First meeting of District Planning Committee to discuss the guidelines and constituting Sectoral Sub-Committees for preparation of District Vision and perspective plan	June 2006
3.	Formulation of District Vision	By July 2006
4.	Approval of District Vision by DPC and sending the same to all LB's	July 2006
5.	District Level Workshops	August 2006
6.	Block Level Workshop	August 2006
7.	Meeting of Local Bodies to discuss the guidelines and constituting Working Groups	September 2006
8.	Formulation of Local Bodies Vision	September 2006
9.	Approval in the General Body meeting ofLBs	October 2006
10.	Conducting Grama Sabha/Ward Sabha	October-November 2006
11.	Development Seminars	November-December 2006
12.	Preparation of Final Local Bodies Five Year Plans by Working Groups	January 2007
13.	Consolidation of Final Local Bodies' Five Year Plans	January 2007
14.	Submission of Local Bodies Five Year Plans to DPCs	January 2007

(*Contd.*)

S. No.	Activity	Activity to be Completed (Period or by the Date)
15.	Discussion with representatives of Local Bodies and approval by DPCs	February 2007
16.	Approval by DPCs	March 2007
17.	Bringing out Development perspective of the District and Local Bodies' Five Year Plans and Annual Plan 2007-08.	March 2007

STRENGTHENING THE SYSTEM FOR PLANNING FROM BELOW

District Planning Committees

Planning for economic development and social justice is a mandated function of local governments and the District Planning Committees (DPC) have a crucial role to play in the process. Under Article 243ZD of the Constitutión of India, a District Planning Committee shall be constituted at the district level in every State to consolidate the plans prepared by the Panchayats and the Municipalities in the district and to prepare a draft development plan for the district. The Constitution therefore enjoins upon the DPCs two specific responsibilities. In preparing the draft development plan, the DPC shall have regard to matters of common interest between the Panchayats and the Municipalities including spatial planning, sharing of water and other physical and natural resources, the integrated development of infrastructure and environmental conservation and the extent and type of available resources, both financial or otherwise. The DPC in this endeavour, is also mandated to consult such institutions and organizations as may be specified. In order that the plans at different levels are prepared as envisaged in the previous chapter, there is need to strengthen the system comprising the machinery of planning and the process of consolidation of plans at the district level.

There is often confusion as to whether the DPC is to be established as a separate and permanent office or whether it denotes only a meeting that is periodically called and which can be serviced by a part-time secretariat. There is a feeling that the DPC ought not to emerge as yet another layer of bureaucracy to vet people's plans. At the same time, the fact that the DPC is held intermittently and without permanent support undermines its effectiveness as a constitutional institution and a coordinating mentor. On balance, the group feels that the DPC merits the status of a permanent institution, with adequate Secretariat to service it at the District level. It could also be provided the means of drawing experts to assist it whenever required.

Status of DPCs at Present

All States and Union Territories except Meghalaya, Mizoram, Nagaland, J&K and NCT of Delhi are required to set up District Planning Committees in accordance with Article 243ZD of the Constitution of India. Bihar, Chhattisgarh, Goa, Haryana, Himachal Pradesh, Karnataka, Kerala, Madhya Pradesh, Orissa, Rajasthan, Sikkim, Tamil Nadu, West Bengal and the Union Territories of Andaman and Nicobar, Dadra and Nagar Haveli, Daman & Diu and Lakshadweep have constituted District Planning Committees in all districts. Manipur has constituted DPCs in four Valley districts. District Planning Committees have not been constituted in Jharkhand and Pondicherry where elections to Panchayats are yet to be held. Uttar Pradesh has enacted legislation for District Planning Committees but is yet to issue the notification constituting these bodies. Uttaranchal, which inherited the UP Panchayati Raj Act, has also not notified or constituted the DPCs. Maharashtra, has not constituted DPCs in accordance with Article 243ZD of the Constitution. All three—Uttar Pradesh, Uttaranchal and Maharashtra—have District Planning and Development Councils headed by a Minister, including nominated members from Panchayats and Municipalities. Andhra Pradesh has issued an Ordinance in September, 2005 for the Constitution of DPCs pending the passage of the relevant bill in the Legislative Assembly. Punjab has enacted legislation on the Constitution of DPCs in October, 2005. The Union Territory of Chandigarh has informed that since it comprises just one District, the planning function can be carried out at the territorial level.

The Current Status of DPCs in States is as Follows:

Table 1

Sl. No.	*States/UTs*	*Status of Constitution of DPCs*
1.	Andhra Pradesh	Not yet constituted.
2.	Arunachal Pradesh	Not yet constituted.
3.	Assam	Not yet constituted.
4.	Bihar	Constituted in all 38 districts. Chairman ZP is the Chairman of DPCs.
5.	Chhattisgarh	Constituted, Minister is Chairpersons of DPC.
6.	Goa	Constituted. President of ZP is the Chairperson of DPC.
7.	Gujarat	Not yet constituted.
8.	Haryana	Constituted in all 19 Districts.
9.	Himachal Pradesh	Constituted in 12 districts, Minister is Chairperson of DPC.
10.	Karnataka	Yes. In all Districts, President, ZP is Chairman of DPC.
11.	Jharkhand	Panchayat Elections yet to be held.
12.	Kerala	Yes, Chairman of District Panchayat (DP) is Chairman of DPC.
13.	Madhya Pradesh	Yes. District in-charge Ministers are Chairpersons.
14.	Maharashtra	Not yet constituted.
15.	Manipur	Yes in 4 districts, Adhyaksha, DP is Chairperson.
16.	Orissa	26 Districts, Minister is Chairperson of DPC.
17.	Punjab	Not yet constituted.
18.	Rajasthan	Yes, Chairman of DP is Chairman of DPC.
19.	Sikkim	Yes.
20.	Tamil Nadu	Yes, Chairperson, DP is Chairperson.
21.	Tripura	Not yet constituted.
22.	Uttar Pradesh	DPCs are not notified or constituted, even though legal provision exists.
23.	Uttaranchal	DPCs are not notified or constituted, even though legal provision exists.
24.	West Bengal	Yes, Chairperson, DP is Chairperson of DPC.
25.	A&N Islands	Yes, Chairperson of DP is Chairman of DPC.
26.	Chandigarh	Not yet constituted.
27.	D&N Haveli	Yes, Chairman, DP is Chairman of DPC
28.	Daman & Diu	Yes, Chairman, DP is Chairman of DPC
29.	Lakshadweep	Yes, Collector cum Dev. Commissioner is Chairperson.
30.	Pondicherry	Not yet constituted.

An analysis of the functioning of DPCs and the formulation and implementation of 'district plans' in 14 States reveals the following:

- In most States DPCs are yet to function as envisaged in the Constitution. They neither consolidate nor prepare draft district developmental plans.
- Very few States are preparing district plans even though some of them allocate funds to the district sector.
- In several States, where there is no separation of the budget into District and State sectors, allocation of funds to Panchayats does not match the legislative devolution of functions to them.
- Funds given to Panchayats are tied down to schemes, thus limiting the scope for determining and addressing local priorities through a planning exercise. In this regard, CSSs pertaining to functions devolved to Panchayats now constitute the largest element of such tied funds.
- Actual provision in State budgets also differs from the gross outlays communicated. Some States do not provide matching funds to Centrally Sponsored Schemes, reducing the actual flow of funds for such Schemes to local governments.
- Planning' is of poor quality and is generally a mere collection of schemes and works, many of the works suggested by elected panchayat members themselves is an ad-hoc manner. Integration of Gram and Taluk Panchayat plans into the District plan, even when done, also tends to be mere summation and not a synergistic integration. This is further distorted by placing funds with MPs and MLAs, whose utilization falls outside the pale of any planning.
- Since the so-called planning exercise follows certain chain of events at the State level as regards finalisation of budgets and plans, its quality suffers seriously for lack of sufficient time. Thus detailed guidelines regarding consultation, consideration and decision-making at different levels remain largely on paper and the planning process does not stir meaningful debate in Panchayats.

- In the absence of a well-functioning District Planning machinery, taking decisions on the priorities of a district is often left to officials, guided by district development committees, which consist largely of elected representatives of legislatures and Members of Parliament and some nominated members, sometimes including elected representatives of Panchayats.

It is clear that the steps taken to operationalise the provisions of Article 243 ZD by the States have been far from satisfactory. While several aspects of how the shortcomings ought to be dealt with are described in other Chapters, we here make recommendations aimed at ensuring that the DPC becomes the fulcrum of the planning effort in the district, and has the capacity to undertake the tasks expected of it.

Establishment of DPCs in Accordance with Article 243 ZD of the Constitution

The first step is to ensure that DPCs are set up in all States in accordance with Article 243 ZD of the Constitution. In spite of the resolutions of the Second Round Table to set up DPCs as mandated by the Constitution and efforts by the Ministry of Panchayati Raj to persuade all States, some States are still dragging their feet in this regard. The Ministry of Panchayati Raj addressed all Secretaries of Panchayati Raj in States on 30th May, 2005 requesting them to constitute DPCs in their respective States if the same had not been constituted. Their attention was also drawn to the meeting of the Committee of Chief Secretaries and Secretaries of Panchayati Raj in the States/Union Territories held on 11th April, 2005 wherein the Ministry of Panchayati Raj had communicated that the States that had not constituted DPCs in accordance with Article 243ZD of the Constitution should do so before 31st October, 2005. However, this was not achieved. The steps taken by this Expert Group and the circular issued by the Planning Commission to all States regarding formulation of the Annual Plans of States has already been referred.

While the circular marks an important step forward and would give an impetus to the endeavour to establish and strengthen District Planning Committees, it is suggested that detailed instructions need to be issued to all States and Central Ministries prior to Eleventh Plan discussions on the following points:

- CSS guidelines that entrust the task of district level planning and implementation to parallel bodies, such as DRDAs and District Health Societies, need to be modified to incorporate the District Planning Committee in the process of District level planning.
- The Planning Commission could inform States that the DPC would be the sole body that is entrusted with the task of consolidating plans at the district level.
- The Planning Commission could specify a time frame within which States will need to issue detailed instructions covering the manner in which the DPC would perform its functions.

Support to DPCs

The need to provide professional support to the DPC cannot be overstated. Though several States have provided staff from the State level on deputation to District Panchayats for the purpose of undertaking planning, such Staff are overburdened and ill equipped. There is a need to create, preferably within the District Panchayat, a separate cell to service the District Planning Committee. The Cell could have five separate and distinct sections, namely, dealing with Municipal Plans, District Panchayat Plans, Intermediate Panchayat Plans, Village Panchayat Plans and one for maintenance of data and undertake research, with the necessary support in terms of IT and qualified research assistants.

- There must be a full time professionally qualified District Planning Officer to head the District Planning Unit. If such persons are unavailable in the government, appointments of professionals on contract or outsourcing are options to be considered and acted upon.
- Institutional support through universities and research institutions, both at the District and State level, could be identified for assisting the DPC in planning, monitoring and evaluation.

- The Planning Commission should continue to provide the required support for district planning as was done earlier, except that this would now be provided to the DPC.

Experts to Support the District Planning Committee

The aim of drawing experts is to assist the local governments concerned (Panchayats and Urban Local Bodies) in both forming a vision and designing strategies to attain that vision. Advice of the experts would be based on experience, expertise and the field position, as revealed from ground data. Special efforts ought to be made by States to ensure that the best talent and the most motivated are invited to participate as experts. The following points are recommended to guide the drawing of experts to support the DPC:

- Experts could be assigned to work either individually or in teams. They could be taken on a part time basis, an assignment basis or full time, if the need arises.
- It is for the State to determine the number of experts that can be drawn to assist the DPC. This could depend upon the extent of devolution in each State.
- Though ideally they are best drawn locally, experts can be drawn even from outside the jurisdiction of the district, if required. Care must be taken to ensure that participation is voluntary, above partisan politics and able to respect different points of view.
- With growing urbanization of smaller and intermediate sized towns, there is need to especially draw in experts on municipal matters and the urban rural interphase to assist the DPC in planning for local resource sharing, area planning, solid waste and sewage disposal and other such matters which call for close coordination between Panchayats and Municipalities.

The DPC could also constitute a few sectoral sub-committees for both the envisioning and the consolidation processes. The task of sectoral Sub-Committees is to go into the details of each development sector assigned, such as proper quantification and description of service available in the sector, whether these meet the norms prescribed, the gaps that need to be filled and track data availability, in consultation with local Bodies, public and private organizations before finalizing the vision of that Sector. Once the Sectoral Vision document is prepared, it shall be submitted to the DPC. Sectoral sub-committees could also give suggestions for innovative plans and integrated projects, which local governments may accept if they so desire.

Assisting Panchayats in Planning

One of the primary tasks of the DPC would be to build capacity for decentralized planning in the district. A major impediment to proper planning is the lack of personnel providing planning support and availability of good and comprehensible information at the Intermediate and Gram Panchayat levels.

Provision of support for planning at the Intermediate Panchayat level:

> It is strongly recommended that each Intermediate Panchayat be provided a planning and data unit, which could also be integrated into the larger concept of having a Resource Centre at each Intermediate Panchayat level, to provide a basket of pooled services, such as for engineering, agriculture, watershed development, women and child care, public health etc., which Gram Panchayats can draw upon for support in planning and implementation.

A Generic Set of Guidelines for the DPCs

The DPC should be entrusted with anchoring the preparation of the vision document, the maintenance of databases, training of planners, evaluation of outcomes, internal monitoring of performance and independent evaluation of outcomes. Guidelines for planning would need to cover both public participation and technical scrutiny. The guidelines will need to cover the visioning exercise, listing of needs through participation and the technical examination. The end product will therefore contain well prepared projects/schemes with technical details and estimates of expenditure (projectisation) so that local bodies are able to adopt and implement them. The plan as prepared by the local body concerned would have clear targets, describing both outputs and outcomes and would have matched the plan to all available resources, which would mean, in addition to the devolved funds, whether they be plan or non-plan, own funds, beneficiary contribution, community contribution and institutional finance. Some States have issued detailed and meaningful guidelines for the functioning of DPCs and they could be used as models for adoption.

Consolidation of Panchayat and Local Body Plans by District Planning Committee

In the realization of the district vision, district plans will need to put together resources channelised from all sources including district segments to the State Plan, CSSs, Special Programmes such as Employment Guarantee, *Sarva Shiksha Abhiyaan*, Rural Health Mission, Grants-in-aid for specific purposes from Finance Commission, Bharat Nirman etc. Therefore, consolidation is a task that goes much beyond compilation and connotes a degree of value addition through integration of local plans. There are several aspects of integration of plans that have to be considered in the preparation of the draft development plan. The different dimensions of integration have been discussed very succinctly in the planning guidelines for local bodies in Kerala as detailed below and could be adapted for general use:

- *Spatial Integration*: This would mean integration of schemes such as roads that run through one or more Panchayats. Such kinds of Multi-Panchayat infrastructure projects could be taken up with proportionate contributions from the Panchayats concerned dovetailed into the funding available from above and entrusted to one local government for execution.
- *Sectoral Integration*: This relates to the integration that takes place within a sector. For instance, an integrated approach to agricultural development would require the integration of several schemes relating to agriculture, such as horticulture, drip irrigation, high yielding varieties and integrated pest management.
- *Cross-sectoral integration*: To ensure maximum impact from different interventions, it is necessary to design

approaches that draw resources from various schemes. For instance, a good approach to public health would require inputs from water and sanitation allocations and health programme allocations. Again, a typical watershed management programme would comprise of soil conservation, water harvesting, micro-irrigation, bio-mass generation, fisheries, animal husbandry, agro-processing and micro-enterprise components, all properly sequenced.

- *Vertical Integration*: This is based on the precept that District and Intermediate Panchayats ought to perform activities which have the advantages of scale and which cannot be done by the lower tiers of local government. This will require that Block Panchayats have a clear idea as to what the draft plans of Village Panchayats will contain. Similarly the District Panchayats would need to consider the approved plans of Village and Block Panchayats before finalizing theirs.
- *Integration of Resources*: There are several schemes both Centrally sponsored and State sponsored which Panchayats can utilize, integrate into local plans and to which they can contribute additional resources. This would comprise of two aspects, as below:
- *Integration with State Plans*: There are several State Plans, which as implemented can be strengthened by increased allocation from Panchayat funds. In some cases a component having a complementary nature could be added to the State Plan Scheme. For instance, the drawing of electric wires to villages could be complemented by the Panchayat taking up the wiring of BPL houses.
- *Integration of Centrally Sponsored Schemes with Local Plans*: It is important that in the interest of efficient use of resources, there ought to be only one development plan for the local government prepared through a common planning process and not a set of separate plans prepared in accordance with the guidelines of each programme. Thus once priorities and works are identified and prioritized through a single planning process, components pertaining to a particular sector could be taken up through schemes, including CSSs while still keeping within the guidelines of those schemes.

- *Integration with Local Resources*: Planning can provide for local investments to be catalysed through local resources or initiatives. For example, village knowledge centers and Rural business Hubs could be catalysed by Panchayats. This is also possible by extending the concept of Pura to encompass the concept of rural business hubs. By this, we do not meant that Panchayats ought to run industry locally, but that it catalogs local skills and natural resource endowments and facilitate the development of business linkages.

Rural Urban Integration

Integration of urban-rural plans, which is particularly important in the light of increasing urbanization, is an area where the District Planning Committee could contribute a great deal. The DPC should work out mechanisms of joint programmes to be financed by State Government institutions and joint contributions by urban and rural local bodies.

Issue of Detailed Guidelines by Each State Government Regarding Preparation of Draft District Plan

Each State Government may issue guidelines regarding the components of a draft district plan, which will need to be sent to the State level for approval. The focus of these guidelines is to be on the planning process as detailed in this Report rather than the nature, structure and details of the plans themselves.

Maintenance and Use of Data for Preparation of the Vision Document and Planning

There is a need for collection and computerization of habitation wise information on a large number of parameters.* Data available from several sources, either computerized or otherwise, will need to be integrated. Such data is available through the census, BPL

* Several States have provided matrices for the same. Karnataka's samanya mahithi, comprises of more than 350 parameters tracked for each habitation and enabled to be sorted on the basis of Gram Panchayats.

census and other censuses conducted by the Department of Animal Husbandry, Department of Statistics, Education and Health Departments. Much of this data can be compiled on a village-wise basis. Alongside, more general data such as State or District level economic data at a Glance, Inter-state, District and Block level Socio Economic Indicators and State and District Income details could be collected. Line department's publications, reports of task forces and working groups, may suggest various approaches and reforms in the sectors assigned to them. Planning Department and Line Departments often bring out evaluation reports of different schemes, which can go into a database for planning.

In this connection it is noted that in keeping with the need to prepare detailed databases at the Block level, the National Sample Survey should be taken to all blocks in the country in the Eleventh plan period.

Capacity Building for Planning

The DPC could be given a coordinating role in capacity building efforts at the district level. Capacity building would go beyond training to encompass provisioning of staff and providing a framework for outsourcing of technical support. Even as volunteers and experts are brought into the district planning effort, there will be a need for familiarizing them with the processes involved with participatory planning from below. The following principles are essential to a training strategy:

- Training cannot be envisaged as a single one-time intervention and must be periodically repeated as a longer and continuous process of transformation and development.
- The focus of training is not upon a one way information flow alone. It is a process involving both trainers and participants in a common inter-learning situation. Trainers should be objective and non-judgmental in outlook and ought to evoke and stimulate thinking.
- Training cannot provide ready-made answers but must provide space and time for 'trainees' to reflect on and analyze their situation and seek solutions to their problems.

- Learning occurs best in an non-threatening environment which encourages people to be active.
- Participants come to the training programme with significant pre-knowledge, experience and native wisdom, which needs to be recognized and its full potential realized.
- Training Content will need to cover the background and ethos of participatory planning, the operational processes involved as also issues relating to gender and disadvantaged sections of society.
- Building of awareness regarding human rights, rights of women, children, disabled, dalits and tribes, right to information and regarding responsibilities as citizens of a pluralistic, democratic society is an essential part of training.
- Persons to be covered will include all elected Panchayat Representatives and office bearers at each level of Panchayat. It will also need to cover all Panchayat secretaries, other staff field staff of line departments and Accounts and Auditing staff. Training should also be in mixed groups to promote greater interaction and cross learning. Emphasis needs to be placed on the attitudes and skills necessary to interact and work with other peoples organizations like Cooperatives, NGOs, Self-Help Groups and Users' Associations.

Training could be a mix of face-to-face and distance learning, through either satellite or video-conferencing. Both means would require the creation of a pool of resource persons, through a cascading process. Four levels of cascading could be considered, namely, the National, State, District and Block levels. Care will need to be taken to specially identify people with the right mindset, commitment and drive as Trainers and Resource persons. They could also be specially identified, screened and drawn from Panchayat members themselves (or ex-members) and NGOs, or could be government servants.

In the case of Distance training using Satellite or video-conferencing, care must be taken to ensure a full utilization of the interactivity provided by the system. A mix of satellite technology and participatory training techniques, which allows for training to reach out to large number of people cost effectively, in a short period of time would be ideal.

The training of Panchayat members and Staff can be complemented by a large scale community mobilization programme, through the performance of *kalajatha nataks* and evocative songs on a variety of themes, which form the subject of planning for development and social justice.

Even after training of all stakeholders, there would be need to provide a speedy channel of clarification and information to those involved in the implementation of the programme. While in the long-term, IT would provide this interactive mechanism, a more immediate approach is to set up telephone help lines. Timings of the helpline must be convenient and wide publicity needs to be given to the helpline telephone numbers in all communications of the government.

Training of the magnitude envisaged will require the development of a variety of print material, which ought to be easy on the eye, preferably well illustrated. Print material could be of Reference handbooks for Panchayat members, staff and other stakeholders, which is best arranged in the form of answers to frequently asked questions. Charts, wall newspapers and posters can be displayed in Panchayat offices and other public places.

Training Programme Management can be decentralized and adapted for local needs. A core team of full time managers of training can be located at the State level, preferably at the SIRD. Separate groups could oversee specific aspects of programme management could also be set up, to look at curricula, monitoring, evaluation and documentation.

Many line departments still adopt systems of hierarchical technical guidance, which have to be modified and simplified, Creating a pool of technically competent staff or other agencies at the Intermediate Panchayat level is an essential part of capacity creation for decentralized planning.

DPC's Role in the National Evaluation and Monitoring Mechanism

Monitoring progress in planning and implementation has been attempted only down to the district level. With increasing computerization and connectivity, it is time that block level monitoring be adopted. Since there are about 6100 Intermediate Panchayats in the country, keeping track of the progress of planning at that level is practicable at the National level. At the district level, this task can be entrusted to the DPC, which could function as part of a national planning network, at the apex of which will be the Planning Commission. Participatory monitoring at the local level is best undertaken through a system of peer reviews, through which Panchayats undertake monitoring of each other and rank themselves through a transparent system. Several states have experimented with peer reviews in individual programmes, but this idea needs to be broad based to cover all local participatory evaluation. The system of peer reviews could also be undertaken at higher levels of planning so that eventually all second stage monitoring is based on the data thrown up through such reviews.

Training itself will require monitoring and periodic evaluation. The quality of facilitation provided to Panchayats, particularly Gram Panchayats, in undertaking their responsibilities, will need to be evaluated. It will specifically have to be assessed how training has enabled more effective community participation, with reference to the conduct of Gram Sabhas, Ward Sabhas and Social Audits; how it has affected the functioning of standing committees in the Panchayats how it has catalyzed partnering amongst functionaries, Panchayat elected representatives and people, how it has addressed gender issues and other aspects of social justice and how it has facilitated effective organization of planning and implementation by Panchayats.

WAYS AND MEANS OF STRENGTHENING THE DELIVERY SYSTEM FOR SERVICES AND DEVELOPMENT INITIATIVES THROUGH PANCHAYATI RAJ INSTITUTIONS

Article 243G of the Constitution provides for devolution to empower Panchayati Raj Institutions (PRIs) to function as institutions of self-government for the twin purposes of (*i*) *making plans* for economic development and social justice for their respective areas as regards subjects devolved to them and (*ii*) *implementing* these plans subject to such conditions as the State may, by law, specify. For effective service delivery by Panchayats, there is need to define the scope and ambit of such devolution. In several States, the incompleteness and ineffectiveness of devolution is manifested by merely stating loosely in the legislation the functions that are devolved to Panchayats without a more exact assignment of activities relating to the devolved functions to each level of Panchayats. In addition, funds relating to the devolved activities continue to be with line departments. In the absence of fiscal devolution to match functional devolution, employees with State departments oppose their being placed in or made accountable to Panchayats.

Such incomplete devolution places upon Panchayats the burden of having to perform several service delivery and economic development functions without adequate finances and staff support. Incomplete devolution induces in the Panchayats habits of sidestepping their responsibilities and becoming yet another petitioner to higher departmental authorities—hardly the kind of role that one would expect a local self-government to play.

The critical steps that need to be taken to ensure that Panchayats become effective in service delivery are:

- Ensuring that clearly demarcated roles are assigned to Panchayats, through activity mapping.
- Confining centrally sponsored and state schemes to a small number of important programmes to achieve declared national and state goals.
- Undertaking a well structured process of fiscal devolution that matches the fund availability at each level of Panchayat with the functions assigned to it.
- Providing capacity to the Panchayats, in the widest sense of the term to perform their responsibilities effectively.
- Ensuring benchmarking of services so that Panchayats can be clearly judged in terms of outcomes.
- Putting in place systems of accountability so that citizens, the ultimate recipient of services from Panchayats, are enabled to hold them to account for any inadequacies in service delivery.
- Spreading Public spiritedness on the part of all concerned.

Role Clarity for Panchayats

Activity Mapping

Activity mapping is the key to the effective devolution of functions to Panchayats. The first Round Table of State Ministers of Panchayati Raj held at Kolkata in July 2004 resolved that activities related to the devolved functions ought to be identified with a view to attributing each of them to the appropriate tier of the 3-tier system, through the application of the principle of subsidiarity. It also resolved that with a view to promoting a measure of irrevocability of devolved functions, devolution may be routed through legislative measures or, alternatively, by providing a strong framework for devolution through executive orders. Though the Ministry of Panchayati Raj agreed that it could furnish technical assistance and expertise to State Govts./UT Administrations to accomplish activity mapping and also suggested that the model as evolved in the Ministry of Rural Development in the Report of the Task Force on Devolution of Powers and Functions upon Panchayati Raj Institutions 2001, could be used for guidance, it is seen that very few States took concrete steps in this direction within the time-frame indicated.

In some States, while the preliminary work has been completed in terms of the assignment of functions to the three levels of Panchayats, the matter is pending at the stage of being considered and finalized by the Government. Since Activity Mapping is the trigger for the devolution of finances and functionaries, States have to expedite operationalising the same. We suggest that the stage of activity mapping may be specifically reviewed by the Planning Commission when draft State plans are discussed. We have also suggested the institution of a Panchayati Raj Incentive Scheme, in which a key element would be the completion of activity mapping by the State Government.

Devolution of Funds to Match Activity Mapping

The Kolkata Round Table also resolved that devolution of finances to the three-tier of the Panchayati Raj System should be patterned on activity mapping. The essential steps in this direction are for State Governments to undertake a detailed analysis of their annual budgets both non-plan and plan, with a view to separating out the allocations that would need to be transferred to Panchayats in accordance with the activities devolved to them. This exercise would require a reworking of the formats for the preparation of State budgets to provide for a 'Panchayat Sector' which can be structured as an annex to the budget. The Panchayat sector budget would then give details of the fund transfers that would go to Panchayats. To make it easier to trace the funds down to each Panchayat level, a 'link document' could be provided, which further assigns these allocations to the Panchayats in each district. We recommend that in the first instance, the link document could provide district-wise details of the allocations that are budgeted by the State for the three-tiers of Panchayats in the district. However, within the district itself, a further district link document could be provided, which separates out the allocations made to each Panchayat within the district. Such a disaggregation of the budget would give a clear idea of funds allocated to each Panchayat from the State budget. Such a system has been in vogue in some States that have gone ahead substantially on Panchayati Raj and could be adopted by all States.

Mode of Release of Funds to Panchayats

Stating out financial allocations to Panchayats in the manner outlined above is only part of the story. For fiscal devolution to work, it must be ensured that these funds are released to Panchayats through routes that are clearly known. As a rule it should be ensured that funds pass through as few channels as possible in reaching the Panchayats. We give below certain do's and don'ts for running such a system effectively:

- Funds pertaining to the same sector could be released to Panchayats through one route alone. Different line items and schemes ought not to have different means of release. This change will give clarity regarding release of funds to Panchayats.
- Fund release need not be from each State level department to Panchayats. The Panchayat sector budget is best operated by one department, say the Finance Department, which can release these funds to Panchayats in a periodic

fashion, preferably once a month, through a composite order, listing out the line items in respect of which funds are released.

- It must be ensured that each Panchayat has a fund repository, a Tanchayat fund', as mandated by Article 243H of the Constitution, into which the funds transferred from the State budget will be deposited.
- A computerized treasury system would allow for easy placing of funds into Panchayat accounts and tracking of Panchayat transactions. However, for the tracking process to be complete it is also essential that Panchayat accounts are computerized, compatibly with treasury computerization. This will ensure that there is no problem of reconciliation of accounts and balances between the two accounts, a phenomenon that results in several downstream problems, particularly delays in completion and certification of Panchayat accounts.
- The practice of Central Ministries releasing funds for Centrally Sponsored Schemes (CSSs) directly to separate project implementing agencies set up in the districts or State level should be given up and funds transferred to State Consolidated funds from where they pass down directly to each level of Panchayat.

Transferring Funds to Panchayats without Delay or Diversion

Though the Constitution establishes the Panchayats at the District, Intermediate and Village levels as institutions of local self-government and authorizes States to enact laws through which these bodies were to be endowed with powers so as to enable them to functions as such institutions, bodies that became parallel to the Panchayat set-up such as DRDAs have continued as recipients of funds from the Central Government. Far from withering away the practice of sending money directly to a district or state level project implementing agency is now also followed by other Central Ministries like Education and Health in relation to the schemes administered by them. Setting up such parallel bodies goes against the letter and spirit of the 73rd Amendment. They particularly undermine Panchayats empowered under the law to undertake several functions, considerably weakens the Central Government's persuasion of States to move ahead on empowering Panchayats and acts as a strong disincentive to States which want to go ahead on empowering Panchayats.

States have demanded that funds ought to be released by the Central Government to Panchayats only through the Consolidated Funds of the States. Vide Office Memorandums (OMs) dated 13/1/2003 and 6/02/2003, the Ministry of Finance, Government of India intimated Central Ministries that in the meeting of Chief Ministries held on 18/10/2002 at New Delhi under the Chairmanship of the Prime Minister, there was a consensus that henceforth all releases under CSSs should be made through the Consolidated Fund of the States and not directly to the project implementing agencies set up by the Central Ministries. It was also agreed that as a pre-condition, the States would pass on the funds to the end users within a stipulated time of three weeks and inform the administrative Central Ministry concerned in the Government of India of having done so. Accordingly, all Central Ministries were advised by Ministry of Finance to re-classify their budgetary provisions so that the funds from Centrally Sponsored Schemes would go as grants-in-aid to State Governments. However, these OMs were withdrawn by the Ministry of Finance vide OM dated 11/06/2003.

In order to put in place a mechanism of transfer of funds pertaining to Centrally Sponsored Schemes to PRIs that is quick, transparent, easy to track and not subject to diversion, action ought to be taken to operationalise the decision of the NDC that funds for CSSs will be credited to the Consolidated Funds of States, on the guarantee that States will pass on the funds to Panchayati Raj Institutions within a stipulated time. It may be noted that such a system has been mandated for sending Twelfth Finance Commission grants to Panchayats. A credible and transparent monitoring mechanism will have to be put in place to ensure that the stipulated limit for transfer of funds to PRIs is guaranteed. The basic prerequisite for routing these funds through State Consolidated funds to Panchayats is introduction of foolproof treasury arrangements under which money meant for them cannot be held back to meet State overdraft needs when cheques are presented for encashment. This can be done by providing that CSS fund instalments are sent to a dedicated Panchayats' account in the treasury, over which State Finance departments do not exercise release restrictions.

In most States, the operations of District Panchayats and Intermediate Panchayats are already carried out through fund accounts under Public Account opened in treasuries. These fund accounts of each District and Intermediate Panchayat can be split into three distinct accounts, namely.

- Fund-I, which accounts for all receipts and expenditure of Central Plan and Centrally Sponsored Schemes including their State share, non-plan Central Grants and grants under Finance Commission's recommendations.
- Fund-II, which accounts for all receipts and expenditure in respect of all State Plan schemes, other than matching share of Central Plan and Centrally Sponsored Schemes and all non-plan assistance received from State Government.
- Fund-III, which accounts for all receipts and expenditure in respect of own funds of the Panchayat concerned under Tax or Non-Tax Revenue, Earnest Money and Security Deposits.

Separating the three "funds" in the Public Accounts of District and Intermediate Panchayats is possible when State treasuries are computerized as is happening all over the country. If computerization with budget control is introduced, treasury cheques issued by panchayats can be routinely encashed by them within the provided line item. This can be a win-win game for all participants, since up to the date of drawal, such funds will prop up the ways and means position of the States, when today they are being kept out of State treasuries in toto. This is a strong incentive for States to introduce these arrangements.

Since the total number of District and Intermediate Panchayats in the country are just 6800, it is practically possible to set up a monitoring mechanism at the Central level to track and ensure that funds have been transferred to each such District and Intermediate Panchayat, in a particular state. The monitoring mechanism and authority would have a permanent data base of all PRIs at the intermediate and district level.

Transfer of Funds to Village Panchayats

With respect to Village Panchayats, given the constraints of connectivity and the fact that all Gram Panchayats may not have convenient access to Treasuries, to put in place a system of treasury transfer of founds to them. However, it is possible to put in place a two-tier system, based on bank accounts. Each State could maintain a database of bank accounts of all Village Panchayats, a task that is already being undertaken by several of them for sending Twelfth Finance Commission devolutions to all Panchayats within the stipulated time of 15 days. Once such a database is created, funds can be directly transferred to them through the core banking system wherever available. In case these facilities are not available, telegraphic transfers or other modes of electronic transfers could also be adopted. In the long-term, with the spread of the core banking system to cover more bank branches, even such transfers of funds from account to account might become notional—Panchayats could be assigned "Special Drawing Rights" (SDRs) from the single line account concerned, which enables them to make payments on account of the scheme concerned to the limit prescribed in the SDR. This system, which is in effect to have a single operating account with multiple operators, could put an end to the entire issue of inter-account reconciliation, which is the bane of multiple-tier accounting that is now such an essential feature of fiscal transfers to Panchayats.

Effectively Providing Capacity to Panchayats to Perform Activities Entrusted to Them

An important aspect of provision of capacity is the devolution of staff to Panchayats, or enabling them to secure their own staff. Logic dictates that for Panchayats to function effectively, they should ultimately be vested with powers to recruit their staff and exercise control over them. However, government itself has a large number of staff that would be rendered surplus in case local bodies are given full powers to recruit their own cadres of officials. Purely as a transitional measure, it will be necessary to fill up all PRI posts, barring those at lower levels, through deputation of government employees to them. However, these transitional arrangements cannot be allowed to became permanent, because as long as officials do not belong to a local body and have the option to revert to his original cadre, true control cannot be there. The creation of local cadres through administrative and legislative measures is essential so that Panchayats can function effectively, execute schemes and are accountable to the people. As stated by elected representatives in several discussions, it would also reduce staff costs.

Unfortunately, it is not easy to find lasting solutions without tackling the issue of how to manage the transition. Movement of staff to Panchayats is also likely to meet with resistance as the two groups that matter, namely, the elected representatives of PRIs and the officials who work under them, harbour persistent misgivings about each other. However, it is illogical for officials to accept on the one hand that as civil servants they are accountable to the State legislature, which is also an elected representative body, but then express misgivings about coming under the control of elected representatives at the PRI level.

While moving from a system of deputation to one of local cadres, the compartmentalization of Government into departments could also be re-examined, so that this is maintained only to the extent required to undertake specialized departmental responsibilities. There is an opportunity for facilitating cross-departmental movement of staff. Since with full devolution, Panchayats will end up handling functions related to a large number of departments, inter-departmental movement of general purpose staff should be encouraged so as to address local staff shortages. A framework for lateral movement of staff is detailed in the table overleaf:

Level	*Work description*	*Propensity for convergence*
Group D Group C ministerial	General Purpose	These staff ought to be a common pool for all departments. General qualifications could be prescribed for recruitment and could be shared between departments within the district.
Junior Technical level		Technical staff will have to be recruited in a department specific manner as they are to perform departmental technical activities.
Senior Technical Staff	Specific Purpose	These persons could either rise from the junior technical staff or be directly recruited in a department specific manner. However, they would also have the opportunity to rise to occupy largely administrative positions within the department concerned.
Policy Making Staff	General Purpose	When persons have gained enough experience at the departmental level, they graduate further to the position of becoming policy makers, where again there is convergence between departments.

Thus except for technical staff, convergence is easily possible. Even in the case of specialized cadres, lateral movement should be encouraged. Since policy making staff is not required in great numbers at the decentralized administration level, convergence at that level is largely not relevant in the PRI context. However, the applicability of the convergence principle to the Group 'D' and the Group 'C' ministerial levels would be of great benefit at the PRI level. Appropriate mechanisms should be put into place at the earliest to ensure that such convergence and cross-departmental movement is possible.

One fear is that decentralized recruitment into local cadres limits exposure and thereby restricts the possibility of enriching experience elsewhere. In order to tackle this, we suggest that arrangements can be made for staff to be exchanged through a process of deputations between Districts, thus ensuring that staff gets opportunities to appreciate newer ideas and learn from new experiences. We also suggest that while creating local cadres, a system of transfers that ensure a prescribed mandatory level of cross-district experience should be introduced.

A major issue concerning district level recruitments and cadres is that since these cadres are smaller, opportunities of growth through promotions tend to be restricted. While designing local cadres, we must ensure that opportunities are provided for the good to rise to higher levels. Doing so through time bound and routine promotions reduces the incentive to perform well. The system must allow stars to rise, provided that they do so through adherence to excellence. The idea would be to have an independent board that works in a similar manner as the Public Enterprises Recruitment Board of the Government of India. We recommend that above certain levels, posts can be reserved only for direct recruitment, with the option for those within or outside the government to apply for recruitment. Such a system would allow those with the necessary ability currently occupying a lower level in the hierarchy, to climb faster. Such a system will also expose in-house staff to the pressure of competition with outsiders for higher jobs on a sustained basis.

Decentralising Technical Guidance

With greater devolution of functions, powers and responsibilities to PRIs, departmental processes ought to local officials to deal with local needs. However, many departments still rely on hierarchical technical guidance guided by rigid rules. Greater transparency through Panchayati Raj requires corresponding transparency and simplification of internal processes. This could be better achieved through rewriting technical scrutiny rules to make them more transparent, simple and provide for situations where projects are taken up with peoples' participation. Since people are increasingly contributing in greater proportion to such projects, they must be given the right to decide what should be done, how to do it and at what cost. In addition, securing technical guidance ought to be broadbased, so as to go beyond line departments. Panchayats at all levels ought to be provided the leeway to secure the services of qualified technical personnel to undertake their works.

Strengthening the Supervisory Powers of Gram Panchayats Over Local Staff

In the ultimate analysis, all officials in the rural sector work in one or the other Gram Panchayat jurisdiction. There are some field level functionaries whose work touches the lives of almost every person in the village more than the rest, such as Teachers, Doctors, ANMs, Anganwadi Workers, Agricultural Assistants, Veterinary Doctors and Electricity department linemen. These functionaries, whose work is vital at the Gram Panchayat. The attendance of such field level workers should be monitored by Gram Panchayats, regardless of which tier to which they answer. During the Eleventh Plan, all States may progressively ensure that salaries to such departmental functionaries are paid through Gram Panchayats. Till such time, it may be provided that such officials need to get attendance certificates issued by the Gram Panchayat concerned before they can draw their salaries. Where officials have jurisdictions larger than that of an individual Grama Panchayat, the Intermediate Panchayat could monitors attendance. In addition, at the Gram Panchayat level, there ought to be sufficient full time staff, consisting at the minimum of a full time secretary, an accountant and at least two assistants, one for field work and one for office work. These could be provided either through re-deployment or Gram Panchayats could be given powers to recruit such staff on contract basis. Currently, though almost 40 per cent of Panchayat members are women, there are hardly any women posted to executive jobs, such as secretaries of Gram Panchayats, in most States. This imbalance results in gender insensitivity in the preparation of decentralized plans and their execution and needs to be corrected through an emphasis in recruitment of women to such posts. The Group recommends that all aspects of this important question of 'functionaries' may be taken up by the Ministry of Panchayati Raj for detailed discussions with the States so that certain common approaches regarding the transition may be evolved. The implementation of such measures could be one of the parameters in the Incentive Scheme.

Eschewing Restrictive Administrative Instructions

Even in States that have gone far on empowering Panchayats, over time, administrative instructions progressively restricting the independence of elected PRI office-bearers and members in decision-making are adopted. Similarly, with corporate practice, we can have a system where the local body itself can vote on the essential expenditure limits given to office bearers and members, provided that the expenditure incurred on this behalf is disclosed in the Annual Report.

Ensuring Smooth Coordination between Departments

A high degree of coordination between departments to ensure effective convergence of government activities is required for a well functioning Panchayati Raj System. However, at the district level too, departments still tend to work in isolation. Some departments such as those dealing with watershed development, created their own systems for convergence, by having in-house agriculture, forest, horticulture and soil conservation staff. However, duplication of skills is not a solution for coordination and convergence. We suggest that departments ought to converge around scheme related and untied fund outcomes. Broadly, the system could revolve around Standing Committees of the ZP assisted by departmental officials.

ICT for Better Monitoring of Service Delivery Through Panchayats

ICT is also going to become increasingly important in the context of greater transparency in government processes, greater openness to the public, greater streamlining of procurement procedures, taking analytical decisions, helping the DPC to plan better, informing elected representatives of works taken up and undertaking evaluation studies. Computerisation of Panchayats will involve considerable creation and maintenance of updated databases. While initial steps in this direction could be centralized, by computerizing large volumes of data available, for the system to be sustainable, those who must use the data must feel that they own it. Therefore, ultimately, data collecting and updating ought to be at the lowest level possible. Each Panchayat will need to be provided support for data collection and storage for what comes within its sphere and to make use of this data for their own benefit and efficiency. This will involve improving monitoring systems, maintaining and updating baseline data and disclosure of information under the Right to Information Act. Disclosure of information would particularly focus on beneficiary lists and information on plans and schemes, including the publication of social audit reports, and estimates and inspection reports of works.

Improving internal housekeeping systems is another aspect calling for rapid reform. This would entail the computerisation of Panchayat accounts, maintenance of correspondence, minutes of meetings, notices to members and correspondence to higher authorities, computerisation of routine civic activities such as issue of bills and computerisation of cash books, social audit formats and reports. Evolution of the above independent processes could then result in their eventual networking with other computerization initiatives. Linking PRI accounts computerization systems with treasury computerization will help in easier disbursements of money, tracking of expenditure and reconciliation of vouchers, leading to greater control and monitoring of expenditure. This will also involve re-designing procedures and rewriting manuals and instructions appropriately. *We suggest that these objectives have to be met within a specified time frame, say over the next three years.*

Fiscal Information System for Panchayats

State Governments have hardly put in efforts to compile the information system to aid the planning process. Even the State Finance Commissions in most States have not compiled economic, demographic and fiscal information at the local body level and have often made their recommendations without recourse to any analysis of expenditures, standards of services or revenue collections.

An information system for grassroot level planning has to be put in place for urban and rural local bodies at village, block and district levels. Remote sensing satellites would provide information on natural resources, forest cover, minerals, cropping pattern, water bodies etc. Such data will have to be supplemented by information available from the census, economic census, district industries centres, urban local bodies, state statistical bureaus and similar other agencies. It would be desirable to have a statistical department adequately equipped to compile the information system at the district level.

The most important and difficult information to compile is on fiscal variables. The Eleventh Finance Commission expressed serious concern about the non-availability of data on local body finances. In order to strengthen preparation of database on Panchayat finances, it recommended computerization and networking through V-SAT and recommended high level coordination at the level of Chief Secretaries of States. The C&AG's office was asked to design standard formats for data collection, so as to ensure inter-state comparability. To achieve these objectives, the Commission recommended a grant of Rs. 200 crore, of which Rs. 197 crore was for rural local bodies. However, the situation had hardly improved when the Twelfth Finance Commission reviewed the situation. It reported that of the Rs. 200 crore allocated, only Rs. 93 crore was utilized. Noting that the data collected was quite poor in quality, it reiterated that an appropriate system be put in place at the grassroot level to facilitate realistic assessment of the needs of the panchayats and municipalities for basic civic and developmental functions. It remarked that the "absence of data necessary for a rational determination of the gap between the cost of service delivery and the capacity to raise resources makes the task of recommending measures for achieving equalisation of services almost impossible." *It therefore recommended that rural and urban local bodies should give high priority to expenditure on creation of data base and maintenance of accounts through the use of modern technology and management systems.*

Strategy for Building Information System

The first task therefore is to design a common accounting system for three levels of Panchayats and urban local bodies, adopting the accounting system designed by the Comptroller and Auditor General as a standard. The second task is to set up a system of collecting information right from the village Panchayat level. Gram panchayats will need to maintain their accounts in the standard formats and detailed data on various items of revenues, transfers under various heads and different items of expenditures will need to be regularly transmitted to the Intermediate Panchayats for compilation and forward to the District Panchayats, along with their own financial information. The District Planning Office under

Statistical Information System for Decentralised Planning

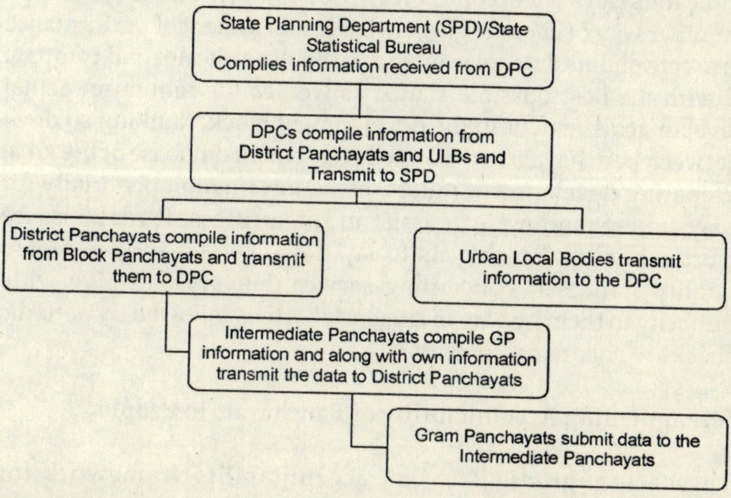

the District Panchayat should have a well equipped statistical cell, which could also be entrusted with the task of compiling data from Urban Local Bodies. Data could be sent to a data repository at the

State level. The Fiscal Cell recommended to be set up at the State level by the Twelfth Finance Commission could be entrusted the task of maintaining data. This data could also be integrated with the data on natural resources, economic, social and demographic data. Apart from giving raw data in the public domain, the State Statistical Bureau could also compile and publish detailed data. The details of the information and data flow are given in the Chart.

The Planning Commission should earmark necessary funds for the purpose. Once formats are finalized, the entire exercise can be conducted within a month. In the process, it should be possible to get the last three years' information, which should form the basis of building the information system for future.

Laying Down Standards for Benchmarking Quality of Services

To ensure effective service delivery, Panchayats' performance has to be closely monitored. The best way of doing this is to fully involve PRIs at all levels in the monitoring process. This can be done through the development of yardsticks for monitoring through discussion at the Panchayat level. The development of indicators can itself become a very good capacity building exercise. Another way of encouraging such self-assessment of performance is to consolidate data relevant to a particular indicator and compare it with the best possible status, as well as the minimum actual level of achievement in the development block. Ranking so done between panchayats provides a development database of the area. Preparing development radars, using information pictorially for easy understanding, can assist in this process. It may also be worthwhile for Panchayats to lay down certain fully accepted quality standards concerning service delivery and give wide publicity to them by way of citizens' charters, followed by periodic checks to ensure conformity.

Strengthening Accountability of Panchayats to People

The basic ingredients of an accountability framework for Panchayats are:

- A Panchayat Raj Act and rules relating to conduct of business by Panchayats, such as how often and how meetings are to be conducted, records maintained and disclosed.

- State Panchayat Raj legislation empowering Gram Sabhas to approve plans, select beneficiaries, monitor plan implementation, approve payment and conduct social audit.
- A framework for social audit.
- A clear structure of budgeting of the Panchayats.
- Legislative provisions for a right to information and a structure to govern periodic disclosure of information.
- Legislative provisions for an ombudsman-like authority.

In order to enforce accountability, the following have to be ensured so that there is no room for alibi:

- A minimum staffing pattern particularly at the Village level.
- An administrative mechanism for providing adequate technical assistance and support to the panchayats.
- Legislative or administrative provisions which permit Panchayats to form networks or associations to undertake tasks that are beyond the individual jurisdiction of each, but still fall within their functional mandate.
- Legislative or administrative provisions for scaling down, which enable Panchayats to forge links and provide support to local citizens associations and user groups.
- A well functioning system of Standing Committees operating at every Panchayat level, which ensures that decisions are committee based.
- Comprehensive databases that can be used by panchayats for their own functioning and decision-making.
- A working plan for training village panchayat members, functionaries and departments (as already detailed).
- Several of these points have been dealt with earlier in this chapter and the following recommendations are made only in respect of those not dealt with so far.

A Grievance Redressal Mechanism; the Local Body Ombudsman

With increased devolution to Panchayats, there is a need for an institution for independent complaint investigation and grievance redressal against decisions of Panchayats. Establishing an Ombudsman system can provide a convenient and relatively low-cost mechanism to deal with such complaints. The work of the Ombudsman would be essentially investigative in character looking at both reasonableness of a decision as also due process being disregarded in rendering a service or deciding on a claim. The Ombudsman could look at matters relating to internal administration. The Ombudsman could consist of both Judicial and Administrative Officers of appropriate seniority. In States where the institution of Lok-Ayukta has been established, it could function as the local body Ombudsman. A critical test of success of the Ombudsman would be the speed with which appeals are heard and disposed. Such speed can be attained by combining relatively simple procedures of an executive authority with the advantages of an independent judicial system. For this reason we suggest that time limits may be imposed for completing the Ombudsman's investigation into a complaint.

Putting in Place Baseline Standards on Accounting and Auditing

As already mentioned, the C&AG recommended certain standardised formats for PRI accounts. States may be persuaded to universally adopt them. Auditing of Panchayats will also need to be closely monitored and it is recommended that States can establish a separate Public Accounts Committee as recommended by the Eleventh Finance Commission for monitoring the completion of audits of accounts and examining action taken on audit observations and reports.

Social Audit

Institutionalising a system of social audit is essential for improving local service delivery. An effective system of social audit will have to be based on two precepts, first, that service standards are made public through citizens' charters and second, that periodic suo moto disclosure is made on attainment of service delivery standards by Panchayats. Social audit processes are also important to ensure effectiveness. Some do's and don'ts in this regard are suggested below:

- Social audit ought not to be individually prescribed for each scheme implemented by Panchayats. A multiplicity of social audits separately prescribed for each scheme undermines the importance of the process.
- Adequate publicity will need to be given for social audit.
- It may be a good idea to provide nodal officers to assist Panchayats in the proper conduct of social audit. However, care must be taken to ensure that such support does not give the impression that the Panchayat can sidestep its own accountability.
- Social audit "action taken reports" have to be time bound and placed in the public domain. It is a good idea to precede a social audit with the action taken on the previous social audit.
- Opportunity has to be given to people to inspect the records of the Panchayat, particularly their documentation on property lists, tax assessments and tax collected, measurement books and muster rolls.
- It would be a good idea for a higher level of Panchayat, such as the intermediate panchayat, to provide details of the comparative performance of all Panchayats falling within its jurisdiction, so that people can get an idea of where their Panchayat stands in respect of each service delivered.

A system of social audit at the intermediate and district Panchayat levels is also required.

Index